BROWNIES & BARS

TASTE OF HOME BOOKS
RDA ENTHUSIAST BRANDS, LLC
MILWAUKEE, WI

Taste of Home

EDITORIAL

Editor-in-Chief: Catherine Cassidy
Vice President, Content Operations: Kerri Balliet
Creative Director: Howard Greenberg

Managing Editor, Print & Digital Books: Mark Hagen
Associate Creative Director: Edwin Robles Jr.

Editor: Amy Glander
Art Director: Maggie Conners
Layout Designer: Catherine Fletcher
Editorial Services Manager: Dena Ahlers
Editorial Production Coordinator: Jill Banks
Copy Chief: Deb Warlaumont Mulvey
Copy Editors: Dulcie Shoener (senior), Ronald Kovach,
Chris McLaughlin, Ellie Piper
Contributing Copy Editor: Kristin Sutter
Editorial Services Administrator: Marie Brannon

Content Director: Julie Blume Benedict
Food Editors: Gina Nistico; James Schend; Peggy Woodward, RDN
Recipe Editors: Sue Ryon (lead), Irene Yeh
Senior Digital Editor: Kelsey Mueller
Associate Digital Editor: Nicole Doster

Test Cooks: Nicholas Iverson (lead), Matthew Hass
Food Stylists: Kathryn Conrad (lead), Lauren Knoelke,
Shannon Roum
Prep Cooks: Bethany Van Jacobson (lead), Melissa Hansen,
Aria C. Thornton
Culinary Team Assistant: Maria Petrella

Photography Director: Stephanie Marchese
Photographers: Dan Roberts, Jim Wieland
Photographer/Set Stylist: Grace Natoli Sheldon
Set Stylists: Melissa Franco (lead), Stacey Genaw,
Dee Dee Schaefer
Set Stylist Assistant: Stephanie Chojnacki

Business Architect, Publishing Technologies:
Amanda Harmatys
Business Analyst, Publishing Technologies: Kate Unger
Junior Business Analyst, Publishing Technologies:
Shannon Stroud

Editorial Business Manager: Kristy Martin
Rights & Permissions Associate: Samantha Lea Stoeger
Editorial Business Associate: Andrea Meiers

BUSINESS

Vice President, Group Publisher: Kirsten Marchioli
Publisher: Donna Lindskog
Business Development Director, Taste of Home Live:
Laurel Osman
Strategic Partnerships Manager, Taste of Home Live:
Jamie Piette Andrzejewski

TRUSTED MEDIA BRANDS, INC.

President & Chief Executive Officer: Bonnie Kintzer
Chief Financial Officer: Dean Durbin
Chief Marketing Officer: C. Alec Casey
Chief Revenue Officer: Richard Sutton
Chief Digital Officer: Vince Errico
Senior Vice President, Global HR & Communications:
Phyllis E. Gebhardt, SPHR; SHRM-SCP
General Counsel: Mark Sirota
Vice President, Magazine Marketing: Christopher Gaydos
Vice President, Product Marketing: Brian Kennedy
Vice President, Operations: Michael Garzone
Vice President, Consumer Marketing Planning: Jim Woods
Vice President, Digital Product & Technology: Nick Contardo
Vice President, Financial Planning & Analysis: William Houston

For other *Taste of Home* books and products, visit us at
tasteofhome.com.

International Standard Book Number: 978-1-61765-606-4
Library of Congress Control Number: 2016954575

Pictured on front cover (from top left):
Raspberry Pecan Squares, page 96; German Chocolate Dump
Cake, page 155; Loaded M&M Oreo Cookie Bars, page 102;
Fudgy S'mores Brownies, page 61

Pictured on title page: Fudge-Topped Brownies, page 57

Pictured on back cover (from left): Peanut Butter Brownie
Trifle, page 241; Cream Cheese Swirl Brownies, page 147;
Banana Cream Brownie Dessert, page 226

Printed in China
1 3 5 7 9 10 8 6 4 2

GET SOCIAL WITH US

To find a recipe tasteofhome.com
To submit a recipe tasteofhome.com/submit
To find out about other *Taste of Home* products shoptasteofhome.com

LIKE US
facebook.com/tasteofhome

PIN US
pinterest.com/taste_of_home

FOLLOW US
@tasteofhome

TWEET US
twitter.com/tasteofhome

BROWNED BUTTER
CEREAL BARS, 219

PICNIC BARS, 121

RHUBARB
CUSTARD BARS, 176

FROSTED PISTACHIO
BARS, 175

CONTENTS

Love at **First Bite**

From timeless chip-filled delights to indulgent chocolate sensations, brownies and bars are the perfect bite-sized treat. That's because these scrumptious goodies are big on finger-licking satisfaction and low on time and effort. They're great for bake sales, potlucks, classroom treats, lunchboxes, or as an anytime snack when a craving calls. It's no wonder they're ranked as all-time favorites with bakers (and tasters!) everywhere.

Brownies and bars are easy to make but difficult to define; they can be made in endless variations.

They can be crisp with a rich, buttery shortbread crust, cakelike or fudgy. They can have layers, fruit, jam or a cooked filling and be topped with a dreamy frosting or a delicate glaze. Best of all, they can steal the show in an elegant trifle—or be as deliciously humble as a chocolate chip cookie bar.

Before you whip up a big batch of from-scratch goodness, brush up on these helpful tips and tricks to ensure good and consistent baking results. Follow these guidelines and you're guaranteed your best baked wonders!

**FROSTED FUDGE
BROWNIES, PAGE 183**

AT-A-GLANCE ICONS IN THIS BOOK:

BIG BATCH
Recipes that yield 4 dozen or more.

⑤INGREDIENTS
Recipes that use 5 or fewer ingredients. Recipes may also call for water, salt, pepper, and canola or olive oil.

EASY LEMON
CURD BARS, PAGE 92

CHERRY-COCONUT
CHOCOLATE TORTE,
PAGE 234

BAKING 101

Read the entire recipe before you begin. Make sure you understand the baking and/or cooking techniques and have the necessary equipment and bakeware.

Check to see that you have all the required ingredients.

Choose the right size baking pan. If you choose to use a pan size other than the one the recipe calls for, you may need to adjust the baking time.

Prepare the ingredients before you start mixing. Let butter soften, chop the nuts, toast the coconut...

Measure the ingredients carefully, using the proper techniques and measuring utensils.

Test the accuracy of your oven's heat setting with an oven thermometer. Preheat the oven to the desired temperature. Place the thermometer on the center rack. Close the oven door, leaving the oven at the set temperature. After 15 minutes, check the oven thermometer. If it does not agree with the set temperature, the thermometer is correct and the oven temperature setting is inaccurate. Then adjust the setting accordingly, raising or lowering the heat.

Follow recipe directions to prepare the food.

Time the baking accurately with a kitchen timer.

Cool baked goods on a wire rack to allow air to circulate around the food.

BROWNIE & BAR CONUNDRUMS

Baked unevenly
- The batter wasn't spread evenly in the pan.
- The oven rack wasn't level.

Are overbaked
- A pan larger than the recipe calls for was used, causing the batter to be thin and bake dry.
- The oven temperature was too high.
- Baking time was too long; next time, check the bars 5 minutes sooner than the recipe says.

Have a soggy crust
- The crust was not baked long enough before placing the filling on top.

Have a crumbly crust
- Next time, cut in a little more butter so that the crust will hold together better.

Crumble when they are cut
- Cool the bars completely before cutting them.
- Warm the knife blade in hot water, dry with a towel, then cut the brownies or bars. Clean and rewarm the knife after each cut.
- Use a sawing motion when cutting.

TOP 10 SECRETS
for Successful Brownies & Bars

1 **Use butter**, stick margarine (with at least 80% oil) or shortening. Whipped, tub, soft, liquid or reduced-fat products contain air and water and will produce flat, tough bars or brownies.

2 **Measure ingredients** accurately.

3 **Avoid overmixing** the batter. If it's handled too much, gluten in the flour will develop, and the bars or brownies will be tough.

4 **Use dull aluminum** baking pans or glass dishes. Dark-colored pans may cause overbrowning.

5 **Grease the pan** with shortening or coat with nonstick cooking spray.

6 **Line the bottom of the pan** with foil, then grease, to remove bars and brownies from a pan even more easily. Add the batter and bake as directed.

7 **Spread batter evenly** in the pan. If one corner is thinner than another, it will bake faster and be overbaked when the rest of the pan is done.

8 **Center the pan** in the middle of the rack placed in the middle of the oven.

9 **Use a kitchen timer.** Check bars when the minimum baking time has been reached, baking longer if needed.

10 **Cut after cooling completely** on a wire rack for most bars and brownies. However, crisp bars should be cut while still slightly warm.

LEBKUCHEN, PAGE 110

BONUS BROWNIE POINTS

LAYERED BROWNIE DESSERT, PAGE 222

PEPPERMINT BROWNIE CUPS, PAGE 226

CUTTING BROWNIES & BARS

With a knife, use a gentle sawing motion. Remove the corner piece first. Then the remaining bars will be easier to remove.

For perfectly even bars, lay a clean ruler on top of the bars and make cut marks with the point of a knife. Use the edge of the ruler as a cutting guide.

For basic bars and brownies (those without soft fillings or toppings), line the pan with foil before baking. When cool, lift the foil from the pan. Trim the edges of the bars or brownies, then cut into bars, squares or diamonds. The scraps can be crumbled and used as a topping for ice cream or pudding.

How many pieces? An 8-inch square pan will yield 16 pieces when cut four rows by four rows. A 13x9-inch pan will yield 48 pieces when cut six rows by eight rows.

STORING BROWNIES & BARS

Cover a pan of uncut brownies and bars with foil or put the pan in a large resealable plastic bag.

If made with perishable ingredients, like cream cheese, they should be covered and refrigerated.

Once the bars are cut, always store them in an airtight container.

Most bars and brownies freeze well for up to 3 months. To freeze a pan of uncut bars, place in an airtight container or resealable plastic bag. You can also wrap individual bars in plastic wrap and stack in an airtight container. Thaw at room temperature before serving.

SEPARATING EGGS

Place an egg separator over a custard cup; crack egg into the separator. As each egg is separated, place the yolk in one bowl and egg white into another. It is easier to separate eggs when they are cold.

SOFTENING BUTTER

To cream butter, it should first be softened. (You should be able to make an indentation in a stick of butter with your finger, and a table knife should glide through it.) But to cut butter into a mixture, it generally should be cold from the refrigerator.

CHOCOLATE BUTTERMILK
SQUARES, PAGE 17

Prizewinning Delights

Everyone at the table wins big when you serve these first-rate favorites from *Taste of Home* baking contests.

GLAZED APPLE-MAPLE BLONDIES

My young son and I created this recipe to use up the last of the apples we picked at our local orchard. To make the blondies extra special, serve them warm with a dollop of whipped cream.
—**HEATHER BATES** ATHENS, ME

PREP: 25 MIN.
BAKE: 25 MIN. + COOLING
MAKES: 2 DOZEN

- 1⅓ cups packed brown sugar
- ½ cup butter, melted and cooled
- ½ cup maple syrup
- 2 teaspoons vanilla extract
- 2 large eggs
- 2 cups all-purpose flour
- ¾ teaspoon salt
- ¼ teaspoon baking soda
- 3 cups chopped peeled apples (about 3 medium)

GLAZE
- ¼ cup butter, cubed
- ½ cup maple syrup
- ¼ cup packed brown sugar

1. Preheat oven to 350°. Line a 13x9-in. baking pan with parchment paper, letting ends extend up sides.

2. In a large bowl, beat brown sugar, melted butter, syrup and vanilla until blended. Beat in eggs. In another bowl, whisk flour, salt and baking soda; gradually beat into brown sugar mixture. Stir in apples (batter will be thick).

3. Transfer to prepared pan. Bake 25-30 minutes or until golden brown and a toothpick inserted in center comes out with moist crumbs.

4. Meanwhile, in a small saucepan, melt butter over medium-low heat; stir in syrup and brown sugar. Bring to a boil over medium heat; cook and stir 2-3 minutes or until slightly thickened. Remove from heat; cool slightly.

5. Pour glaze over warm blondies. Cool completely in pan on a wire rack. Cut into bars.

GLAZED APPLE-MAPLE BLONDIES

SOUR CREAM & CRANBERRY BARS

I put an unexpected spin on sour cream raisin pie by turning it into a cookie bar with a crunchy oatmeal crust, custard-style cranberry filling and crisp topping.

—SHELLY BEVINGTON
HERMISTON, OR

PREP: 35 MIN.
BAKE: 35 MIN. + COOLING
MAKES: 2 DOZEN

- 3 **large egg yolks**
- 1½ **cups (12 ounces) sour cream**
- 1 **cup sugar**
- 3 **tablespoons cornstarch**
- ⅛ **teaspoon salt**
- 1 **cup dried cranberries**
- 1 **teaspoon vanilla extract**

CRUST

- 1 **cup butter, softened**
- 1 **cup sugar**
- 2 **teaspoons vanilla extract**
- 1¾ **cups all-purpose flour**
- 1⅓ **cups quick-cooking oats**
- 1 **teaspoon salt**
- 1 **teaspoon baking soda**
- 1 **cup flaked coconut**

1. Preheat oven to 350°. In top of a double boiler or a metal bowl over simmering water, whisk the first five ingredients until blended; stir in cranberries. Cook and stir 15-20 minutes until mixture is thickened. Remove from heat; stir in vanilla.

2. Meanwhile, in a large bowl, cream butter and sugar until light and fluffy. Beat in vanilla. In another bowl, whisk flour, oats, salt and baking soda; gradually beat into creamed mixture. Stir in coconut. Reserve half of the dough for topping. Press remaining onto bottom of a greased 13x9-in. baking dish. Bake 8-10 minutes or until set.

3. Spread sour cream mixture over crust; crumble reserved dough over top. Bake 25-30 minutes or until the filling is set and top is golden brown. Cool in pan on a wire rack. Cut into bars.

SOUR CREAM & CRANBERRY BARS

FIVE-STAR BROWNIES

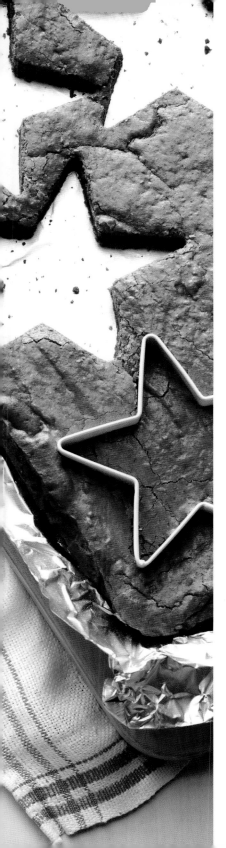

FIVE-STAR BROWNIES

When I entered these treats in the 1990 state fair, Kansas was celebrating the 100th birthday of Five-Star U.S. General and 34th President Dwight D. Eisenhower, who grew up in the central Kansas town of Abilene. So I renamed my brownies in honor of the rank he'd achieved as a general, and cut them out with a star-shaped cookie cutter. They won a blue ribbon!

—**PAM BUERKI ROGERS** VICTORIA, KS

PREP: 15 MIN.
BAKE: 30 MIN. + COOLING
MAKES: 1 DOZEN

- 3 **large eggs**
- 2 **cups sugar**
- 1½ **teaspoons vanilla extract**
- ½ **cup butter, melted**
- ¼ **cup shortening, melted**
- 1½ **cups all-purpose flour**
- ¾ **cup baking cocoa**
- ¾ **teaspoon salt**
- 1 **cup chopped nuts, optional**

1. In a large bowl, beat the eggs, sugar and vanilla until blended. Beat in butter and shortening until smooth. Combine the flour, cocoa and salt; gradually add to egg mixture. Stir in nuts if desired.
2. Line a 13x9-in. baking pan with foil and grease the foil; pour the batter into pan. Bake at 350° for 30 minutes or until a toothpick inserted near the center comes out clean. Cool in pan on a wire rack.
3. Using foil, lift brownies out of pan. Discard foil. Cut brownies with a 3-in. star-shaped cookie cutter or into bars.

TOP TIP

BROWNIE PIECES

Cut leftover brownie scraps into small pieces and sprinkle them on top of an ice cream sundae.

BIG BATCH
SACHER BARS

This rich take on the traditional Viennese torte calls for apricot preserves and chocolate. It left our taste testers speechless— unless you count "*mmm*." Is your mouth watering yet?

—**LORRAINE CALAND** SHUNIAH, ON

PREP: 30 MIN.
BAKE: 15 MIN. + COOLING
MAKES: 6¼ DOZEN

- ¾ **cup butter, cubed**
- 3 **ounces unsweetened chocolate, chopped**
- 3 **large eggs**
- 1½ **cups sugar**
- 1½ **teaspoons vanilla extract**
- 1¼ **cups all-purpose flour**
- ¾ **cup apricot preserves**
- 2 **ounces semisweet chocolate, chopped**

1. Preheat oven to 325°. Line a greased 15x10x1-in. baking pan with waxed paper. Grease and flour the paper; set aside. In a microwave, melt butter and unsweetened chocolate; stir until smooth. In a large bowl, beat eggs and sugar. Stir in vanilla and chocolate mixture. Gradually add flour.
2. Transfer to prepared pan. Bake 15-20 minutes or until a toothpick inserted near the center comes out clean (do not overbake). Cool 10 minutes before removing from pan to a wire rack to cool completely.
3. In a microwave, heat preserves until melted. Cut cake into four 7½x5-in. rectangles. Spread half of the preserves over two rectangles. Top each with remaining cake and spread with remaining preserves. Cut into bars.
4. In a microwave, melt semisweet chocolate; stir until smooth. Drizzle over bars. Let stand until set. Store in an airtight container in the refrigerator.

RUSTIC NUT BARS

Folks love crunching into the shortbreadlike crust and nutty topping on these chewy, gooey bars. This recipe is a keeper!

—BARBARA DRISCOLL WEST ALLIS, WI

PREP: 20 MIN.
BAKE: 35 MIN. + COOLING
MAKES: ABOUT 3 DOZEN

- 1 tablespoon plus ¾ cup cold butter, divided
- 2⅓ cups all-purpose flour
- ½ cup sugar
- ½ teaspoon baking powder
- ½ teaspoon salt
- 1 large egg, lightly beaten

TOPPING

- ⅔ cup honey
- ½ cup packed brown sugar
- ¼ teaspoon salt
- 6 tablespoons butter, cubed
- 2 tablespoons heavy whipping cream
- 1 cup chopped hazelnuts, toasted
- 1 cup salted cashews
- 1 cup pistachios
- 1 cup salted roasted almonds

1. Preheat oven to 375°. Line a 13x9-in. baking pan with foil, letting ends extend over sides by 1 inch. Grease foil with 1 tablespoon butter.
2. In a large bowl, whisk flour, sugar, baking powder and salt. Cut in remaining butter until mixture resembles coarse crumbs. Stir in egg until blended (mixture will be dry). Press firmly onto bottom of prepared pan.
3. Bake 18-20 minutes or until edges are golden brown. Cool on a wire rack.
4. In a large heavy saucepan, combine honey, brown sugar and salt; bring to a boil over medium heat, stirring frequently to dissolve sugar. Boil 2 minutes, without stirring. Stir in butter and cream; return to a boil. Cook and stir 1 minute or until smooth. Remove from heat; stir in nuts. Spread over crust.

5. Bake 15-20 minutes or until topping is bubbly. Cool completely in pan on a wire rack. Lifting with foil, remove from pan. Discard foil; cut into bars.
NOTE *To toast nuts, bake in a shallow pan in a 350° oven for 5-10 minutes or cook in a skillet over low heat until lightly browned, stirring occasionally.*

BIG BATCH
PECAN SHORTBREAD DIAMONDS

My mother and I used to make these rich, buttery shortbread cookies every year around the holidays, both to enjoy at home and to give as gifts. With a hint of chocolate and a chewy pecan filling, they are exceptionally good. The diamond shape adds a special touch.

—JANE ELLEN BENROTH
BLUFFTON, OH

PREP: 40 MIN.
BAKE: 20 MIN. + COOLING
MAKES: 5 DOZEN

- ¾ cup butter, softened
- ½ cup confectioners' sugar
- 2 cups all-purpose flour
- ½ teaspoon salt

FILLING

- 2 ounces unsweetened chocolate, chopped
- 4 large eggs
- 1½ cups packed brown sugar
- 2 teaspoons vanilla extract
- ½ teaspoon salt
- 3 cups chopped pecans

1. In a large bowl, cream butter and confectioners' sugar until light and fluffy. Combine flour and salt; gradually add to creamed mixture and mix well. Press into an ungreased 15x10x1-in. baking pan. Bake at 375° for 12-15 minutes or until lightly browned. Cool for 5 minutes on a wire rack. Reduce temperature to 350°.
2. To make filling, in a microwave-safe bowl, melt chocolate; stir until smooth. Cool. In a large bowl,

combine the eggs, brown sugar, vanilla, salt and melted chocolate; fold in pecans.
3. Pour filling over crust. Bake for 18-20 minutes or until filling is set. Cool completely on a wire rack. Cut into diamond-shaped bars.

WARREN'S OATMEAL JAM SQUARES

I've lived more than 100 years, and I think baking is one of life's greatest joys. I make these jam-filled bars in my toaster oven for my fellow friends and residents at our assisted living home.

—WARREN PATRICK
TOWNSHEND, VERMONT

PREP: 20 MIN.
BAKE: 25 MIN. + COOLING
MAKES: 16 SQUARES

- 1¼ cups quick-cooking oats
- 1¼ cups all-purpose flour
- ½ cup sugar
- ½ teaspoon baking soda
- ¼ teaspoon salt
- ¾ cup butter, melted
- 2 teaspoons vanilla extract
- 1 jar (10 ounces) seedless raspberry jam or jam of your choice
- 4 whole graham crackers, crushed

1. Preheat oven to 350°. In a large bowl, mix the first five ingredients. In a small bowl, mix melted butter and vanilla; add to oat mixture, stirring until crumbly. Reserve 1 cup mixture for topping.
2. Press remaining mixture onto bottom of a greased 9-in. square baking pan. Spread jam over top to within ½ in. of edges. Add crushed graham crackers to reserved topping; sprinkle over jam.
3. Bake 25-30 minutes or until edges are golden brown. Cool in pan on a wire rack. Cut into squares.

RUSTIC NUT BARS

PECAN SHORTBREAD
DIAMONDS

WARREN'S OATMEAL
JAM SQUARES

BANANA SQUARES

BANANA SQUARES

My husband was in the Navy when we got married. We were stationed in Puerto Rico and had banana trees growing in our yard, so I came up with creative ways to use up dozens of ripe bananas at a time. These yummy squares became a favorite. They freeze well and are a great snack to have on hand when friends drop in to visit.

—SUSAN MILLER RALEIGH, NC

PREP: 20 MIN. • **BAKE:** 45 MIN.
MAKES: 12-16 SERVINGS

- 2 large eggs, separated
- ⅔ cup shortening
- 1½ cups sugar
- 1 cup mashed ripe bananas (2 to 3 medium)
- 1½ cups all-purpose flour
- 1 teaspoon baking soda
- ¼ cup buttermilk
- ½ teaspoon vanilla extract
- ½ cup chopped walnuts, optional
  Whipped cream and sliced bananas, optional

1. In a small bowl, beat egg whites until soft peaks form; set aside. In a large bowl, cream shortening and sugar. Beat in egg yolks; mix well. Add the bananas. Combine the flour and baking soda; add to the creamed mixture alternately with buttermilk, beating well after each addition. Add vanilla. Fold in egg whites. Fold in nuts if desired.
2. Pour into a greased 13x9-in. baking dish. Bake at 350° for 45-50 minutes. Cool on a wire rack.
3. If desired, garnish with whipped cream and a few banana slices.

SUPER BROWNIES

Loaded with macadamia nuts, these chunky bite-size treats never fail to catch attention on a buffet table. If you prefer, replace the macadamia nuts with pecans.

—BERNICE MUILENBURG
MOLALLA, OR

PREP: 20 MIN.
BAKE: 55 MIN. + COOLING
MAKES: ABOUT 3½ DOZEN

- ½ cup butter, cubed
- 1½ cups sugar
- 4⅔ cups (28 ounces) semisweet chocolate chips, divided
- 3 tablespoons hot water
- 4 large eggs
- 5 teaspoons vanilla extract
- 1½ cups all-purpose flour
- ½ teaspoon baking soda
- ½ teaspoon salt
- 2 cups coarsely chopped macadamia nuts or pecans, divided

1. In a large saucepan, melt butter with sugar over medium heat. Remove from the heat; stir in 2 cups chocolate chips until melted.
2. Pour into a large bowl; beat in water. Add eggs, one at a time, beating well after each addition. Add vanilla. Combine the flour, baking soda and salt; beat into the chocolate mixture until blended. Stir in 2 cups chocolate chips and 1 cup nuts.
3. Pour into a greased 13x9-in. baking pan. Sprinkle with remaining chips and nuts. Bake at 325° for 55 minutes or until the center is set (do not overbake). Cool on a wire rack.

CHOCOLATE BUTTERMILK SQUARES

Every time I bring these chocolate goodies to a party or potluck, the pan comes back clean! At home, they disappear as fast as I make them. See photo on page 8.

—CLARICE BAKER STROMSBURG, NE

PREP: 20 MIN. • **BAKE:** 20 MIN.
MAKES: 15 SERVINGS

- 1 cup butter, cubed
- ¼ cup baking cocoa
- 1 cup water
- 2 cups all-purpose flour
- 2 cups sugar
- 1 teaspoon baking soda
- ½ teaspoon salt
- ½ cup buttermilk
- 2 large eggs, beaten
- 1 teaspoon vanilla extract
- 3 to 4 drops red food coloring, optional

FROSTING

- ½ cup butter, cubed
- ¼ cup baking cocoa
- ¼ cup buttermilk
- 3¾ cups confectioners' sugar
- 1 teaspoon vanilla extract
  Dash salt
- ¾ cup chopped almonds, optional

1. In a large saucepan, bring butter, cocoa and water just to a boil. Cool.
2. Meanwhile, in a large bowl, combine the flour, sugar, baking soda and salt. Add cocoa mixture and buttermilk; mix well. Beat in eggs, vanilla and, if desired, food coloring. Pour into a greased and floured 15x10x1-in. baking pan.
3. Bake at 350° for 20 minutes. For frosting, melt cubed butter with cocoa and buttermilk. Stir in confectioners' sugar, vanilla and salt. Spread over warm cake. Garnish with nuts if desired.

TOP TIP

FREEZE EXTRA BANANAS

Peel and mash overripe bananas with 1 teaspoon of lemon juice for each banana used. Freeze in 1- or 2-cup amounts in airtight containers for up to 6 months. About 1⅓ cups mashed bananas equals three medium or four small bananas.

STRAWBERRY-LIME BARS

My family loves fresh strawberries. This yummy layered dessert is a spin on a classic. It boasts the same sweet berries and salty pretzel crust, but with a zesty hint of lime.
—ALEXANDRA BARNETT FOREST, VA

PREP: 25 MIN. + CHILLING
BAKE: 10 MIN. + COOLING
MAKES: 2 DOZEN

- 2 **cups finely crushed pretzels (about 6 ounces)**
- ¾ **cup sugar, divided**
- ¾ **cup butter, melted**
- 2 **cups boiling water**
- 1 **package (6 ounces) strawberry gelatin**
- 1 **pound fresh strawberries, chopped**
- 2 **packages (8 ounces each) cream cheese, softened**
- 1 **tablespoon grated lime peel**
- ¼ **cup lime juice**
- 1 **teaspoon vanilla extract**

1. Preheat oven to 350°. Place crushed pretzels and ¼ cup sugar in a small bowl; stir in melted butter. Spread out in an ungreased 15x10x1-in. baking pan. To toast, bake 9-11 minutes or until golden brown. Cool completely.
2. Meanwhile, in a bowl, add boiling water to gelatin; stir 2 minutes to completely dissolve. Gently stir in strawberries. Cool slightly. Refrigerate 30 minutes.
3. In a large bowl, beat cream cheese, lime peel, lime juice, vanilla and remaining sugar until blended. Stir in cooled pretzel mixture. Spread into an ungreased 13x9-in. baking pan. Top with strawberry mixture. Refrigerate, covered, 2 hours or until firm.

CRANBERRY CLEMENTINE BARS

I love citrus bars, especially around the holidays. Clementines are in abundance that time of year, so I put a slight twist on traditional lemon bars with these refreshing treats. The addition of cranberries adds a lovely pop of color.
—LAURIE LUFKIN ESSEX, MA

PREP: 25 MIN.
BAKE: 35 MIN. + COOLING
MAKES: 2 DOZEN

- 1½ **cups all-purpose flour**
- ½ **cup dried cranberries**
- ¼ **cup confectioners' sugar**
- ½ **teaspoon salt**
- 1 **cup cold butter, cubed**

FILLING

- 5 **large eggs**
- 1¾ **cups sugar**
- 3 **tablespoons cornstarch**
- 2 **tablespoons butter, melted**
- 1 **to 2 tablespoons grated clementine or orange peel**
- ⅓ **cup clementine or orange juice**
- 1 **teaspoon vanilla extract**
- ½ **teaspoon salt**
  Confectioners' sugar

1. Preheat oven to 350°. Line a 13x9-in. baking pan with foil, letting ends extend up sides; grease foil.
2. Place flour, cranberries, confectioners' sugar and salt in a food processor; pulse until blended. Add butter; pulse until butter is the size of peas. Press onto bottom of prepared pan. Bake 14-18 minutes or until edges are golden brown.
3. In a large bowl, whisk eggs, sugar, cornstarch, melted butter, clementine peel, juice, vanilla and salt until blended. Pour over warm crust. Bake 18-22 minutes longer or until filling is set. Cool completely in pan on a wire rack.
4. Dust with confectioners' sugar. Lifting with foil, remove from pan. Cut into bars. Refrigerate leftovers.

STRAWBERRY-LIME BARS

CRANBERRY
CLEMENTINE BARS

S'MORE BARS

S'MORE BARS

These yummy bars will elicit sweet campfire memories, whether they are served for dessert or as a snack.

—**LISA MORIARTY** WILTON, NH

PREP: 20 MIN.
BAKE: 25 MIN. + COOLING
MAKES: 1½ DOZEN

- ½ cup butter, softened
- ¾ cup sugar
- 1 large egg
- 1 teaspoon vanilla extract
- 1⅓ cups all-purpose flour
- ¾ cup graham cracker crumbs
- 1 teaspoon baking powder
- ⅛ teaspoon salt
- 5 milk chocolate candy bars (1.55 ounces each)
- 1 cup marshmallow creme

1. In a large bowl, cream butter and sugar until light and fluffy. Beat in egg and vanilla. Combine the flour, graham cracker crumbs, baking powder and salt; gradually add to creamed mixture. Set aside ½ cup for topping.

2. Press remaining mixture into a greased 9-in. square baking pan. Place candy bars over crust; spread with marshmallow creme. Crumble remaining graham cracker mixture over top.

3. Bake at 350° for 25-30 minutes or until golden brown. Cool on a wire rack. Cut into bars. Store in an airtight container.

TOP TIP

MARSHMALLOW CREME

Marshmallow creme is easy to remove from a jar—just place the jar in a pan of very hot water first. Then, use a wooden spoon to scoop out the creme.

—**MARY F.** PORT ORANGE, FL

BIG BATCH

CHOCOLATE MINT BROWNIES

One of the best things about this recipe is that the brownies get even more tender and moist if you leave them in the refrigerator for a day or two. The problem at our house is that no one can leave them alone for that long!

—HELEN BAINES ELKTON, MD

PREP: 20 MIN.
BAKE: 30 MIN. + CHILLING
MAKES: 5-6 DOZEN

- ½ **cup butter, softened**
- 1 **cup sugar**
- 4 **large eggs**
- 1 **can (16 ounces) chocolate syrup**
- 1 **teaspoon vanilla extract**
- 1 **cup all-purpose flour**
- ½ **teaspoon salt**

FILLING

- ½ **cup butter, softened**
- 2 **cups confectioners' sugar**
- 1 **tablespoon water**
- ½ **teaspoon mint extract**
- 3 **drops green food coloring**

TOPPING

- 1 **package (10 ounces) mint chocolate chips**
- ½ **cup plus 1 tablespoon butter, cubed**

1. Preheat oven to 350°. In a large bowl, cream butter and sugar until light and fluffy. Add eggs, one at a time, beating well after each addition. Beat in syrup and vanilla. Add flour and salt; mix well.

2. Pour into a greased 13x9-in. baking pan. Bake 30 minutes (top of brownies will still appear wet). Cool on a wire rack.

3. For filling, in a small bowl, cream butter and confectioners' sugar; add water, extract and food coloring until blended. Spread over cooled brownies. Refrigerate until set.

4. For topping, melt chocolate chips and butter. Cool 30 minutes, stirring occasionally. Spread over filling. Chill. Cut into bars. Store in refrigerator.

NOTE *If mint chocolate chips are not available, place 2 cups (12 ounces) semisweet chocolate chips and ¼ teaspoon peppermint extract in a plastic bag; seal and toss to coat. Allow chips to stand for 24-48 hours.*

CHOCOLATE MINT BROWNIES

ALMOST A CANDY BAR

I love candy bars and marshmallows, so this recipe was a cinch to create. The bars make great individually wrapped treats for bake sales, picnics, lunch boxes or on-the-go snacking. And with all the different layers and flavors, there's a little something for everyone.

—BARB WYMAN HANKINSON, ND

PREP: 15 MIN.
BAKE: 15 MIN. + CHILLING
MAKES: 3 DOZEN

- 1 tube (16½ ounces) refrigerated chocolate chip cookie dough
- 4 chewy s'mores granola bars, chopped
- 1 package (10 to 11 ounces) butterscotch chips
- 2½ cups miniature marshmallows
- 1 cup chopped walnuts
- 1½ cups miniature pretzels
- 1 package (10 ounces) peanut butter chips
- ¾ cup light corn syrup
- ¼ cup butter, cubed
- 1 package (11½ ounces) milk chocolate chips

1. Preheat oven to 350°. Let dough stand at room temperature for 5-10 minutes to soften. In a large bowl, combine the dough and chopped granola bars. Press into an ungreased 13x9-in. baking pan. Bake, uncovered, 10-12 minutes or until golden brown.

2. Sprinkle with butterscotch chips and marshmallows. Bake 3-4 minutes longer or until marshmallows begin to brown. Sprinkle with walnuts; arrange pretzels over the top. In a small saucepan, melt the peanut butter chips, corn syrup and butter; spoon over bars.

3. In a microwave, melt chocolate chips; stir until smooth. Spread or drizzle over bars. Refrigerate 1 hour or until firm before cutting.

SHORTBREAD LEMON BARS

I've put together two family cookbooks over the years, and this recipe ranks among my favorites. The special lemon bars have a yummy shortbread crust and a refreshing flavor.

—MARGARET PETERSON FOREST CITY, IA

PREP: 25 MIN.
BAKE: 15 MIN. + CHILLING
MAKES: 3 DOZEN

- 1½ cups all-purpose flour
- ½ cup confectioners' sugar
- 1 teaspoon grated lemon peel
- 1 teaspoon grated orange peel
- ¾ cup cold butter, cubed

FILLING
- 4 large eggs
- 2 cups sugar
- ⅓ cup lemon juice
- ¼ cup all-purpose flour
- 2 teaspoons grated lemon peel
- 2 teaspoons grated orange peel
- 1 teaspoon baking powder

TOPPING
- 2 cups (16 ounces) sour cream
- ⅓ cup sugar
- ½ teaspoon vanilla extract

1. In a food processor, combine the flour, confectioners' sugar, and lemon and orange peel. Add butter; cover and process until mixture forms a ball.

2. Pat into a greased 13x9-in. baking pan. Bake at 350° for 12-14 minutes or until set and the edges are lightly browned.

3. In a large bowl, combine all the filling ingredients. Pour over hot crust. Bake for 14-16 minutes or until set and lightly browned.

4. In a small bowl, combine the topping ingredients. Spread over filling.

5. Bake 7-9 minutes longer or until topping is set. Cool on a wire rack. Refrigerate overnight. Cut into bars just before serving. Store in the refrigerator.

SHORTBREAD LEMON BARS

WINNING APRICOT BARS

WINNING APRICOT BARS

This recipe is down-home baking at its best. It has won blue ribbons at county fairs and cookie contests in several states!

—JILL MORITZ IRVINE, CA

PREP: 15 MIN.
BAKE: 30 MIN. + COOLING
MAKES: 2 DOZEN

- ¾ cup butter, softened
- 1 cup sugar
- 1 large egg
- ½ teaspoon vanilla extract
- 2 cups all-purpose flour
- ¼ teaspoon baking powder
- 1⅓ cups flaked coconut
- ½ cup chopped walnuts
- 1 jar (10 to 12 ounces) apricot preserves

1. Preheat oven to 350°. In a large bowl, cream butter and sugar until light and fluffy. Beat in egg and vanilla. In a small bowl, whisk flour and baking powder; gradually add to creamed mixture, mixing well. Fold in coconut and walnuts.
2. Press two-thirds of dough onto the bottom of a greased 13x9-in. baking pan. Spread with preserves; crumble remaining dough over preserves. Bake 30-35 minutes or until golden brown. Cool completely in pan on a wire rack. Cut into bars.

TOP TIP

REFRESH FLAKED COCONUT

It's easy to make frozen or dried-out flaked coconut fresh again. Simply place the amount you need in a bowl, and sprinkle it with a few drops of water. Cover and microwave until warm.

—SANDRA S. GAINESVILLE, FL

BIG BATCH
CARAMEL HEAVENLIES

My mom made these goodies for cookie exchanges when I was little, and she let me sprinkle on the almonds and coconut. They're easy to fix and they make a big batch, so they're perfect when you're crunched for time during the holidays.

—DAWN BURNS LAKE ST. LOUIS, MO

PREP: 20 MIN.
BAKE: 15 MIN. + COOLING
MAKES: ABOUT 6 DOZEN

- 12 whole graham crackers
- 2 cups miniature marshmallows
- ¾ cup butter, cubed
- ¾ cup packed brown sugar
- 1 teaspoon ground cinnamon
- 1 teaspoon vanilla extract
- 1 cup sliced almonds
- 1 cup flaked coconut

1. Preheat oven to 350°. Line a 15x10x1-in. baking pan with foil, letting foil extend over sides by 1 in.; lightly coat foil with cooking spray. Arrange graham crackers in prepared pan; sprinkle with marshmallows.
2. In a small saucepan, combine butter, brown sugar and cinnamon; cook and stir over medium heat until butter is melted and sugar is dissolved. Remove from heat; stir in vanilla.
3. Spoon butter mixture over marshmallows. Sprinkle with almonds and coconut. Bake 14-16 minutes or until browned. Cool completely in pan on a wire rack.
4. Using foil, lift cookies out of pan. Cut into triangles; discard foil.

CARAMEL HEAVENLIES

COCONUT CITRUS BARS

Sweet oranges are the secret to my amazing bars with loads of orange flavor in every bite. The crunchy crust and triple-citrus zing make them stand apart from traditional lemon bars.

—HEATHER ROTUNDA ST. CLOUD, MN

PREP: 30 MIN.
BAKE: 20 MIN. + COOLING
MAKES: 2 DOZEN

¾ cup butter, softened
⅓ cup confectioners' sugar
1½ cups all-purpose flour
½ cup crisp rice cereal

FILLING

4 large eggs
1½ cups sugar
1 cup flaked coconut
⅓ cup orange juice
¼ cup lemon juice
2 tablespoons lime juice
2 tablespoons all-purpose flour
3 teaspoons grated orange peel
2 teaspoons grated lemon peel
1½ teaspoons grated lime peel
Confectioners' sugar

1. Preheat oven to 350°. In a small bowl, cream softened butter and confectioners' sugar until light and fluffy; gradually beat in flour until crumbly. Stir in cereal. Press into a greased 13x9-in. baking pan. Bake 18-22 minutes or until lightly browned.
2. Meanwhile, in a large bowl, beat eggs, sugar, coconut, juices, flour and peels until frothy. Pour over hot crust. Bake 18-22 minutes longer or until lightly browned. Cool on a wire rack. Dust with confectioners' sugar; cut into bars. Store in the refrigerator.

RASPBERRY COCONUT BARS

I've been layering these delicious bars for years, and now my young daughter joins me in the fun. We bake them every Christmas and have received many compliments and recipe requests. The chocolate drizzle adds a pretty touch.

—BARB BOVBERG FORT COLLINS, CO

PREP: 20 MIN.
BAKE: 20 MIN. + CHILLING
MAKES: 3 DOZEN

1⅔ cups graham cracker crumbs
½ cup butter, melted
2⅔ cups flaked coconut
1 can (14 ounces) sweetened condensed milk
1 cup seedless raspberry preserves
⅓ cup chopped walnuts, toasted
½ cup semisweet chocolate chips
¼ cup white baking chips

1. In a small bowl, combine cracker crumbs and butter. Press into a 13x9-in. baking dish coated with cooking spray. Sprinkle with coconut; drizzle with milk.
2. Bake at 350° for 20-25 minutes or until lightly browned. Cool completely on a wire rack.
3. Spread preserves over crust. Sprinkle with walnuts. In a microwave, melt chocolate chips; stir until smooth. Drizzle over walnuts. Repeat with white chips. Cut into bars. Refrigerate for 30 minutes or until chocolate is set.

HONEY-PECAN SQUARES

When we left Texas to move north, a neighbor gave me so many pecans from his trees that the trunk of my car was bulging at the seams. So I brought these treats for him when we went back to visit. He loved them!

—LORRAINE CALAND SHUNIAH, ON

PREP: 15 MIN. • **BAKE:** 30 MIN.
MAKES: 2 DOZEN

1 cup unsalted butter, softened
¾ cup packed dark brown sugar
½ teaspoon salt
3 cups all-purpose flour

FILLING

½ cup unsalted butter, cubed
½ cup packed dark brown sugar
⅓ cup honey
2 tablespoons sugar
2 tablespoons heavy whipping cream
¼ teaspoon salt
2 cups chopped pecans, toasted
½ teaspoon maple flavoring or vanilla extract

1. Preheat oven to 350°. Line a 13x9-in. baking pan with parchment paper, letting ends extend up sides of pan. In a large bowl, cream the butter, brown sugar and salt until light and fluffy. Gradually beat in flour. Press onto bottom of prepared pan. Bake 16-20 minutes or until lightly browned.
2. In a small saucepan, combine the first six filling ingredients; bring to a boil. Cook 1 minute. Remove from the heat; stir in pecans and maple flavoring. Pour over crust.
3. Bake 10-15 minutes or until bubbly. Cool in pan on a wire rack. Lifting with parchment paper, transfer to a cutting board; cut into bars.
NOTE *To toast nuts, bake in a shallow pan in a 350° oven for 5-10 minutes or cook in a skillet over low heat until lightly browned, stirring occasionally.*

COCONUT
CITRUS BARS

RASPBERRY
COCONUT BARS

HONEY-PECAN SQUARES

RASPBERRY PATCH
CRUMB BARS

RASPBERRY PATCH CRUMB BARS

Add a sprinkle of nuts to the yummy crumb topping to give these fresh and fruity bars even more crunch. Everyone will want to indulge.

—LEANNA THORNE LAKEWOOD, CO

PREP: 30 MIN.
BAKE: 35 MIN. + COOLING
MAKES: 3 DOZEN

- 3 cups all-purpose flour
- 1½ cups sugar, divided
- 1 teaspoon baking powder
- ¼ teaspoon salt
- ¼ teaspoon ground cinnamon
- 1 cup shortening
- 2 large eggs, lightly beaten
- 1 teaspoon almond extract
- 1 tablespoon cornstarch
- 4 cups fresh or frozen raspberries

1. In a large bowl, combine the flour, 1 cup sugar, baking powder, salt and cinnamon. Cut in the shortening until mixture resembles coarse crumbs. Stir in eggs and extract. Press two-thirds of the mixture into a greased 13x9-in. baking dish.
2. In a large bowl, combine the cornstarch and remaining sugar; add berries and gently toss. Spoon over crust. Sprinkle with remaining crumb mixture.
3. Bake at 375° for 35-45 minutes or until bubbly and golden brown. Cool on a wire rack. Cut into bars. Store in the refrigerator.
NOTE *If using frozen raspberries, do not thaw before tossing with cornstarch mixture.*

BIG BATCH
WINNING CRANBERRY DATE BARS

I enjoy making these when the cranberry season arrives. The recipe is a cinch, which is perfect for busy parents like me.

—RICHARD GRAMS LACROSSE, WI

PREP: 20 MIN.
BAKE: 30 MIN. + COOLING
MAKES: 4 DOZEN

- 1 package (12 ounces) fresh or frozen cranberries
- 1 package (8 ounces) chopped dates
- 1 teaspoon vanilla extract
- 2 cups all-purpose flour
- 2 cups quick-cooking oats
- 1½ cups packed brown sugar
- ½ teaspoon baking soda
- ¼ teaspoon salt
- 1 cup butter, melted

ORANGE GLAZE
- 2 cups confectioners' sugar
- 2 to 3 tablespoons orange juice
- ½ teaspoon vanilla extract

1. In a large saucepan, combine cranberries and dates. Cover and cook over low heat for 15 minutes or until berries pop, stirring often. Remove from the heat and stir in vanilla; set aside.
2. In a large bowl, combine the flour, oats, brown sugar, baking soda and salt. Stir in the melted butter until crumbly. Press half into an ungreased 13x9-in. baking pan. Bake at 350° for 8 minutes. Spoon cranberry mixture over the crust; spread gently. Sprinkle with remaining crumb mixture; pat down gently.
3. Bake at 350° for 20-25 minutes or until golden brown. Cool on a wire rack. Combine the glaze ingredients; drizzle over bars.

PECAN DREAM BARS

These ooey-gooey cake bars are a baker's dream come true. They pull ever so gently from the pan and hold a firm cut. Best of all, they taste delicious!

—CAY KEPPERS NISSWA, MN

PREP: 15 MIN.
BAKE: 20 MIN. + COOLING
MAKES: 2 DOZEN

- 1 package yellow cake mix (regular size)
- ½ cup butter, softened
- 1 large egg
FILLING
- 1 can (14 ounces) sweetened condensed milk
- 1 large egg
- 1 teaspoon vanilla extract
- 1 cup chopped pecans
- ½ cup brickle toffee bits

1. Preheat oven to 350°. In a large bowl, beat cake mix, butter and egg until crumbly. Press mixture onto the bottom of a greased 13x9-in. baking pan.
2. In a small bowl, beat milk, egg and vanilla until combined. Stir in pecans and toffee bits. Pour over crust.
3. Bake 20-25 minutes or until golden brown. Cool on a wire rack. Cut into bars.

DID YOU KNOW?

SWEETENED CONDENSED MILK

Sweetened condensed milk is made with cow's milk. Water is removed and sugar is added to yield a thick, sweet liquid that's conveniently packaged in a can. It's used most often in candy and dessert recipes.

COOKIE DOUGH BROWNIES

When I take these rich brownies to a get-together, I carry the recipe, too, because I always get requests for it. Children of all ages love the tempting "cookie dough" filling, so these brownies never sit on the buffet table for long!
—**WENDY BAILEY** ELIDA, OH

PREP: 20 MIN. + CHILLING
BAKE: 30 MIN. + COOLING
MAKES: 3 DOZEN

- 4 large eggs
- 1 cup canola oil
- 2 cups sugar
- 2 teaspoons vanilla extract
- 1½ cups all-purpose flour
- ½ cup baking cocoa
- ½ teaspoon salt
- ½ cup chopped walnuts, optional

FILLING

- ½ cup butter, softened
- ½ cup packed brown sugar
- ¼ cup sugar
- 2 tablespoons 2% milk
- 1 teaspoon vanilla extract
- 1 cup all-purpose flour

GLAZE

- 1 cup (6 ounces) semisweet chocolate chips
- 1 tablespoon shortening
- ¾ cup chopped walnuts

1. Preheat oven to 350°. In a large bowl, beat eggs, oil, sugar and vanilla until well blended. Combine flour, cocoa and salt; gradually beat into egg mixture. Stir in walnuts if desired.

2. Pour into a greased 13x9-in. baking pan. Bake 30 minutes or until a toothpick inserted in center comes out with moist crumbs. Cool completely.

3. For filling, in a large bowl, cream butter and sugars until light and fluffy. Beat in milk and vanilla. Gradually beat in flour. Spread over brownies; chill until firm.

4. For glaze, in a microwave, melt chocolate chips and shortening; stir until smooth. Spread over filling. Immediately sprinkle with nuts, pressing down slightly. Let stand until set.

ZUCCHINI DESSERT SQUARES

We planted one too many zucchini plants a few summers ago and harvested a lot of zucchinis that year. I needed tasty ways to use them all up. This delicious dessert is one of my favorite creations.
—**NANCY MORELLI** LIVONIA, MI

PREP: 30 MIN. • **BAKE:** 40 MIN.
MAKES: 16-20 SERVINGS

- 4 cups all-purpose flour
- 2 cups sugar
- ½ teaspoon ground cinnamon
- ½ teaspoon salt
- 1½ cups cold butter

FILLING

- 8 to 10 cups cubed seeded peeled zucchini (4 to 5 pounds)
- ⅔ cup lemon juice
- 1 cup sugar
- 1 teaspoon ground cinnamon
- ½ teaspoon ground nutmeg

1. In a large bowl, combine the flour, sugar, cinnamon and salt. Cut in butter until crumbly; reserve 3 cups. Pat remaining crumb mixture into a greased 13x9-in. baking pan. Bake at 375° for 12 minutes.

2. Meanwhile, for filling, place zucchini and lemon juice in a large saucepan; bring to a boil. Reduce heat; cover and cook for 6-8 minutes or until zucchini is crisp-tender. Stir in the sugar, cinnamon and nutmeg; cover and simmer for 5 minutes (mixture will be thin).

3. Spoon over crust; sprinkle with the reserved crumb mixture. Bake at 375° for 40-45 minutes or until golden.

COOKIE DOUGH BROWNIES

ZUCCHINI DESSERT
SQUARES

**COCONUT-PINEAPPLE
RHUBARB BARS**

COCONUT-PINEAPPLE RHUBARB BARS

I make this crunchy, buttery dessert bar with homegrown rhubarb. It's great served warm with a scoop of frozen yogurt or ice cream.

—RAYMONDE BOURGEOIS
SWASTIKA, ON

PREP: 25 MIN.
BAKE: 40 MIN. + COOLING
MAKES: 2 DOZEN

- 3 **cups chopped fresh or frozen rhubarb (about ¾ pound)**
- 1 **cup coarsely chopped fresh pineapple**
- ½ **cup packed brown sugar**
- 4 **tablespoons water, divided**
- 1 **teaspoon lemon juice**
- 2 **tablespoons cornstarch**
- ½ **teaspoon coconut extract, optional**

CRUST AND TOPPING

- 2 **cups old-fashioned oats**
- 1½ **cups all-purpose flour**
- 1 **cup flaked coconut**
- ½ **cup packed brown sugar**
- ½ **teaspoon salt**
- 1 **cup butter, melted**

1. Preheat oven to 350°. In a large saucepan, combine the rhubarb, pineapple, brown sugar, 1 tablespoon water and lemon juice; bring to a boil. Reduce heat; simmer, uncovered, 4-5 minutes or until rhubarb is tender.
2. In a small bowl, mix cornstarch and remaining water until smooth; stir into rhubarb mixture. Return to a boil; cook and stir 1-2 minutes or until thickened. Remove from heat; if desired, stir in extract.
3. In a large bowl, mix oats, flour, coconut, brown sugar and salt; stir in melted butter until crumbly. Press 3 cups crumb mixture onto bottom of a greased 13x9-in. baking dish. Spread with rhubarb mixture. Sprinkle with remaining crumb mixture.
4. Bake 40-45 minutes or until golden brown. Cool in pan on a wire rack. Cut into bars.

MAPLE-GLAZED CINNAMON CHIP BARS

Cinnamon chips and a maple glaze add fabulous flavor. When I make these, the kitchen smells just like Christmas. The glaze fancies them up a bit.

—**LYNDI PILCH** SPRINGFIELD, MO

PREP: 20 MIN. • **BAKE:** 20 MIN.
MAKES: 2 DOZEN

- 1 **cup butter, softened**
- 2 **cups packed brown sugar**
- 2 **large eggs**
- 2 **teaspoons vanilla extract**
- 2⅔ **cups all-purpose flour**
- 2 **teaspoons baking powder**
- 1 **teaspoon salt**
- ¾ **cup cinnamon baking chips**
- 1 **tablespoon cinnamon-sugar**

GLAZE
- ½ **cup confectioners' sugar**
- 3 **tablespoons maple syrup**
- ½ **teaspoon vanilla extract**

1. Preheat oven to 350°. In a large bowl, cream butter and brown sugar until well blended. Beat in eggs and vanilla. In another bowl, mix flour, baking powder and salt; gradually beat into creamed mixture. Stir in cinnamon chips.

2. Spread into a greased 13x9-in. baking pan. Sprinkle with the cinnamon-sugar. Bake for 20-25 minutes or until golden brown and a toothpick inserted in center comes out clean. Cool completely in pan on a wire rack.

3. In a small bowl, mix all glaze ingredients until smooth; drizzle over top. Cut into bars. Store in an airtight container.

MAPLE-GLAZED CINNAMON CHIP BARS

BUTTERY COCONUT BARS

My coconut bars are an American version of a Filipino coconut cake called *bibingka*. These are a crispier, sweeter take on the Christmas tradition I grew up with.
—**DENISE NYLAND** PANAMA CITY, FL

PREP: 20 MIN. + COOLING
BAKE: 40 MIN. + COOLING
MAKES: 3 DOZEN

- 2 cups all-purpose flour
- 1 cup packed brown sugar
- ½ teaspoon salt
- 1 cup butter, melted

FILLING

- 3 large eggs
- 1 can (14 ounces) sweetened condensed milk
- ½ cup all-purpose flour
- ¼ cup packed brown sugar
- ¼ cup butter, melted
- 3 teaspoons vanilla extract
- ½ teaspoon salt
- 4 cups flaked coconut, divided

1. Preheat oven to 350°. Line a 13x9-in. baking pan with parchment paper, letting ends extend up sides.
2. In a large bowl, mix flour, brown sugar and salt; stir in 1 cup melted butter. Press onto bottom of prepared pan. Bake 12-15 minutes or until light brown. Cool 10 minutes on a wire rack. Reduce oven setting to 325°.
3. In a large bowl, whisk the first seven filling ingredients until blended; stir in 3 cups coconut. Pour over crust; sprinkle with remaining coconut. Bake 25-30 minutes or until light golden brown. Cool in pan on a wire rack. Lifting with parchment paper, remove from pan. Cut into bars.

MILLION DOLLAR PECAN BARS

Invest 15 minutes of your time and enjoy a big payoff when you pull these rich bars of golden layered goodness from your oven.
—**LAURA DAVIS** RUSK, TX

PREP: 15 MIN. • **BAKE:** 20 MIN.
MAKES: 2 DOZEN

- ¾ cup butter, softened
- ¾ cup packed brown sugar
- 2 large eggs
- 2 teaspoons vanilla extract
- 1 package butter pecan cake mix (regular size)
- 2½ cups quick-cooking oats

FILLING

- 1 can (14 ounces) sweetened condensed milk
- 2 cups milk chocolate chips
- 1 cup butterscotch chips
- 1 tablespoon butter
- 1 teaspoon vanilla extract
- 1½ cups chopped pecans

1. In a large bowl, cream butter and brown sugar until light and fluffy. Add eggs, one at a time, beating well after each addition. Beat in vanilla. Add cake mix just until blended. Stir in oats. Press 3 cups onto the bottom of a greased 13x9-in. baking pan.
2. In a large microwave-safe bowl, combine milk and chips. Microwave, uncovered, on high for 2 minutes; stir. Cook 1-2½ minutes longer or until chips are melted, stirring every 30 seconds. Stir in butter and vanilla until melted. Stir in pecans. Spread over crust.
3. Crumble remaining oat mixture; sprinkle over top. Bake at 350° for 20-25 minutes or until topping is golden brown. Cool on a wire rack. Cut into bars.

GOOEY BUTTERSCOTCH BARS

These bars are a butterscotch lover's dream. Try my recipe or have fun experimenting with different flavors of pudding, chips and cookie mix. So many possibilities!
—**CAROL BREWER** FAIRBORN, OH

PREP: 20 MIN.
BAKE: 20 MIN. + COOLING
MAKES: ABOUT 3 DOZEN

- 1 package (17½ ounces) sugar cookie mix
- 1 package (3.4 ounces) instant butterscotch pudding mix
- ½ cup butter, softened
- 1 large egg
- 1 package (14 ounces) caramels
- ½ cup evaporated milk
- 2 cups mixed nuts
- 1 teaspoon vanilla extract
- 1 cup butterscotch chips

1. In a large bowl, combine the sugar cookie mix, pudding mix, butter and egg. Press into an ungreased 13x9-in. baking pan. Bake at 350° for 20-25 minutes or until set.
2. In a large saucepan, combine caramels and milk. Cook and stir over medium-low heat until melted. Remove from the heat. Stir in nuts and vanilla. Pour over crust. Sprinkle with butterscotch chips.
3. Cool completely. Cut into bars. Store in an airtight container.

TOP TIP

BUTTERSCOTCH FLAVOR ENHANCER
Whenever I make anything with butterscotch, I replace the vanilla extract (if called for) with almond extract to take the flavor up a notch.
—**DANA W.** LADYSMITH, WI

BUTTERY COCONUT BARS

MILLION DOLLAR PECAN BARS

GOOEY BUTTERSCOTCH BARS

FROSTED BANANA BARS

FROSTED BANANA BARS

These bars are always a hit at potlucks in the small rural farming community where my husband and I live. I also serve them at coffee hour after church. They're so moist and delicious that wherever I take them, they don't last long.

—**KAREN DRYAK** NIOBRARA, NE

PREP: 15 MIN.
BAKE: 20 MIN. + COOLING
MAKES: 3 DOZEN

- ½ cup butter, softened
- 2 cups sugar
- 3 large eggs
- 1½ cups mashed ripe bananas (about 3 medium)
- 1 teaspoon vanilla extract
- 2 cups all-purpose flour
- 1 teaspoon baking soda
  Dash salt

FROSTING

- 1 package (8 ounces) cream cheese, softened
- ½ cup butter, softened
- 4 cups confectioners' sugar
- 2 teaspoons vanilla extract

1. In a large bowl, cream butter and sugar until light and fluffy. Beat in the eggs, bananas and vanilla. Combine the flour, baking soda and salt; stir into creamed mixture just until blended.

2. Transfer mixture to a greased 15x10x1-in. baking pan. Bake at 350° for 20-25 minutes or until a toothpick inserted near the center comes out clean. Cool in pan on a wire rack.

3. For frosting, in a small bowl, beat cream cheese and butter until fluffy. Add confectioners' sugar and vanilla; beat until smooth. Frost bars.

CHERRY COCONUT TREATS

My great-grandmother created this recipe more than 100 years ago, so it's made many appearances at family parties. Make the treats even more fun for the holidays by using both red and green maraschino cherries.

—**ANNE MULLEN** WINDSOR, ON

PREP: 15 MIN.
BAKE: 35 MIN. + CHILLING
MAKES: 2 DOZEN

- 1½ cups all-purpose flour
- 1 cup graham cracker crumbs
- ⅔ cup packed brown sugar
- 1 teaspoon baking powder
- ½ teaspoon salt
- 1 cup butter, melted

FILLING

- 4 cups finely shredded unsweetened coconut
- 2 cans (14 ounces each) sweetened condensed milk
- 2 jars (10 ounces each) maraschino cherries, drained and chopped
- 2 teaspoons vanilla extract
- 1 teaspoon almond extract

1. Preheat oven to 325°. In a small bowl, mix the first five ingredients; stir in melted butter. Press onto bottom of a greased 13x9-in. baking pan.

2. In another bowl, mix filling ingredients; pour over crust. Bake 35-40 minutes or until edges are lightly browned. Cool on a wire rack 1 hour. Refrigerate, covered, 4 hours before cutting. Store in an airtight container in the refrigerator.

NOTE *Look for unsweetened coconut in the baking or health food section.*

CHERRY COCONUT TREATS

CHOCOLATE TOFFEE DELIGHTS

I combined my favorite shortbread recipe with some ingredients I had on hand, and these wonderful bars were the result. They remind me of my favorite Girl Scout cookie.

—SHANNON KOENE BLACKSBURG, VA

PREP: 15 MIN.
BAKE: 30 MIN. + COOLING
MAKES: 3 DOZEN

- 1 **cup butter, softened**
- ½ **cup plus 2 tablespoons sugar, divided**

- ¾ **teaspoon almond extract**
- ½ **teaspoon coconut extract**
- 2 **cups all-purpose flour**
- ¼ **teaspoon salt**
- ¼ **teaspoon baking powder**
- ½ **cup flaked coconut**
- ½ **cup sliced almonds, toasted and cooled**
- 1 **jar (12¼ ounces) caramel ice cream topping**
- ¾ **cup dark chocolate chips**

1. Preheat oven to 350°. In a small bowl, cream butter and ½ cup sugar until light and fluffy. Beat in extracts. Combine flour, salt and baking powder; gradually add to creamed mixture and mix well.

2. Press into a greased 13x9-in. baking pan. Bake 10 minutes. Prick crust with a fork; sprinkle with remaining sugar. Bake 15 minutes longer or until set.

3. Meanwhile, place coconut and almonds in a food processor; cover and process until finely chopped. Transfer to a small bowl; stir in ice cream topping. Spread over crust. Bake 5-10 minutes or until edges are bubbly. Cool on a wire rack.

4. In a microwave, melt chocolate chips; stir until smooth. Drizzle over caramel mixture. Let stand until chocolate is set. Cut into bars. Store in an airtight container.

CHOCOLATE TOFFEE DELIGHTS

HUMBLE BUMBLE CRUMBLE BARS

I needed a yummy treat for my bingo group. I asked my hubby for ideas, and he suggested a fruit bar. These berry-topped bars are slightly sweet and easy to make.

—NANCY PHILLIPS PORTLAND, ME

PREP: 30 MIN.
BAKE: 45 MIN. + COOLING
MAKES: 15 SERVINGS

- ½ cup butter, softened
- ¾ cup sugar
- 1 large egg
- 2½ cups all-purpose flour
- ½ teaspoon baking powder
- ¼ teaspoon salt
- ¼ cup packed brown sugar
- 1 teaspoon ground cinnamon

FILLING

- 2 cups chunky applesauce
- ½ teaspoon ground cinnamon
- ⅛ teaspoon ground nutmeg
- 2 cups fresh blackberries
- 2 cups fresh raspberries

1. Preheat oven to 350°. In a large bowl, cream butter and sugar until light and fluffy. Beat in egg. In another bowl, whisk flour, baking powder and salt; gradually beat into creamed mixture. Reserve ½ cup crumb mixture for topping. Press remaining mixture onto bottom of a greased 13x9-in. baking pan. Bake 12-15 minutes or until lightly browned. Cool on a wire rack.

2. Stir brown sugar and cinnamon into reserved topping; set aside. In a large bowl, combine the applesauce, cinnamon and nutmeg until blended. Spread over crust; top with berries and reserved topping. Bake 30-35 minutes or until golden brown. Cool in pan on a wire rack. Cut into bars.

HUMBLE BUMBLE CRUMBLE BARS

FUDGY S'MORES
BROWNIES, PAGE 61

Chocolate Sensations

Surrender to your deepest chocolate craving with these treats. They're a chocolate lover's dream come true!

LUSCIOUS FUDGY BROWNIES

I'm always especially careful not to overbake this favorite after-dinner treat because I love the ooey-gooey middle in these brownies.

—KRISTA FRANK
RHODODENDRON, OR

PREP: 15 MIN.
BAKE: 20 MIN. + COOLING
MAKES: 16 BROWNIES

- 1 **cup sugar**
- 3 **tablespoons butter, melted**
- 3 **tablespoons reduced-fat vanilla yogurt**
- 1 **teaspoon vanilla extract**
- 1 **large egg, lightly beaten**
- ¾ **cup all-purpose flour**
- ⅓ **cup baking cocoa**
- ⅛ **teaspoon salt**

1. In a small bowl, combine the sugar, butter, yogurt and vanilla. Stir in egg until blended. Combine the flour, cocoa and salt; stir into the sugar mixture. Transfer to an 8-in. square baking dish coated with cooking spray.
2. Bake at 350° for 20-25 minutes or until a toothpick inserted in the center comes out clean and brownies begin to pull away from sides of pan. Cool on a wire rack. Cut into eight pieces, then cut each diagonally in half.

BEST FUDGY BROWNIES

I love to bake treats like these delish brownies to share with my friends and co-workers. I grew up on a farm, and I helped my mother make yummy desserts like this—and meals, too—for our family of eight.

—JUDY CUNNINGHAM MAX, ND

PREP: 15 MIN.
BAKE: 25 MIN. + COOLING
MAKES: 2½ DOZEN

- 1⅓ **cups butter, softened**
- 2⅔ **cups sugar**
- 4 **large eggs**
- 3 **teaspoons vanilla extract**
- 2 **cups all-purpose flour**

- 1 **cup baking cocoa**
- ½ **teaspoon salt**
  Confectioners' sugar, optional

1. In a large bowl, cream butter and sugar until light and fluffy. Beat in eggs and vanilla. Combine the flour, cocoa and salt; gradually add to the creamed mixture.
2. Spread into a greased 13x9-in. baking pan. Bake at 350° for 25-30 minutes or until the top is dry and the center is set. Cool completely. Dust brownies with confectioners' sugar if desired.

LAYERED PEANUT BUTTER BROWNIES

The classic combo of chocolate and peanut butter makes these crowd-pleasing brownies stand out. They even won a ribbon at a local fair. You'll love them, too!

—MARGARET MCNEIL
GERMANTOWN, TN

PREP: 15 MIN.
BAKE: 35 MIN. + COOLING
MAKES: 3 DOZEN

- 3 **large eggs**
- 1 **cup butter, melted**
- 2 **teaspoons vanilla extract**
- 2 **cups sugar**
- 1¼ **cups all-purpose flour**
- ¾ **cup baking cocoa**
- ½ **teaspoon baking powder**
- ¼ **teaspoon salt**
- 1 **cup milk chocolate chips**

FILLING

- 16 **ounces cream cheese, softened**
- ½ **cup creamy peanut butter**
- ¼ **cup sugar**
- 1 **large egg**
- 2 **tablespoons 2% milk**

1. In a large bowl, beat the eggs, butter and vanilla until smooth. Combine the dry ingredients; gradually add to egg mixture. Stir in the chocolate chips. Set aside 1 cup for the topping. Spread the

remaining batter into a greased 13x9-in. baking pan.
2. In a small bowl, beat the cream cheese, peanut butter and sugar until smooth. Beat in egg and milk on low just until combined. Carefully spread over batter. Drop reserved batter by tablespoonfuls over filling. Cut through batter with a knife to swirl.
3. Bake at 350° for 35-40 minutes or until a toothpick inserted in the center comes out clean (do not overbake). Cool on a wire rack. Chill until serving.
NOTE *Reduced-fat peanut butter is not recommended for this recipe.*

⑤ INGREDIENTS *BIG BATCH*

DOUBLE CHOCOLATE BARS

A few years ago, a friend brought over some fudgy bars to tempt me with yet another chocolate treat. They're simple to make, and clean up is a breeze. The bars are rich so a small piece will satisfy.

—NANCY CLARK ZEIGLER, IL

START TO FINISH: 25 MIN. + COOLING
MAKES: ABOUT 4 DOZEN

- 1 **package (15½ ounces) Oreo cookies, crushed**
- ¾ **cup butter, melted**
- 1 **can (14 ounces) sweetened condensed milk**
- 2 **cups (12 ounces) miniature semisweet chocolate chips, divided**

1. Combine cookie crumbs and butter; pat onto the bottom of an ungreased 13x9-in. baking pan.
2. In a microwave, heat milk and 1 cup of chocolate chips; stir until smooth. Pour over crust. Sprinkle with remaining chips.
3. Bake at 350° for 10-12 minutes or until chips begin to melt but do not lose their shape. Cool on a wire rack.

LUSCIOUS FUDGY BROWNIES

BEST FUDGY BROWNIES

LAYERED PEANUT BUTTER BROWNIES

MERINGUE-TOPPED
CHOCOLATE BARS

MERINGUE-TOPPED CHOCOLATE BARS

I was first introduced to this tasty treat at a friend's house in 1956. Since then I have made these bars too many times to count! The secret to neatly slicing the bars is using a hot, wet knife.

—ALICE MCMASTERS OXFORD, FL

PREP: 20 MIN.
BAKE: 15 MIN. + COOLING
MAKES: 8 SERVINGS

- ⅔ cup milk chocolate chips
- 1 teaspoon plus 3 tablespoons shortening, divided
- 2 tablespoons sugar
- 2 tablespoons plus ⅓ cup packed brown sugar, divided
- 1 large egg, separated
- ½ teaspoon vanilla extract
- ½ cup all-purpose flour
- ¼ teaspoon baking powder
  Dash salt

1. In a microwave, melt milk chocolate chips and 1 teaspoon shortening; stir until smooth. Set aside. In a small bowl, cream sugar, 2 tablespoons brown sugar and remaining shortening until light and fluffy. Beat in egg yolk and vanilla. Combine the flour, baking powder and salt; gradually add to creamed mixture and mix well. Spread into an ungreased 9x5-in. loaf pan. Spread chocolate evenly over crust.
2. In a small bowl, beat egg white on medium speed until soft peaks form. Gradually beat in remaining brown sugar, 1 tablespoon at a time, beating on high until stiff glossy peaks form and sugar is dissolved, about 6 minutes.
3. Carefully spread meringue over chocolate layer. Bake at 350° for 15-18 minutes or until top is dry. Cool on a wire rack. Cut into bars; refrigerate leftovers.

BIG BATCH
FUDGE-FILLED BROWNIE BARS

I make sure to always have on hand the ingredients I need to whip up these soft chewy bars whenever the craving calls. They've been a hit at many potlucks, and someone always asks for the recipe.

—NOLA BURSKI LAKEVILLE, MN

PREP: 10 MIN.
BAKE: 30 MIN. + COOLING
MAKES: 4 DOZEN

- 1½ cups all-purpose flour
- ¾ cup packed brown sugar
- ¾ cup butter, softened
- 1 large egg yolk
- ¾ teaspoon vanilla extract

FILLING
- 1 package fudge brownie mix (13x9-inch pan size)
- 1 large egg
- ⅓ cup water
- ⅓ cup canola oil

TOPPING
- 1 package (11½ ounces) milk chocolate chips, melted
- ¾ cup chopped walnuts, toasted

1. In a large bowl, combine the first five ingredients. Press onto the bottom of a greased 15x10x1-in. baking pan. Bake at 350° for 15-18 minutes or until golden brown.
2. Meanwhile, in a large bowl, combine the filling ingredients. Spread over hot crust. Bake for 15 minutes or until set. Cool on a wire rack for 30 minutes.
3. Spread melted chocolate over filling; sprinkle with walnuts. Cool completely. Cut into bars.

CHOCOLATE-DIPPED BROWNIES

My family calls these bars "the world's chocolatiest brownies," and they are more than happy to gobble up a batch whenever I make them. They're a deliciously jolly part of our Christmas cookie collection, too.

—JACKIE ARCHER CLINTON, IA

PREP: 30 MIN. + FREEZING
BAKE: 35 MIN. + COOLING
MAKES: 3 DOZEN

- ¾ cup sugar
- ⅓ cup butter, cubed
- 2 tablespoons water
- 4 cups (24 ounces) semisweet chocolate chips, divided
- 1 teaspoon vanilla extract
- 2 large eggs
- ¾ cup all-purpose flour
- ½ teaspoon salt
- ¼ teaspoon baking soda
- 2 tablespoons shortening
  Chopped pecans, jimmies and/ or nonpareils, optional

1. In a large saucepan, bring the sugar, butter and water to a boil over medium heat. Remove from the heat; stir in 1 cup chocolate chips and vanilla until smooth. Cool for 5 minutes. Beat in eggs. Combine the flour, salt and baking soda; add to the chocolate mixture. Stir in 1 cup chocolate chips.

2. Pour into a greased 9-in. square baking pan. Bake the brownies at 325° for 35 minutes or until set. Cool completely on a wire rack.

3. Place in the freezer for 30-40 minutes or until firm (do not freeze completely). Cut into bars.

4. In a microwave-safe bowl, melt remaining chips and shortening; stir until smooth. Using a small fork, dip brownies to completely coat; allow excess to drip off. Place on waxed paper-lined baking sheets. Sprinkle with pecans, jimmies and/or nonpareils if desired. Let stand until set. Store in an airtight container.

ULTIMATE DOUBLE CHOCOLATE BROWNIES

I live in the city, but within just a block of my house, I can see cattle grazing in a grassy pasture. Growing up in the country I learned to appreciate nature and the simple life, and that inspired my love of down-home, made-from-scratch recipes like these brownies.

—CAROL PREWETT CHEYENNE, WY

PREP: 15 MIN. • **BAKE:** 35 MIN.
MAKES: 3 DOZEN

- ¾ cup baking cocoa
- ½ teaspoon baking soda
- ⅔ cup butter, melted, divided
- ½ cup boiling water
- 2 cups sugar
- 2 large eggs
- 1⅓ cups all-purpose flour
- 1 teaspoon vanilla extract
- ¼ teaspoon salt
- ½ cup coarsely chopped pecans
- 2 cups (12 ounces) semisweet chocolate chunks

1. Preheat oven to 350°. In a large bowl, combine cocoa and baking soda; blend in ⅓ cup of melted butter. Add boiling water; stir until well blended. Stir in the sugar, eggs and remaining butter. Add the flour, vanilla and salt. Stir in the pecans and chocolate chunks.

2. Pour into a greased 13x9-in. baking pan. Bake 35-40 minutes or until brownies begin to pull away from sides of pan. Cool.

CHOCOLATE-DIPPED BROWNIES

**ULTIMATE DOUBLE
CHOCOLATE BROWNIES**

GERMAN CHOCOLATE BROWNIES

GERMAN CHOCOLATE BROWNIES

As a young girl, I loved going through recipe books in search of something new to make. That's how I came across these brownies, which became a family favorite. They capture the rich flavor of traditional German chocolate cake with a few easy steps. Broiling the sweet coconut topping adds an extra layer of goodness.

—**KAREN GRIMES** STEPHENS CITY, VA

PREP: 20 MIN.
BAKE: 25 MIN. + COOLING
MAKES: 16 BROWNIES

- ½ cup butter, cubed
- 4 ounces German sweet chocolate, coarsely chopped
- 2 large eggs, lightly beaten
- ½ cup sugar
- 1 teaspoon vanilla extract
- 1 cup all-purpose flour
- ½ teaspoon baking powder
- ¼ teaspoon salt

TOPPING
- 2 tablespoons butter, melted
- ½ cup packed brown sugar
- 1 cup flaked coconut
- ½ cup chopped pecans
- 2 tablespoons corn syrup
- 2 tablespoons 2% milk

1. Preheat the oven to 350°. In a microwave, melt butter and chocolate; stir until smooth. Cool slightly. In a large bowl, beat eggs and sugar. Stir in the vanilla and chocolate mixture. Combine flour, baking powder and salt; gradually add to mixture.
2. Pour into a greased 9-in. square baking pan. Bake 18-22 minutes or until a toothpick inserted in the center comes out clean (do not overbake the brownies).
3. For the topping, combine butter and brown sugar in a large bowl. Add coconut, pecans, corn syrup and milk; mix well. Drop by teaspoonfuls onto warm brownies; spread evenly.
4. Broil 6 in. from heat 2-4 minutes or until top is browned and bubbly. Cool on a wire rack. Cut into bars.

CHOCOLATE TEMPTATION BROWNIES

Chocolate lovers will stand in line for these rich, three-layer squares that have a peanut butter filling and decadent glaze. They're heavenly!

—**IOLA EGLE** BELLA VISTA, AR

PREP: 20 MIN.
BAKE: 25 MIN. + CHILLING
MAKES: 3 DOZEN

- 1 **cup butter, cubed**
- 1 **ounce bittersweet chocolate, chopped**
- ¾ **cup sugar**
- ¾ **cup packed light brown sugar**
- 2 **teaspoons vanilla extract**
- 3 **large eggs**
- 1¼ **cups all-purpose flour**
- ¾ **teaspoon salt**
- 1 **cup chopped salted peanuts**

PEANUT BUTTER FILLING
- 12 **ounces cream cheese, softened**
- 1 **cup creamy peanut butter**
- 1 **cup confectioners' sugar**

CHOCOLATE GLAZE
- 8 **ounces bittersweet chocolate, finely chopped**
- ¼ **cup butter, cubed**
- ½ **cup heavy whipping cream**
- ½ **cup confectioners' sugar**

1. Preheat the oven to 350°. In a large saucepan, melt the butter and chocolate over medium heat. Remove from the heat; stir in sugars and vanilla. Add eggs, one at a time, stirring well after each addition. Combine flour and salt; stir into butter mixture just until combined. Stir in peanuts.

2. Transfer to a greased 13x9-in. baking pan. Bake 25-30 minutes or until a toothpick inserted in the center comes out clean. Cool completely on a wire rack.

3. In a small bowl, beat the cream cheese, peanut butter and confectioners' sugar until light and fluffy; spread over brownie layer. Chill until firm.

4. In a microwave, melt chocolate and butter with cream; stir until smooth. Stir in confectioners' sugar. Spread over peanut butter layer. Chill until firm.

CHOCOLATE
TEMPTATION BROWNIES

CRANBERRY-PORT FUDGE BROWNIES

Port wine adds a sophisticated flavor to this dessert. Maybe that's why my friend Krysta ranks these brownies among her favorites.

—KELLY HEFT SOMERSVILLE, MA

PREP: 25 MIN.
BAKE: 30 MIN. + COOLING
MAKES: 16 SERVINGS

- 4 ounces unsweetened chocolate, chopped
- ½ cup butter, cubed
- 1½ cups sugar
- ½ teaspoon vanilla extract
- 2 large eggs
- ¾ cup all-purpose flour
- ¼ teaspoon salt
- ½ cup dried cranberries
- ½ cup tawny port wine

1. In a small saucepan, melt the chocolate and butter; stir until smooth. Remove from the heat; stir in sugar and vanilla. Add eggs, one at a time, stirring well after each addition. Stir in flour and salt just until blended. In a another small saucepan, combine cranberries and wine. Bring to a boil over medium heat; cook until liquid is reduced to a thin syrupy consistency (about 3 minutes). Stir into batter.
2. Transfer to a greased 9-in. square baking pan. Bake at 325° for 30-35 minutes or until a toothpick inserted in the center comes out clean (do not overbake). Cool on a wire rack.

2 A.M. FEEDING SNACK BARS

I assured my friend that she didn't have to wait to try one of these scrumptious brownies until she got up in the middle of the night to feed the baby. But the chocolaty treats are a perfect pick-me-up any time, and not just for new parents short on sleep and energy.

—AME ANDREWS LITTLE ROCK, AR

PREP: 10 MIN.
BAKE: 25 MIN. + COOLING
MAKES: 2 DOZEN

- 1⅓ cups all-purpose flour
- 1¼ cups sugar
- ½ cup baking cocoa
- 1 teaspoon baking powder
- ½ teaspoon salt
- 4 large eggs, lightly beaten
- ¾ cup butter, melted
- ½ cup each milk chocolate chips, semisweet chocolate chips and vanilla or white chips
- 3 Snickers candy bars (2.07 ounces each), cut into ¼-inch pieces

1. In a large bowl, combine the flour, sugar, cocoa, baking powder and salt. In a small bowl, combine the eggs and butter; add to the dry ingredients and mix well. Stir in chocolate chips.
2. Transfer to a greased 13x9-in. baking pan. Bake at 350° for 25-30 minutes or until a toothpick inserted in the center comes out clean. Immediately sprinkle with candy bar pieces. Cool on a wire rack. Cut into bars.

⑤ INGREDIENTS
CHOCOLATE & PEANUT BUTTER CRISPY BARS

To make a dairy-free dessert, I created chocolate peanutty bars. My kids and their friends gobble them up, as I mention in my blog, *joyfulscribblings.com.*

—DAWN PASCO OVERLAND PARK, KS

PREP: 15 MIN.
BAKE: 25 MIN. + CHILLING
MAKES: 2 DOZEN

- 1 package fudge brownie mix (13x9-inch pan size)
- 1½ cups chunky peanut butter
- 2 cups (12 ounces) semisweet chocolate chips
- 1 cup creamy peanut butter
- 3 cups Rice Krispies

1. Line a 13x9-in. baking pan with parchment paper, letting the ends extend up sides. Prepare and bake brownie mix according to package directions, using the prepared pan. Cool the brownies on a wire rack for 30 minutes. Refrigerate until cold.
2. Spread chunky peanut butter over brownies. Place the chocolate chips and creamy peanut butter in a large microwave-safe bowl. Microwave in 30-second intervals until melted; stir the mixture until smooth. Stir in the Rice Krispies; spread over chunky peanut butter layer. Refrigerate, covered, at least 30 minutes or until set.
3. Lifting with parchment paper, remove brownies from pan. Cut into bars. Store in an airtight container in the refrigerator.

TOP TIP

FANCY SPIN ON BROWNIES

Adding wine gives Cranberry-Port Fudge Brownies an elegant twist. They would make a special treat to serve at a wine-tasting party or other dressy event. If you're hosting a fondue party, cut the brownies into cubes to dunk in any sweet dip.

CHOCOLATE & PEANUT
BUTTER CRISPY BARS

COCONUT CHIP
NUT BARS

CHOCOLATE STRAWBERRY
TRUFFLE BROWNIES

RICH CHOCOLATE BROWNIES

COCONUT CHIP NUT BARS

There's something for everyone in these delectable bars—coconut, chocolate chips, walnuts and toffee. You might even want to double the recipe, they're so popular with kids and adults alike. You'll be amazed how fast they vanish from your goodie tray.

—JUDITH STROHMEYER
ALBRIGHTSVILLE, PA

PREP: 15 MIN. • **BAKE:** 20 MIN.
MAKES: 3 DOZEN

- 1¾ cups all-purpose flour
- ¾ cup confectioners' sugar
- ¼ cup baking cocoa
- 1¼ cups cold butter, cubed
- 1 can (14 ounces) sweetened condensed milk
- 2 cups (12 ounces) semisweet chocolate chips, divided
- 1 teaspoon vanilla extract
- 1 cup chopped walnuts
- ½ cup flaked coconut
- ½ cup English toffee bits or almond brickle chips

1. Preheat oven to 350°. In a small bowl, combine the flour, sugar and cocoa. Cut in the butter until the mixture resembles coarse crumbs. Press firmly into a greased 13x9-in. baking pan. Bake 10 minutes.
2. Meanwhile, in a small saucepan, combine milk and 1 cup chocolate chips; cook and stir over low heat until smooth and chips are melted. Stir in vanilla.
3. Pour over crust. Sprinkle with walnuts and remaining chocolate chips. Top with coconut and toffee bits. Gently press topping down into chocolate layer. Bake 18-20 minutes longer or until firm. Cool on a wire rack. Cut into bars.

CHOCOLATE STRAWBERRY TRUFFLE BROWNIES

Every summer I make strawberry jam, and one day I decided to add some to a batch of brownies. They were a hit with my family. I also treat the students in my special ed classes to these delectable treats.

—TERESA JANSEN ADVANCE, MO

PREP: 30 MIN.
BAKE: 30 MIN. + CHILLING
MAKES: ABOUT 2 DOZEN

- 1¼ cups semisweet chocolate chips
- ½ cup butter, cubed
- ¾ cup packed brown sugar
- 2 large eggs
- 1 teaspoon instant coffee granules
- 2 tablespoons water
- ¾ cup all-purpose flour
- ½ teaspoon baking powder

TRUFFLE FILLING
- 1 cup (6 ounces) semisweet chocolate chips
- ¼ teaspoon instant coffee granules
- 8 ounces cream cheese, softened
- ⅓ cup strawberry jam or preserves
- ¼ cup sifted confectioners' sugar

GLAZE
- ¼ cup semisweet chocolate chips
- 1 teaspoon shortening

1. In a microwave, melt chocolate and butter; stir until smooth. Cool slightly. In a large bowl, beat brown sugar and eggs. Stir in chocolate mixture. Dissolve coffee in water; add to chocolate mixture. Combine flour and baking powder; gradually add to batter.
2. Spread evenly in a greased and floured 9-in. square baking pan. Bake at 350° for 30-35 minutes or until a toothpick inserted in the center comes out clean. Cool.
3. Meanwhile, for filling, melt chocolate chips and coffee granules; stir until smooth. Set aside.

4. In a small bowl, beat the cream cheese until smooth. Add jam and confectioners' sugar; mix well. Beat in the melted chocolate until well blended. Spread over brownies.
5. For glaze, in a microwave, melt chocolate and shortening; stir until smooth. Drizzle over filling. Chill at least 1 hour.

RICH CHOCOLATE BROWNIES

I looked high and low for a rich brownie recipe that used cocoa instead of chocolate squares, and this is it. These treats never last more than a day at our house.

—KAREN TRAPP
NORTH WEYMOUTH, MA

PREP: 15 MIN.
BAKE: 25 MIN. + COOLING
MAKES: 12 SERVINGS

- 1 cup sugar
- 2 large eggs
- ½ teaspoon vanilla extract
- ½ cup butter, melted
- ½ cup all-purpose flour
- ⅓ cup baking cocoa
- ¼ teaspoon baking powder
- ¼ teaspoon salt

FROSTING
- 3 tablespoons baking cocoa
- 3 tablespoons butter, melted
- 2 tablespoons warm water
- 1 teaspoon instant coffee granules
- 1½ cups confectioners' sugar

1. In a large bowl, beat the sugar, eggs and vanilla. Beat in butter. Combine the flour, cocoa, baking powder and salt; gradually add to batter and mix well.
2. Pour into a greased 8-in. square baking dish. Bake at 350° for 25-30 minutes or until a toothpick inserted in the center comes out clean. Cool on a wire rack.
3. For frosting, combine the cocoa and butter. Combine the water and coffee granules; add to the cocoa mixture. Stir in sugar until smooth. Frost brownies.

BIG BATCH

CHOCOLATE MINT TREASURES

I love chocolate and mint together. These bars win rave reviews for taking that winning combination up a notch by using dark, milk and white chocolate.

—SHERRY JOHNSTON
GREEN COVE SPRINGS, FL

PREP: 45 MIN.
BAKE: 20 MIN. + COOLING
MAKES: 4 DOZEN

FIRST LAYER
- ½ cup butter, softened
- ½ cup sugar
- 1 large egg
- ½ teaspoon vanilla extract
- 1 cup all-purpose flour
- ¼ cup baking cocoa
- ⅛ teaspoon salt

SECOND LAYER
- ½ cup butter, softened
- ½ cup sugar
- 1 large egg
- ½ teaspoon vanilla extract
- 1¼ cups all-purpose flour
- ⅛ teaspoon salt
- 1 package (7.05 ounces) After Eight thin mints

DRIZZLE
- 3 ounces bittersweet chocolate, chopped
- 1 tablespoon butter
- 2 ounces white baking chocolate

1. In a large bowl, cream butter and sugar until light and fluffy. Beat in egg and vanilla. Combine the flour, cocoa and salt; gradually add to creamed mixture and mix well. Spread into a greased 13x9-in. baking pan. Chill 15 minutes.

2. Meanwhile, for second layer, in a large bowl, cream butter and sugar until light and fluffy. Beat in egg and vanilla. Combine the flour and salt; gradually add to creamed mixture and mix well. Gently spread over chocolate layer.

3. Bake at 350° for 16-20 minutes, until edges are golden brown.

Remove from the oven; top with mints. Bake 1-2 minutes or until mints begin to melt; carefully spread mints evenly over the top. Cool completely.

4. In a microwave, melt the bittersweet chocolate and butter; stir until smooth. Drizzle or spread over bars. Grate white chocolate or make chocolate curls to decorate top. Chill until set. Cut the bars into triangles.

FUDGE-FILLED BARS

I appreciate the ease of baking oat bars on a busy day, and my children love the fudgy filling. With colorful candies on top, the sweet squares are sure to sell at bake sales.

—RENEE ZIMMER GIG HARBOR, WA

PREP: 20 MIN. • **BAKE:** 20 MIN.
MAKES: 2½ DOZEN

- 2 cups quick-cooking oats
- 1½ cups all-purpose flour
- 1 cup packed brown sugar
- ¾ teaspoon salt
- 1 cup butter, melted
- 1 cup chopped pecans
- 1 can (14 ounces) sweetened condensed milk
- 1 cup (6 ounces) semisweet chocolate chips
- 2 tablespoons shortening
- 1 cup milk chocolate M&M's

1. In a large bowl, combine the oats, flour, brown sugar and salt. Add butter and mix until crumbly. Stir in pecans. Set aside 1½ cups for topping. Press the remaining crumb mixture into a greased 13x9-in. baking pan.

2. In a large saucepan, combine the milk, chocolate chips and shortening. Cook and stir over low heat until chips are melted; stir until smooth.

3. Spread over the crust; sprinkle with the reserved crumb mixture. Top with M&M's. Bake at 350° for 20-25 minutes or until the edges are golden brown.

CHOCOLATE MINT TREASURES

FUDGE-FILLED BARS

**TRIPLE FUDGE
BROWNIES**

⑤INGREDIENTS *BIG BATCH*

TRIPLE FUDGE BROWNIES

When you're in a hurry to make dessert, here's a "mix of mixes" that's convenient and quick. The result is a big pan of very rich, fudgy brownies. Friends who ask me for the recipe are amazed that it's so easy to make.

—**DENISE NEBEL** WAYLAND, IA

PREP: 10 MIN. • **BAKE:** 30 MIN.
MAKES: 4 DOZEN

- 1 package (3.9 ounces) instant chocolate pudding mix
- 1 package chocolate cake mix (regular size)
- 2 cups (12 ounces) semisweet chocolate chips
  Confectioners' sugar
  Vanilla ice cream, optional

1. Prepare pudding according to package directions. Whisk in dry cake mix. Stir in chocolate chips.
2. Pour into a greased 15x10x1-in. baking pan. Bake at 350° for 30-35 minutes or until the top springs back when lightly touched.
3. Dust with confectioners' sugar. Serve with ice cream if desired.

TOP TIP

BROWNIES EVEN BETTER

It's a snap to take a regular pan of brownies from ordinary to extraordinary... even if you rely on a boxed mix. Simply stir a handful of chocolate or butterscotch chips into the batter, or add a little mint extract. If the recipe calls for water, replace some with cooled coffee for a mocha twist.

BIG BATCH
FUDGE-TOPPED BROWNIES

Why have either brownies or fudge when you can have them both in the ultimate chocolate dessert?

—JUDY OLSON WHITECOURT, AB

PREP: 25 MIN.
BAKE: 25 MIN. + FREEZING
MAKES: ABOUT 10 DOZEN

- 1 **cup butter**
- 4 **ounces unsweetened chocolate, chopped**
- 2 **cups sugar**
- 2 **teaspoons vanilla extract**
- 4 **large eggs**
- 1½ **cups all-purpose flour**
- 1 **teaspoon baking powder**
- ½ **teaspoon salt**
- 1 **cup chopped walnuts**

TOPPING
- 4½ **cups sugar**
- 1 **can (12 ounces) evaporated milk**
- ½ **cup butter, cubed**
- 1 **package (12 ounces) semisweet chocolate chips**
- 1 **package (11½ ounces) milk chocolate chips**
- 1 **jar (7 ounces) marshmallow creme**
- 2 **teaspoons vanilla extract**
- 2 **cups chopped walnuts**

1. In a heavy saucepan or the microwave, melt butter and chocolate; stir until smooth. Remove from the heat; blend in sugar and vanilla. Add eggs; mix well. Combine the flour, baking powder and salt; add to chocolate mixture. Stir in walnuts. Pour into a greased 13x9-in. baking pan. Bake at 350° for 25-30 minutes or until the top springs back when lightly touched. Cool on a wire rack while preparing topping.

2. Combine the sugar, milk and butter in a large heavy saucepan; bring to a boil over medium heat. Reduce heat; simmer, uncovered, for 5 minutes, stirring constantly. Remove from the heat. Stir in the chocolate chips, marshmallow creme and vanilla until smooth. Add walnuts. Spread over warm brownies. Freeze for 3 hours or until firm. Cut into 1-in. squares. Store in the refrigerator.

FUDGE-TOPPED BROWNIES

TRUFFLE RASPBERRY BROWNIES

Each of these rich, fudgelike brownies is bursting with plump red raspberries and topped with a dreamy bittersweet ganache—perfection!
—AGNES WARD STRATFORD, ON

PREP: 30 MIN.
BAKE: 25 MIN. + CHILLING
MAKES: 1 DOZEN

- 6 ounces bittersweet chocolate, chopped
- ½ cup butter, cubed
- 2 large eggs
- 1 cup sugar
- 1 teaspoon vanilla extract
- 1 cup all-purpose flour
- ¼ teaspoon baking soda
- ¼ teaspoon salt
- 1 cup fresh raspberries

FROSTING
- 6 ounces bittersweet chocolate, chopped
- ¾ cup heavy whipping cream
- 2 tablespoons seedless raspberry jam
- 1 teaspoon vanilla extract
- 12 fresh raspberries

1. Preheat the oven to 350°. In a microwave, melt chocolate and butter; stir until smooth. In a large bowl, beat eggs, sugar and vanilla. Stir in chocolate mixture. Combine flour, baking soda and salt; add to the chocolate mixture just until combined. Fold in raspberries.
2. Spread the batter into a greased 9-in. square baking pan. Bake 25-30 minutes or until a toothpick comes out clean. Cool on a wire rack.
3. For frosting, in a microwave-safe bowl, combine chocolate, cream and jam. Microwave at 50% power for 2-3 minutes or until smooth, stirring twice. Transfer to a bowl; stir in vanilla. Place in a bowl of ice water; stir 3-5 minutes. With a hand mixer, beat on medium speed until soft peaks form.
4. Cut small hole in corner of a heavy-duty resealable plastic bag; insert a #825 star tip. Fill with ½ cup frosting. Spread remaining frosting over brownies. Cut into 12 bars; pipe a rosette in center of each; top with a raspberry. Cover and refrigerate 30 minutes or until set. Refrigerate leftovers.

FUDGE-NUT OATMEAL BARS

When I make these bars for lunches and snacks, they're gone in a jiffy!
—KIM STOLLER SMITHVILLE, OH

PREP: 20 MIN. • **BAKE:** 20 MIN.
MAKES: 2½ DOZEN

- 1 cup butter, softened
- 2 cups packed brown sugar
- 2 large eggs
- 2 teaspoons vanilla extract
- 3 cups quick-cooking oats
- 2½ cups all-purpose flour
- 1 teaspoon baking soda
- 1 teaspoon salt

FUDGE FILLING
- 1 can (14 ounces) sweetened condensed milk
- 2 cups (12 ounces) semisweet chocolate chips
- 2 tablespoons butter
- ½ teaspoon salt
- 1 cup chopped walnuts
- 2 teaspoons vanilla extract

1. In a bowl, cream butter and brown sugar until light and fluffy. Add eggs and vanilla; mix well. Combine the oats, flour, baking soda and salt; add to the creamed mixture. Spread two-thirds into an ungreased 15x10x1-in. baking pan; set aside.
2. For the filling, heat the milk, chocolate chips, butter and salt in a microwave-safe bowl until chips are melted. Remove from the heat; stir in walnuts and vanilla. Spread over top. Drop remaining oat mixture by tablespoonfuls over chocolate.
3. Bake at 350° for 20 to 25 minutes. Cool on a wire rack.

PEPPERMINT BROWNIES

My grandmother encouraged me to enter these brownies in our county fair some years ago, and they earned top honors. The colorful crushed mint candy makes them a great treat to serve during the holidays.
—MARCY GREENBLATT REDDING, CA

PREP: 15 MIN. • **BAKE:** 35 MIN.
MAKES: 2 DOZEN

- ¾ cup canola oil
- 2 cups sugar
- 2 teaspoons vanilla extract
- 4 large eggs
- 1⅓ cups all-purpose flour
- 1 cup baking cocoa
- 1 teaspoon baking powder
- 1 teaspoon salt
- ¾ cup crushed peppermint candy, divided

GLAZE
- 1 cup (6 ounces) semisweet chocolate chips
- 1 tablespoon shortening

1. Line a 13x9-in. baking pan with foil; grease foil and set aside. In a large bowl, beat oil and sugar until blended. Beat in vanilla. Add eggs, one at a time, beating well after each addition. Combine the flour, cocoa, baking powder and salt; gradually add to the oil mixture. Set aside 2 tablespoons peppermint candy for garnish; stir in remaining candy. Spread into prepared pan.
2. Bake at 350° for 35-40 minutes or until a toothpick inserted in the center comes out clean. Cool on a wire rack.
3. For glaze, in a microwave, melt chocolate chips and shortening; stir until smooth. Spread over the brownies; sprinkle the glaze with reserved candy.

PEPPERMINT
BROWNIES

**DOUBLE CHOCOLATE
ORANGE BROWNIES**

DOUBLE CHOCOLATE ORANGE BROWNIES

Since we dearly love the pairing of chocolate and orange, my husband suggested I put them together in brownie. These rich treats do our favorite flavor combination proud.

—ELINOR TOWNSEND
NORTH GRAFTON, MA

PREP: 15 MIN.
BAKE: 30 MIN. + COOLING
MAKES: 2 DOZEN

- ¾ **cup butter, cubed**
- 4 **ounces unsweetened chocolate, chopped**
- 3 **large eggs**
- 2 **cups sugar**
- 1 **teaspoon orange extract**
- 1 **cup all-purpose flour**
- 1 **cup (6 ounces) semisweet chocolate chips**
  Confectioners' sugar

1. In a microwave, melt butter and chocolate; stir until smooth. Cool slightly. In a large bowl, beat eggs and sugar. Stir in chocolate mixture. Beat in extract. Gradually add flour to chocolate mixture.

2. Pour into a greased 13x9-in. baking dish. Sprinkle with the chocolate chips. Bake at 350° for 30-35 minutes or until a toothpick inserted in the center comes out clean (do not overbake).

3. Cool completely on a wire rack. Cut brownies into squares. Just before serving, sprinkle with the confectioners' sugar.

FUDGY S'MORES BROWNIES

I combined the classic summertime campfire treat with my favorite brownie recipe to get a dessert that's sure to wow at your next party. See them on page 40.

—JUDY CUNNINGHAM MAX, ND

PREP: 15 MIN.
BAKE: 25 MIN. + COOLING
MAKES: 1 DOZEN

- 1⅓ **cups butter, softened**
- 2⅔ **cups sugar**
- 4 **large eggs**
- 1 **tablespoon vanilla extract**
- 2 **cups all-purpose flour**
- 1 **cup baking cocoa**
- ½ **teaspoon salt**
- 1 **cup Golden Grahams, coarsely crushed**
- 1¾ **cups miniature marshmallows**
- 4 **ounces milk chocolate, chopped**

1. Preheat oven to 350°. In a large bowl, cream butter and sugar until light and fluffy. Beat in eggs and vanilla. In a bowl, mix flour, cocoa and salt; gradually beat into the creamed mixture.

2. Spread into a greased 13x9-in. baking pan. Bake 25-30 minutes or until a toothpick inserted in center comes out with moist crumbs (do not overbake).

3. Preheat broiler. Sprinkle the baked brownies with cereal and marshmallows; broil 5-6 in. from heat 30-45 seconds or until the marshmallows are golden brown. Immediately sprinkle with chopped chocolate. Cover with foil and let stand 5 minutes or until chocolate begins to melt. Remove foil and cool completely in pan on a wire rack. Cut into bars.

ULTIMATE FUDGY BROWNIES

Coffee granules bump up the chocolate flavor in these ultra fudgy brownies. Sprinkle some chocolate chips into the batter and you've got pure yum!

—SARAH THOMPSON GREENFIELD, WI

PREP: 20 MIN.
BAKE: 40 MIN. + COOLING
MAKES: 16 SERVINGS

- 1 cup sugar
- ½ cup packed brown sugar
- ⅔ cup butter, cubed
- ¼ cup water
- 2 teaspoons instant coffee granules, optional
- 2¾ cups bittersweet chocolate chips, divided
- 4 large eggs
- 2 teaspoons vanilla extract
- 1½ cups all-purpose flour
- ½ teaspoon baking soda
- ½ teaspoon salt

1. Preheat oven to 325°. Line a 9-in. square baking pan with parchment paper, letting ends extend up sides. In a large heavy saucepan, combine sugars, butter, water and, if desired, coffee granules; bring to a boil, stirring constantly. Remove from heat; add 1¾ cups chocolate chips and stir until melted. Cool slightly.

2. In a large bowl, whisk eggs until foamy, for about 3 minutes. Add the vanilla; gradually whisk in the chocolate mixture. In another bowl, whisk flour, baking soda and salt; stir into chocolate mixture. Fold in remaining chocolate chips.

3. Pour into prepared pan. Bake on a lower oven rack 40-50 minutes or until a toothpick inserted in the center comes out with moist crumbs (do not overbake). Cool completely in pan on a wire rack.

4. Lifting with parchment paper, remove brownies from pan. Cut into squares.

ULTIMATE FUDGY
BROWNIES

CHOCOLATE FUDGE BROWNIES

These brownies are so moist and rich, you won't even miss the icing.

—**HAZEL FRITCHIE** PALESTINE, IL

PREP: 15 MIN.
BAKE: 35 MIN. + COOLING
MAKES: 16 SERVINGS

- 1 **cup butter, cubed**
- 6 **ounces unsweetened chocolate, chopped**
- 4 **large eggs**
- 2 **cups sugar**
- 1 **teaspoon vanilla extract**
- ½ **teaspoon salt**
- 1 **cup all-purpose flour**
- 2 **cups chopped walnuts**
  Confectioners' sugar, optional

1. Preheat the oven to 350°. In a small saucepan, melt the butter and chocolate over low heat. Cool mixture slightly.

2. In a large bowl, beat eggs, sugar, vanilla and salt until blended. Stir in chocolate mixture. Add the flour, mixing well. Stir in walnuts.

3. Spread batter into a greased 9-in. square baking pan. Bake for 35-40 minutes or until a toothpick inserted in center comes out with moist crumbs (do not overbake).

4. Cool completely in pan on a wire rack. If desired, dust brownies with confectioners' sugar. Cut into bars.

TOP TIP

EASY CUTTING

To cut brownies or bars into clean-edged pieces, cut downward with a serrated knife. Avoid sawing motions. When slicing frosted treats, be sure to wipe the knife clean between cuts. Another easy trick—slice with a pizza cutter treated with nonstick cooking spray.

CHOCOLATE FUDGE BROWNIES

CHOCOLATE CRUNCH BROWNIES

CHOCOLATE SAUCE
BROWNIES

CHOCOLATE NUT BARS

CHOCOLATE CRUNCH BROWNIES

The first time I took these brownies to work, I knew I'd better start making copies of the recipe—they disappeared fast! My husband and kids just devour them, too.
—PAT MUELLER MITCHELL, SD

PREP: 30 MIN.
BAKE: 25 MIN. + CHILLING
MAKES: 3 DOZEN

- 1 cup butter, softened
- 2 cups sugar
- 4 large eggs
- ½ cup baking cocoa
- 1½ cups all-purpose flour
- 2 teaspoons vanilla extract
- ½ teaspoon salt
- 1 jar (7 ounces) marshmallow creme
- 1 cup creamy peanut butter
- 2 cups (12 ounces) semisweet chocolate chips
- 3 cups crisp rice cereal

1. In a large bowl, cream butter and sugar until light and fluffy. Beat in eggs and vanilla. Combine the flour, cocoa and salt; gradually add to creamed mixture until blended.
2. Spread into a greased 13x9-in. baking pan. Bake at 350° for 24-28 minutes or until a toothpick inserted in the center comes out clean (do not overbake brownies). Cool in pan on a wire rack. Spread the marshmallow creme over cooled brownies.
3. In a small saucepan, melt peanut butter and chocolate chips over low heat, stirring mixture constantly until smooth. Remove from the heat; stir in cereal. Spread over top. Refrigerate until set. Cut into bars.

BIG BATCH
CHOCOLATE SAUCE BROWNIES

These moist, cake-like brownies are loaded with crunchy nuts and topped with sweet frosting.
—VICKIE OVERBY WAHPETON, ND

PREP: 20 MIN. • **BAKE:** 20 MIN.
MAKES: 5 DOZEN

- ½ cup butter, softened
- 1 cup sugar
- 4 large eggs
- 1 can (16 ounces) chocolate syrup
- 1 teaspoon vanilla extract
- 1 cup plus 1 tablespoon all-purpose flour
- ½ teaspoon baking powder
- 1 cup chopped pecans or walnuts
FROSTING
- 1 cup sugar
- 6 tablespoons milk
- 6 tablespoons butter
- ½ cup semisweet chocolate chips

1. Preheat oven to 350°. In a bowl, cream butter and sugar. Add eggs, one at a time, beating well after each addition. Stir in chocolate sauce and vanilla. Combine flour and baking powder; add to creamed mixture and mix well. Stir in nuts.
2. Pour into a greased 15x10x1-in. baking pan. Bake 20-25 minutes or until a toothpick inserted in the center comes out clean. Cool on a wire rack.
3. For the frosting, combine the sugar, milk and butter in a heavy saucepan. Bring to a boil over medium heat; boil for 1 minute. Remove from heat. Add chocolate chips; whisk 5 minutes or until smooth. Spread over brownies.

CHOCOLATE NUT BARS

My hubby often asks for these fudgy, nutty bars. They are his all-time favorite treat.
—LISA DARLING SCOTTSVILLE, NY

PREP: 30 MIN.
BAKE: 15 MIN. + COOLING
MAKES: 3 DOZEN

- 1 cup butter, softened
- 2 cups all-purpose flour
- ½ cup sugar
- ¼ teaspoon salt
- 1 can (14 ounces) sweetened condensed milk
- 2 cups (12 ounces) semisweet chocolate chips, divided
- 1 teaspoon vanilla extract
- ½ cup chopped macadamia nuts
- ½ cup chopped walnuts
- ½ cup chopped pecans
- ½ cup milk chocolate chips

1. Preheat oven to 350°. In a large bowl, beat butter until fluffy. Add the flour, sugar and salt; beat just until crumbly. Set aside 1 cup for topping. Press remaining crumb mixture into a greased 13x9-in. baking pan. Bake 10-12 minutes or until set and edges begin to brown.
2. Meanwhile, in a small saucepan, combine the milk and 1½ cups of semisweet chocolate chips. Cook and stir until the chips are melted. Remove from the heat; stir in the vanilla. Spread mixture over crust.
3. Combine the nuts and milk chocolate chips with the remaining semisweet chocolate chips and crumb mixture. Sprinkle over filling. Bake 15-20 minutes or until center is set. Cool on a wire rack. Cut into bars.

TOP TIP

CRUNCHY GOODNESS

If your family members love the crunchy addition of nuts in brownies, bars or even cookies, but someone is allergic to them, substitute granola or crisp rice cereal in the same amount as the nuts called for in your recipes.

HOMEMADE LEMON
BARS, PAGE 87

Fruit-Filled Wonders

These treats will dazzle your taste buds with fresh berry, zesty lemon, tangy orange and other fruity flavors.

MANGO GETAWAY BARS

I've always enjoyed the flavor of mango, so I created this recipe to feature the sweet tropical fruit.

—**PATRICIA HARMON** BADEN, PA

PREP: 25 MIN.
BAKE: 25 MIN. + COOLING
MAKES: 3 DOZEN

- ½ cup macadamia nuts
- 2¼ cups all-purpose flour, divided
- ½ cup confectioners' sugar
- ½ teaspoon salt
- 1 cup cold butter, cubed
- 1 medium mango, peeled and chopped
- ½ cup orange marmalade
- ½ cup sugar
- 4 large eggs
- 1 teaspoon grated lemon peel
- 1 cup flaked coconut

1. Place the nuts in a food processor; cover and process until finely chopped. Add 2 cups flour, confectioners' sugar and salt; cover and process until blended. Add butter; pulse just until mixture is crumbly. Press into an ungreased 13x9-in. baking pan. Bake at 350° for 15-20 minutes or until crust is lightly browned.

2. In a clean food processor, combine the mango and the orange marmalade; cover and process until smooth. Add sugar and remaining flour; process until combined. Add the eggs and lemon peel; process just until combined. Pour over the crust. Sprinkle with coconut.

3. Bake for 23-28 minutes or until golden brown around the edges. Cool on a wire rack. Cut into bars. Refrigerate leftovers.

CRANBERRY-ORANGE BARS

My mother has had this recipe for years. I loved it, too, so she happily passed it on to me. These bars make great snacks, but they can also be served for dessert.

—**MARGARET ADELMAN** BELLINGHAM, MN

PREP: 30 MIN. • **BAKE:** 20 MIN.
MAKES: ABOUT 2½ DOZEN

- 3 cups fresh or frozen cranberries
- 2 large unpeeled oranges, cut into quarters and seeded
- 2½ cups sugar
- 3 tablespoons cornstarch
- 1 teaspoon ground ginger
- ½ cup chopped nuts, optional

CRUST

- 3¼ cups all-purpose flour
- ¾ cup sugar
- 1 tablespoon grated lemon peel
- 1 cup butter, cubed
- 3 large egg yolks
- ¾ teaspoon vanilla extract
- 1 to 2 tablespoons water

1. Grind cranberries and oranges (including peel). Set aside. In a large saucepan, combine the sugar, cornstarch and ginger. Add ground fruit; bring to a boil. Reduce heat; cook and stir for 15 minutes or until thickened. Remove from the heat; stir in nuts if desired. Set mixture aside to cool.

2. Meanwhile, for crust, in a large bowl, combine the flour, sugar and lemon peel. Cut in the butter until coarse crumbs form. Add egg yolks and vanilla. Gradually add water, tossing with a fork until the dough forms a ball.

3. Pat two-thirds of dough into a greased 13x9-in. baking pan. Cover with cranberry-orange mixture. Crumble remaining dough on top. Bake at 425° for 20-25 minutes or until topping is golden brown. Cool on a wire rack; cut into bars.

MANGO GETAWAY BARS

CRANBERRY-ORANGE
BARS

ORANGE NANAIMO BARS

ORANGE NANAIMO BARS
Orange and chocolate layers are as pretty as they are tasty in these bars.
—**DEL MASON** MARTENSVILLE, SK

PREP: 40 MIN. + CHILLING
MAKES: 3 DOZEN

⅓ cup butter, cubed
¼ cup sugar
1 dark chocolate candy bar (3¼ ounces), chopped
1 large egg, beaten
17 shortbread cookies, crushed
½ cup flaked coconut
½ cup finely chopped pecans
1 teaspoon grated orange peel

FILLING
½ cup butter, softened
2 tablespoons instant vanilla pudding mix
2 cups confectioners' sugar
2 tablespoons orange juice
1 teaspoon grated orange peel
1 to 2 drops orange paste food coloring, optional

GLAZE
1 dark chocolate candy bar (3¼ ounces), chopped
1 teaspoon butter

1. In a large heavy saucepan, combine the butter, sugar and candy bar. Cook and stir over medium-low heat until melted. Whisk a small amount of hot mixture into egg. Return all to the pan, whisking constantly. Cook and stir over medium-low heat until mixture reaches 160°.
2. In a large bowl, combine the cookie crumbs, coconut, pecans and orange peel. Stir in the chocolate mixture until blended. Press into a greased 9-in. square baking pan. Refrigerate 30 minutes or until set.
3. For filling, in a large bowl, cream butter and pudding mix. Beat in the confectioners' sugar, orange juice, peel and, if desired, food coloring. Spread over crust. For glaze, melt candy bar and butter in microwave; stir until smooth. Spread over top. Refrigerate until set. Cut into bars.

CHERRY COCONUT BARS

I first came across these bars while stationed at a Michigan Air Force base in 1964 and have been making them ever since. My children think all special events need these bars.
—**MARGUERITE EMERY** ORLAND, CA

PREP: 15 MIN.
BAKE: 30 MIN. + COOLING
MAKES: 3 DOZEN

- 1 **cup all-purpose flour**
- 3 **tablespoons confectioners' sugar**
- ½ **cup cold butter, cubed**

FILLING

- 2 **large eggs**
- 1 **cup sugar**
- 1 **teaspoon vanilla extract**
- ¼ **cup all-purpose flour**
- ½ **teaspoon baking powder**
- ¼ **teaspoon salt**
- ¾ **cup chopped walnuts**
- ½ **cup quartered maraschino cherries**
- ½ **cup flaked coconut**

1. In a small bowl, combine flour and confectioners' sugar; cut in butter until crumbly. Press into a lightly greased 13x9-in. baking pan. Bake crust at 350° for 10-12 minutes or until lightly browned. Cool on a wire rack.

2. For filling, in a small bowl, combine the eggs, sugar and vanilla. Combine flour, baking powder and salt; add to the egg mixture and mix well. Stir in walnuts, cherries and coconut. Spread over crust. Bake for 20-25 minutes or until firm. Cool on a wire rack. Cut into bars.

CHERRY COCONUT BARS

RASPBERRY DELIGHTS

With a rich crust holding the sweet jam topping, these buttery gems are a must-have on every holiday cookie tray I make.

—GEORGIANA HAGMAN LOUISVILLE, KY

PREP: 10 MIN.
BAKE: 25 MIN. + COOLING
MAKES: 3 DOZEN

- 1 cup butter, softened
- 1 cup sugar
- 2 large egg yolks
- 2 cups all-purpose flour
- 1 cup coarsely ground pecans
- 1 cup raspberry jam

1. In a large bowl, cream butter and sugar until light and fluffy. Beat in egg yolks. Gradually add flour and mix well. Stir in the pecans.
2. Spread half into a lightly greased 13x9-in. baking pan. Top with the jam. Drop the remaining dough by teaspoonfuls over jam.
3. Bake at 350° for 25-30 minutes or until top is golden brown. Cool on a wire rack. Cut into bars.

BLUEBERRY CRUMB BARS

Think of these bars as a blueberry crisp turned into a handheld treat. Oats and fresh blueberries are combined for a sweet, no-fuss dish that's perfect for summer.

—BLAIR LONERGAN ROCHELLE, VA

PREP: 20 MIN.
BAKE: 20 MIN. + COOLING
MAKES: 1 DOZEN

- 1 package yellow cake mix (regular size)
- 2½ cups old-fashioned oats
- ¾ cup butter, melted
- 1 jar (12 ounces) blueberry preserves
- ⅓ cup fresh blueberries
- 1 tablespoon lemon juice
- ⅓ cup finely chopped pecans
- 1 teaspoon ground cinnamon

1. Preheat oven to 350°. In a large bowl, combine cake mix, oats and butter until crumbly. Press 3 cups into a greased 9-in. square baking pan. Bake 15 minutes. Cool on a wire rack 5 minutes.
2. Meanwhile, in a small bowl, combine preserves, blueberries and lemon juice. Spread over the crust. Stir the pecans and cinnamon into remaining crumb mixture. Sprinkle over top.
3. Bake 18-20 minutes or until lightly browned. Cool on a wire rack before cutting into bars.

APPLE NUT BARS

These yummy treats pack big apple flavor. As a bonus, you don't have to peel the apples!

—KAREN NELSON SULLIVAN, WI

PREP: 15 MIN. • **BAKE:** 25 MIN.
MAKES: 1 DOZEN

- 2 large egg whites
- ⅔ cup sugar
- ½ teaspoon vanilla extract
- ½ cup all-purpose flour
- 1 teaspoon baking powder
- 2 cups chopped tart apples
- ¼ cup chopped pecans

1. In a large bowl, whisk the egg whites, sugar and vanilla for 1½ minutes or until frothy. Whisk in flour and baking powder until blended. Fold in apples and pecans.
2. Transfer to a 9-in. square baking pan coated with cooking spray. Bake at 350° for 22-28 minutes or until a toothpick inserted in the center comes out clean. Cool on a wire rack. Cut into bars.

TOP TIP

OLD-FASHIONED OATS VS. QUICK-COOKING OATS

Old-fashioned oats and quick-cooking oats are interchangeable, but keep in mind their differences before replacing one with the other. Both have been flattened with large rollers. But because quick-cooking oats are cut into smaller pieces first, they cook faster, and they offer a more delicate texture to baked goods and desserts. If you want a heartier texture, use old-fashioned oats.

RASPBERRY DELIGHTS

BLUEBERRY CRUMB BARS

APPLE NUT BARS

ORANGE CRANBERRY BARS

ORANGE CRANBERRY BARS

My sister, who's a great baker, passed this recipe on to me. The buttery bars are studded with cranberries, pecans and coconut. They're great for fall and pretty enough for Christmas.

—**JUNE WHEELER** WARRENTON, VA

PREP: 10 MIN.
BAKE: 30 MIN. + COOLING
MAKES: 8 BARS

- ¼ **cup all-purpose flour**
- 1½ **teaspoons sugar**
- 2 **tablespoons cold butter**
- 2 **tablespoons chopped pecans**

TOPPING

- 2 **tablespoons beaten egg**
- 1½ **teaspoons whole milk**
- ¾ **teaspoon grated orange peel**
- ¼ **teaspoon vanilla extract**
- ⅓ **cup sugar**
- 1½ **teaspoons all-purpose flour**
- ¼ **cup chopped fresh or frozen cranberries**
- 2 **tablespoons flaked coconut**
- 2 **tablespoons chopped pecans**

1. In a large bowl, combine flour and sugar; cut in the butter until mixture resembles coarse crumbs. Stir in pecans. Press into an 8x4-in. loaf pan coated with cooking spray. Bake at 350° for 15 minutes.
2. Meanwhile, in another bowl, combine the egg, milk, orange peel and vanilla. Combine sugar and flour; gradually add to egg mixture and mix well. Fold in cranberries, coconut and pecans. Spread over the crust.
3. Bake for 15-20 minutes or until golden brown. Cool on a wire rack.

BIG BATCH
CHERRY WALNUT BARS

These nutty fruit bars travel well, so they're perfect when you want to send someone a little cheer. Ever since our cookie-loving son joined the Air Force, I've shipped them as far away as England and Italy. We enjoy them here at home, too.

—**MARGARET ZUBER** MARIETTA, GA

PREP: 15 MIN. • **BAKE:** 40 MIN.
MAKES: 4 DOZEN

- 2¼ **cups all-purpose flour**
- ½ **cup sugar**
- 1 **cup cold butter, cubed**
- 2 **large eggs**
- 1 **cup packed brown sugar**
- ½ **teaspoon salt**
- ½ **teaspoon baking powder**
- ½ **teaspoon vanilla extract**
- 1 **jar (6 ounces) maraschino cherries**
- ½ **cup chopped walnuts**

ICING

- 1 **cup confectioners' sugar**
- 1 **tablespoon butter, softened**
- ½ **cup flaked coconut, toasted, optional**

1. In a large bowl, combine flour and sugar. Cut in the butter until mixture resembles coarse crumbs. Pat into an ungreased 13x9-in. baking pan. Bake at 350° for 18-22 minutes or until edges of the crust are lightly browned.
2. Meanwhile, in a small bowl, combine the eggs, brown sugar, salt, baking powder and vanilla. Drain cherries, reserving 2 tablespoons juice; set juice aside. Chop cherries; add to brown sugar mixture. Stir in walnuts. Pour over crust and spread evenly. Bake 20-25 minutes longer or until set. Cool completely on a wire rack.
3. For the icing, combine the confectioners' sugar and butter in a bowl. Add enough of the reserved cherry juice to achieve the desired consistency; drizzle over bars. If desired, sprinkle with coconut.

CHOCOLATE-DRIZZLED CHERRY BARS

I've been making all kinds of bars since I was in third grade, but these are special. I bake them for my church's Christmas party every year. Folks always rave about them and ask for a copy of the recipe.
—**JANICE HEIKKILA** DEER CREEK, MN

PREP: 35 MIN.
BAKE: 20 MIN. + COOLING
MAKES: 3 DOZEN

- 2   cups all-purpose flour
- 2   cups quick-cooking oats
- 1½ cups sugar
- 1¼ cups butter, softened
- 1   can (21 ounces) cherry pie filling
- 1   teaspoon almond extract
- ¼   cup semisweet chocolate chips
- ¾   teaspoon shortening

1. In a large bowl, combine the flour, oats, sugar and butter until crumbly. Set aside 1½ cups for topping. Press remaining crumb mixture into an ungreased 13x9-in. baking dish. Bake at 350° for 15-18 minutes or until edges of the crust begin to brown.
2. In a small bowl, combine pie filling and extract; carefully spread over crust. Sprinkle with reserved crumb mixture. Bake 20-25 minutes longer or until edges and topping are lightly browned.
3. In a microwave, melt chocolate chips and shortening; stir until smooth. Drizzle over warm bars. Cool completely on a wire rack.

PEACHES 'N' CREAM BARS

Try these easy-to-love bars for a fun spin on peach pie.
—**HUBERT SCOTT** COCKEYSVILLE, MD

PREP: 20 MIN.
BAKE: 25 MIN. + COOLING
MAKES: 2 DOZEN

- 1   tube (8 ounces) refrigerated seamless crescent dough sheet
- 8   ounces cream cheese, softened
- ½   cup sugar
- ¼   teaspoon almond extract
- 1   can (21 ounces) peach pie filling
- ½   cup all-purpose flour
- ¼   cup packed brown sugar
- 3   tablespoons cold butter
- ½   cup sliced almonds

1. Preheat oven to 375°. Unroll the crescent dough sheet into a rectangle. Press dough onto the bottom and slightly up the sides of a greased 13x9-in. baking pan. Bake 5 minutes. Cool completely on a wire rack.
2. In a large bowl, beat cream cheese, sugar and extract until smooth. Spread over crust. Spoon pie filling over cream cheese layer.
3. In a small bowl, whisk flour and brown sugar. Cut in butter until mixture resembles coarse crumbs. Stir in almonds; sprinkle over the peach filling.
4. Bake 25-28 minutes or until edges are golden brown. Cool in pan on a wire rack. Cut into bars. Store the bars in an airtight container in the refrigerator.

RASPBERRY-CHOCOLATE MERINGUE SQUARES

My family loves all sorts of goodies, including this luscious treat with a buttery crust, raspberry jam, chocolate and meringue. Bake it for a buffet, party or anytime snack.
—**NANCY HEISHMAN** LAS VEGAS, NV

PREP: 15 MIN.
BAKE: 20 MIN. + COOLING
MAKES: 9 SERVINGS

- 3   large egg whites, divided
- ¼   cup butter, softened
- ¼   cup confectioners' sugar
- 1   cup all-purpose flour
- ¼   cup sugar
- ½   cup seedless raspberry jam
- 3   tablespoons miniature semisweet chocolate chips

1. Preheat oven to 350°. Place two egg whites in a small bowl; let stand at room temperature 30 minutes. Meanwhile, in a large bowl, cream butter and confectioners' sugar until light and fluffy. Beat in the remaining egg white; gradually add the flour to the creamed mixture, mixing well.
2. Press into a greased 8-in. square baking pan. Bake 9-11 minutes or until lightly browned. Increase the oven setting to 400°.
3. With clean beaters, beat the reserved egg whites on medium speed until foamy. Gradually add sugar, 1 tablespoon at a time, beating on high after each addition until sugar is dissolved. Continue beating until stiff glossy peaks form. Spread jam over crust; sprinkle with chocolate chips. Spread meringue over top.
4. Bake 8-10 minutes or until meringue is lightly browned. Cool completely in pan on a wire rack.

TOP TIP

HOW TO DRIZZLE CHOCOLATE

Melt chocolate according to recipe directions. Transfer to a resealable plastic bag and cut a small hole in one corner. While moving back and forth over the bars, gently squeeze out the melted chocolate. You can also put the melted chocolate in a small bowl and use a spoon or fork to drizzle it.

RASPBERRY-CHOCOLATE
MERINGUE SQUARES

SWEDISH RASPBERRY
ALMOND BARS

SWEDISH RASPBERRY ALMOND BARS

When I was a single mom with a young daughter and on a tight budget, a kind neighbor made me a batch of these bars right before Christmas. We loved them so much that I soon started making them myself. My daughter is in her 30s now, and I still make these amazing treats for us to enjoy.

—MARINA CASTLE KELLEY
CANYON COUNTRY, CA

PREP: 35 MIN.
BAKE: 20 MIN. + COOLING
MAKES: 2 DOZEN

- ¾ cup butter, softened
- ¾ cup confectioners' sugar
- 1½ cups all-purpose flour
- ¾ cup seedless raspberry jam
- 3 large egg whites
- 6 tablespoons sugar
- ½ cup flaked coconut
- 1 cup sliced almonds, divided
  Additional confectioners' sugar, optional

1. Preheat oven to 350°. In a large bowl, cream the butter and the confectioners' sugar until light and fluffy. Gradually add flour and mix well. Press onto the bottom of a greased 13x9-in. baking pan. Bake for 18-20 minutes or until crust is lightly browned.

2. Spread jam over crust. In a large bowl, beat egg whites until soft peaks form. Gradually beat in sugar, 1 tablespoon at a time, on high until stiff peaks form. Fold in the coconut and ½ cup of almonds. Spread over jam. Sprinkle with the remaining almonds. Bake for 18-22 minutes or until golden brown. Cool the bars completely on a wire rack. If desired, dust bars with additional confectioners' sugar.

LEMON COCONUT SQUARES

The tangy citrus flavor of these easy squares seems especially yummy on warm days. It reminds me of when I was a little girl selling lemonade on the sidewalk.

—DONNA BIDDLE ELMIRA, NY

PREP: 25 MIN.
BAKE: 20 MIN. + COOLING
MAKES: 4 DOZEN

- 1½ cups all-purpose flour
- ½ cup confectioners' sugar
- ¾ cup cold butter, cubed
- 4 large eggs
- 1½ cups sugar
- ½ cup lemon juice
- 1 teaspoon baking powder
- ¾ cup flaked coconut

1. In a small bowl, combine flour and confectioners' sugar; cut in the butter until crumbly. Press into a lightly greased 13x9-in. baking pan. Bake at 350° for 15 minutes.

2. Meanwhile, in another small bowl, beat the eggs, sugar, lemon juice and baking powder until combined. Pour over crust; sprinkle with coconut.

3. Bake at 350° for 20-25 minutes or until golden brown. Cool on a wire rack. Cut into squares.

LEMON COCONUT SQUARES

HUNGARIAN STRAWBERRY PASTRY BARS

This Hungarian pastry has always been a family favorite. The dough is rich and soft, and the layers of nuts and jam make a delicious filling. Use a floured pastry cloth when rolling out the dough. It makes placing the dough into the pan easier.

—RONALD ROTH THREE RIVERS, MI

PREP: 45 MIN. + CHILLING
BAKE: 25 MIN. + COOLING
MAKES: 2 DOZEN

- 5 cups all-purpose flour
- 1 cup plus 3 tablespoons sugar, divided
- 4 teaspoons baking powder
- 2 teaspoons baking soda
- ⅛ teaspoon salt
- 1¼ cups shortening
- 4 large egg yolks
- ½ cup sour cream
- ¼ cup water
- 1 teaspoon vanilla extract
- 2½ cups chopped walnuts, divided
- 1 jar (18 ounces) seedless strawberry jam

1. In a large bowl, combine the flour, 1 cup sugar, baking powder, baking soda and salt. Cut in the shortening until mixture resembles coarse crumbs. In a bowl, whisk the egg yolks, sour cream, water and vanilla; gradually add to the crumb mixture, tossing with a fork until the dough forms a ball. Divide into thirds. Chill for 30 minutes.

2. Between two large sheets of waxed paper, roll out one portion of dough into a 15x10-in. rectangle. Transfer rectangle to an ungreased 15x10x1-in. baking pan. Sprinkle dough with 1¼ cups walnuts and 2 tablespoons sugar. Roll out another portion of dough into a 15x10 in. rectangle; place over walnuts. Spread with jam; sprinkle with remaining walnuts and sugar.

3. Roll out remaining pastry; cut into strips. Arrange in a crisscross pattern over filling. Trim and seal edges. Bake at 350° for 25-30 minutes or until golden brown. Cool on a wire rack. Cut into bars.

HUNGARIAN STRAWBERRY PASTRY BARS

BIG BATCH

CHERRY BARS

You can whip together a pan of these festive bars in just 20 minutes with a few pantry staples. They might even become an annual holiday tradition for your family.

—JANE KAMP GRAND RAPIDS, MI

PREP: 20 MIN.
BAKE: 30 MIN. + COOLING
MAKES: 5 DOZEN

- 1 **cup butter, softened**
- 2 **cups sugar**
- 1 **teaspoon salt**
- 4 **large eggs**
- 1 **teaspoon vanilla extract**
- ¼ **teaspoon almond extract**
- 3 **cups all-purpose flour**
- 2 **cans (21 ounces each) cherry pie filling**

GLAZE

- 1 **cup confectioners' sugar**
- ½ **teaspoon vanilla extract**
- ½ **teaspoon almond extract**
- 2 **to 3 tablespoons milk**

1. Preheat oven to 350°. In a large bowl, cream butter, sugar and salt until light and fluffy. Add the eggs, one at a time, beating well after each addition. Beat in extracts. Gradually add the flour.

2. Spread 3 cups of dough into a greased 15x10x1-in. baking pan. Spread with the pie filling. Drop remaining dough by teaspoonfuls over filling. Bake 30-35 minutes or until golden brown. Cool bars completely in pan on a wire rack.

3. In a small bowl, mix the confectioners' sugar, extracts and enough milk to reach desired consistency; drizzle over top.

CHERRY BARS

CRANBERRY BOG BARS

APRICOT SQUARES

BLACK-BOTTOM BANANA BARS

CRANBERRY BOG BARS

These easy treats combine the flavors of oats, cranberries, brown sugar and pecans. I sprinkle them with a light dusting of confectioners' sugar before serving.

—**SALLY WAKEFIELD** GANS, PA

PREP: 25 MIN.
BAKE: 25 MIN. + COOLING
MAKES: 3 DOZEN

- 1¼ cups butter, softened, divided
- 1½ cups packed brown sugar, divided
- 3½ cups old-fashioned oats, divided
- 1 cup all-purpose flour
- 1 can (14 ounces) whole-berry cranberry sauce
- ½ cup finely chopped pecans

1. In a large bowl, cream 1 cup butter and 1 cup brown sugar until light and fluffy. Combine 2½ cups oats and flour. Gradually add to creamed mixture until crumbly. Press into a greased 13x9-in. baking pan. Spread with cranberry sauce.
2. In a microwave-safe bowl, melt remaining butter; stir in the pecans and remaining brown sugar and oats. Sprinkle over cranberry sauce. Bake at 375° for 25-30 minutes or until lightly browned. Cool on a wire rack. Cut into bars.

APRICOT SQUARES

My mom made these goodies for parent-teacher meetings when I was in elementary school more than 40 years ago. Now I serve them for a variety of functions.

—**PAT RUGGIERO** OKEMOS, MI

PREP: 15 MIN.
BAKE: 40 MIN. + COOLING
MAKES: 2 DOZEN

- 1 cup butter, softened
- 1 cup sugar
- 1 large egg
- 1 teaspoon lemon extract
- 3 cups all-purpose flour
- 4 teaspoons grated orange peel
- 1 teaspoon baking powder
- ¼ teaspoon salt

FILLING

- 1 jar (18 ounces) apricot preserves
- 2 teaspoons lemon juice
- 1 teaspoon grated lemon peel

1. In a large bowl, cream butter and sugar until light and fluffy. Beat in egg and extract. Combine the flour, orange peel, baking powder and salt; gradually add to the creamed mixture and mix well. Set aside one-third for the topping.
2. Press the remaining dough into a greased 13x9-in. baking pan. Combine preserves, lemon juice and peel; spread evenly over crust.
3. Crumble reserved dough over filling. Bake at 350° for 40 minutes or until golden brown. Cool on a wire rack. Cut into squares.

BLACK-BOTTOM BANANA BARS

Not only do these bars stay moist, but their rich banana and chocolate flavor is even better the second day. My mother-in-law gave me this recipe, and it's a big favorite with my husband and our two sons.

—**RENEE WRIGHT** FERRYVILLE, WI

PREP: 20 MIN. • **BAKE:** 25 MIN.
MAKES: 2½-3 DOZEN

- ½ cup butter, softened
- 1 cup sugar
- 1 large egg
- 1 teaspoon vanilla extract
- 1½ cups mashed ripe bananas (about 3 medium)
- 1½ cups all-purpose flour
- 1 teaspoon baking powder
- 1 teaspoon baking soda
- ½ teaspoon salt
- ¼ cup baking cocoa

1. In a large bowl, cream butter and sugar until light and fluffy. Beat in egg and vanilla. Stir in the bananas. Combine the flour, baking powder, baking soda and salt; add to the creamed mixture and mix well.
2. Divide the batter in half. Add cocoa to half; spread into a greased 13x9-in. baking pan. Spoon the remaining batter on top. If desired, swirl with a knife to marble batter.
3. Bake at 350° for 25 minutes or until a toothpick inserted near the center comes out clean. Cool on a wire rack.

TOP TIP

TEST BAKING POWDER

The shelf life for baking powder is about 6 months. To test for freshness, place 1 teaspoon baking powder in a cup and add ⅓ cup hot tap water. If it bubbles actively, it's fine to use. If not, replace it.

CHOCOLATE RASPBERRY BARS

I make a lot of cookies and bars, but these special treats are my favorite. My family loves them, too. The chocolate and raspberry jam pair well together, and the bars look so pretty served on a platter.

—KATHY SMEDSTAD SILVERTON, OR

PREP: 20 MIN. + CHILLING
BAKE: 15 MIN. + COOLING
MAKES: 3 DOZEN

- 1 cup all-purpose flour
- ¼ cup confectioners' sugar
- ¼ cup butter, cubed

FILLING

- ½ cup seedless raspberry jam
- 4 ounces cream cheese, softened
- 2 tablespoons 2% milk
- 1 cup white baking chips, melted

GLAZE

- ¾ cup semisweet chocolate chips
- 2 tablespoons shortening

1. In a small bowl, combine flour and confectioners' sugar; cut in butter until crumbly. Press into an ungreased 9-in. square baking pan. Bake at 375° for 15-18 minutes or until browned. Spread jam over warm crust.

2. In a small bowl, beat cream cheese and milk until smooth. Add white chips; beat until smooth. Spread carefully over jam layer. Cool completely. Refrigerate for 1 hour or until set.

3. For glaze, melt chocolate chips and shortening in a microwave; stir until smooth. Spread over filling. Refrigerate for 10 minutes. Cut into bars; chill 1 hour longer or until set. Store in refrigerator.

CHOCOLATE RASPBERRY BARS

RHUBARB DREAM BARS

Dreaming of a different way to use rhubarb? Try these sweet bars. Top a tender shortbread-like crust with rhubarb, walnuts and coconut for delicious results.

—MARION TOMLINSON MADISON, WI

PREP: 15 MIN.
BAKE: 45 MIN. + COOLING
MAKES: 2 DOZEN

- 1¼ cups all-purpose flour, divided
- ⅓ cup confectioners' sugar
- ½ cup cold butter, cubed
- 1¼ to 1½ cups sugar
- 2 large eggs
- 2 cups diced fresh or frozen rhubarb
- ½ cup chopped walnuts
- ½ cup flaked coconut

1. In a large bowl, combine 1 cup flour and the confectioners' sugar. Cut in butter until crumbly. Pat into a lightly greased 13x9-in. baking dish. Bake at 350° for 13-15 minutes or until edges are lightly browned.

2. In a large bowl, combine sugar and remaining flour. Add eggs. Stir in rhubarb, walnuts and coconut; pour over crust. Bake for 30-35 minutes longer or until set. Cool on a wire rack. Cut into bars.

NOTE *If using frozen rhubarb, measure rhubarb while still frozen, then thaw completely. Drain in a colander; do not press liquid out.*

TOP TIP

RHUBARB BASICS

Look for crisp and brightly colored rhubarb stalks. Wrap them tightly in a plastic bag and store in the refrigerator for up to 3 days. Remove the leaves (they're poisonous) and wash stalks before using. One pound of rhubarb yields 3 cups chopped.

RHUBARB DREAM BARS

RED APPLE
BUTTER BARS

RED APPLE BUTTER BARS

I love fall because it means apple-picking time. We make these bars with our fresh-picked apples and apple butter, then top them off with a good crumbly streusel.

—**NANCY FOUST** STONEBORO, PA

PREP: 40 MIN.
BAKE: 35 MIN. + COOLING
MAKES: 2 DOZEN

- 3 **cups all-purpose flour**
- 2 **cups quick-cooking oats**
- 2 **cups packed brown sugar**
- 1½ **teaspoons baking soda**
- ¾ **teaspoon salt**
- ¾ **teaspoon ground cinnamon**
- 1½ **cups butter, melted**
- 2 **medium apples, chopped**
- 1½ **cups apple butter**
- 1 **cup chopped walnuts**

1. Preheat oven to 350°. In a large bowl, combine first six ingredients; stir in the butter. Reserve 1⅓ cups crumb mixture for topping. Press remaining mixture onto bottom of a greased 13x9-in. baking dish. Bake for 15-20 minutes or until crust is lightly browned. Cool completely on a wire rack.

2. Sprinkle apples over crust; spread with apple butter. Stir walnuts into reserved topping; sprinkle over apple butter. Bake 35-40 minutes or until lightly browned. Cool in pan on a wire rack. Cut into bars.

NOTE *This recipe was tested with commercially prepared apple butter.*

HOMEMADE LEMON BARS

My husband remembers these sweet bars from his childhood, and today, our special family meals just aren't complete without them. See the photo on page 66.

—**DENISE BAUMERT** DALHART, TX

PREP: 25 MIN.
BAKE: 20 MIN. + COOLING
MAKES: 9 SERVINGS

- 1 **cup all-purpose flour**
- ⅓ **cup butter, softened**
- ¼ **cup confectioners' sugar**

TOPPING

- 2 **large eggs**
- 1 **cup sugar**
- 2 **tablespoons all-purpose flour**
- 2 **tablespoons lemon juice**
- ¾ **teaspoon lemon extract**
- ½ **teaspoon baking powder**
- ¼ **teaspoon salt**
  Confectioners' sugar
  Orange peel strips (1 to 3 inches), optional

1. Preheat oven to 350°. In a large bowl, beat the flour, butter and confectioners' sugar until blended. Press onto bottom of an ungreased 8-in. square baking dish. Bake 15-20 minutes or until lightly browned.

2. For the topping, in a large bowl, beat eggs, sugar, flour, lemon juice, extract, baking powder and salt until frothy; pour over hot crust.

3. Bake 10-15 minutes longer or until light golden brown. Cool completely in dish on a wire rack. Dust with confectioners' sugar. If desired, sprinkle with orange peel strips.

CHOCOLATE CHIP RASPBERRY BARS

Chocolate and raspberry are a perfect pairing in these bars featuring a buttery shortbread crust. They are a special treat and yet so easy to make.

—**BEV CUDRAK** COALDALE, AB

PREP: 20 MIN.
BAKE: 40 MIN. + COOLING
MAKES: ABOUT 3 DOZEN

- 1¾ cups all-purpose flour
- 1 cup sugar
- 1 cup cold butter, cubed
- 1 large egg
- ½ teaspoon almond extract
- 1 cup seedless raspberry jam
- ½ cup miniature semisweet chocolate chips

1. In a large bowl, combine flour and sugar. Cut in butter until mixture resembles coarse crumbs. Stir in egg and extract just until moistened. Set aside 1 cup crumb mixture for topping.
2. Press the remaining mixture into a greased 11x7-in. baking pan. Bake at 350° for 5 minutes. Spread with jam and sprinkle with reserved crumb mixture. Bake for 35-40 minutes longer or until bars are golden brown.
3. Sprinkle with semisweet chips. Return to the oven for 30 seconds or until the chips are glossy. Cool completely on a wire rack. Cut into bars.

CANDIED ORANGE DATE BARS

A friend gave me the recipe for rich date bars. Chopped candied orange slices are an extra special touch that sets the bars apart. I dip my kitchen shears in hot water to make cutting the orange slices easier.

—**EUNICE STOEN** DECORAH, IA

PREP: 20 MIN.
BAKE: 30 MIN. + COOLING
MAKES: ABOUT 3 DOZEN

- 1 package (7 ounces) orange candy slices
- ½ cup sugar
- 2 tablespoons plus 1¾ cups all-purpose flour, divided
- ½ cup water
- ½ pound chopped dates
- 1 cup butter, softened
- 1 cup packed brown sugar
- 2 large eggs
- 1 teaspoon baking soda
- ½ teaspoon salt
- ½ cup chopped walnuts
  Confectioners' sugar

1. Cut orange slices horizontally in half, then into ¼-in. pieces; set aside. In a saucepan, combine the sugar and 2 tablespoons flour. Stir in water until smooth. Add the dates. Bring to a boil; cook and stir for 2 minutes or until thickened. Remove from the heat; cool.
2. In a large bowl, cream butter and brown sugar until light and fluffy. Add eggs, one at a time, beating well after each addition. Combine the baking soda, salt and remaining flour; add to creamed mixture and mix well. Stir in walnuts.
3. Spread half of the batter into a greased 13x9-in. baking pan. Spread date mixture over batter; sprinkle with reserved orange pieces. Spread remaining batter over the top.
4. Bake at 350° for 30-35 minutes or until a toothpick inserted in the center comes out clean. Cool on a wire rack. Lightly dust the bars with confectioners' sugar.

LEMON CRUMB BARS

I'm always looking for a great new cookie or bar to try, but I often return to this tried-and-true recipe. My husband loves the sweet and salty flavor combination.

—**ANNA MILLER** QUAKER CITY, OH

PREP: 15 MIN.
BAKE: 40 MIN. + COOLING
MAKES: 2 DOZEN

- 1 package lemon cake mix (regular size)
- ½ cup cold butter, cubed
- 1 large egg
- 2 cups crushed saltines (about 60 crackers)
- 3 large egg yolks
- 1 can (14 ounces) sweetened condensed milk
- ½ cup lemon juice

1. In a large bowl, beat the cake mix, butter and egg until crumbly. Stir in cracker crumbs; set aside 2 cups for topping.
2. Press remaining mixture into a 13x9-in. baking dish coated with cooking spray. Bake at 350° for 18-20 minutes or until edges are lightly browned.
3. In a small bowl, beat the egg yolks, milk and lemon juice. Pour over crust; sprinkle with reserved topping. Bake 20-25 minutes longer or until edges are lightly browned. Cool on a wire rack. Cut into bars. Store in the refrigerator.

CHOCOLATE CHIP
RASPBERRY BARS

CANDIED ORANGE
DATE BARS

LEMON CRUMB BARS

ALMOND-COCONUT
LEMON BARS

ALMOND-COCONUT LEMON BARS

Give traditional lemon bars a tasty twist with the addition of almonds and coconut.

—*TASTE OF HOME* TEST KITCHEN

PREP: 10 MIN.
BAKE: 40 MIN. + COOLING
MAKES: 2 DOZEN

- 1½ cups all-purpose flour
- ½ cup confectioners' sugar
- ⅓ cup blanched almonds, toasted
- 1 teaspoon grated lemon peel
- ¾ cup cold butter, cubed

FILLING

- 3 large eggs
- 1½ cups sugar
- ½ cup flaked coconut
- ¼ cup lemon juice
- 3 tablespoons all-purpose flour
- 1 teaspoon grated lemon peel
- ½ teaspoon baking powder
  Confectioners' sugar

1. In a food processor, combine the flour, confectioners' sugar, almonds and lemon peel; cover and process until nuts are finely chopped. Add butter; pulse just until mixture is crumbly. Press the dough into a greased 13x9-in. baking dish. Bake at 350° for 20 minutes.
2. Meanwhile, in a large bowl, whisk eggs, sugar, coconut, lemon juice, flour, lemon peel and baking powder; pour over the hot crust. Bake for 20-25 minutes or until light golden brown. Cool on a wire rack. Dust with confectioners' sugar. Cut into squares.

TOP TIP

LEMON PEEL

To grate lemon peel quickly, slice off big pieces of the colored part and grind for a few seconds in a food processor.

COCONUT RASPBERRY BARS

While mixing a batch of plain bars, I was inspired to add raspberry preserves and flaked coconut to the dough. I wound up with these yummy treats, now a family favorite.

—**AMANDA DENTON** BARRE, VT

PREP: 20 MIN.
BAKE: 30 MIN. + COOLING
MAKES: 3 DOZEN

- ¾ cup butter, softened
- 1 cup sugar
- 1 large egg
- ½ teaspoon vanilla extract
- 2 cups all-purpose flour
- ¼ teaspoon baking powder
- 2 cups flaked coconut, divided
- ½ cup chopped walnuts
- 1 jar (12 ounces) raspberry preserves
- 1 cup white baking chips

1. Preheat oven to 350°. In a large bowl, cream butter and sugar until light and fluffy. Beat in egg and vanilla. Combine flour and baking powder; gradually add to the creamed mixture and mix well. Stir in 1¼ cups coconut and walnuts.
2. Press three-fourths of the dough into a greased 13x9-in. baking pan. Spread with preserves. Sprinkle with chips and remaining coconut. Crumble remaining dough over the top; press lightly.
3. Bake 30-35 minutes or until golden brown. Cool on a wire rack. Cut into bars.

COCONUT RASPBERRY BARS

RHUBARB OAT BARS

These soft rhubarb bars provide just the right balance of tart and sweet. They are simply unbeatable.

—RENETTE CRESSEY FORT MILL, SC

PREP: 20 MIN.
BAKE: 25 MIN. + COOLING
MAKES: 16 BARS

- 1½ **cups chopped fresh or frozen rhubarb**
- 1 **cup packed brown sugar, divided**
- 4 **tablespoons water, divided**
- 1 **teaspoon lemon juice**
- 4 **teaspoons cornstarch**
- 1 **cup old-fashioned oats**
- ¾ **cup all-purpose flour**
- ½ **cup flaked coconut**
- ½ **teaspoon salt**
- ⅓ **cup butter, melted**

1. In a large saucepan, combine the rhubarb, ½ cup brown sugar, 3 tablespoons water and lemon juice. Bring to a boil. Reduce heat to medium; cook and stir for 4-5 minutes or until rhubarb is tender.
2. Combine the cornstarch and remaining water until smooth; gradually stir into rhubarb mixture. Bring to a boil; cook and stir for 2 minutes or until thickened. Remove from the heat; set aside.
3. In a large bowl, combine the oats, flour, coconut, salt and remaining brown sugar. Stir in butter until mixture is crumbly.
4. Press half of the oats mixture into a greased 8-in. square baking dish. Spread with rhubarb mixture. Sprinkle with the remaining oat mixture and press down lightly.
5. Bake at 350° for 25-30 minutes or until golden brown. Cool on a wire rack. Cut into squares.
NOTE *If using frozen rhubarb, measure rhubarb while still frozen, then thaw completely. Drain in a colander; do not press liquid out.*

RASPBERRY PIE SQUARES

Making pie for a crowd may seem impossible, but not when you turn to this crowd-pleasing recipe. The fruity raspberry filling pairs well with the flaky homemade pastry.

—*TASTE OF HOME* TEST KITCHEN

PREP: 40 MIN. + CHILLING
BAKE: 40 MIN. + COOLING
MAKES: 24 SERVINGS

- 3¾ **cups all-purpose flour**
- 4 **teaspoons sugar**
- 1½ **teaspoons salt**
- 1½ **cups cold butter**
- ½ **to 1 cup cold water**

FILLING

- 2 **cups sugar**
- ⅔ **cup all-purpose flour**
- ¼ **teaspoon salt**
- 8 **cups fresh or frozen unsweetened raspberries**
- 1 **tablespoon lemon juice**
- 5 **teaspoons heavy whipping cream**
- 1 **tablespoon coarse sugar**

1. In a large bowl, combine flour, sugar and salt; cut in butter until crumbly. Gradually add water, tossing with a fork until dough forms a ball.
2. Divide dough in half so that one portion is slightly larger than the other; wrap each in plastic wrap. Refrigerate for 1¼ hours or until easy to handle. Preheat oven to 375°. Roll out larger portion of dough between two large sheets of waxed paper into a 17x12-in. rectangle. Transfer to an ungreased 15x10x1-in. baking pan. Press pastry onto the bottom and up the sides of pan; trim pastry even with edges.
3. For the filling, in a large bowl, combine sugar, flour and salt. Add raspberries and lemon juice; toss to coat. Spoon over pastry.
4. Roll out remaining pastry; place over filling. Trim and seal edges. Cut slits in pastry. Brush top with cream and sprinkle with coarse

sugar. Place pan on a baking sheet. Bake 40-45 minutes or until golden brown. Cool completely on a wire rack. Cut into squares.

EASY LEMON CURD BARS

A cup of tea looks lonely without something sweet beside it, like these lovely bars. I'm partial to the combination of the nutty crust and the zesty lemon curd.

—DONNA HARDIN NEW VIRGINIA, IA

PREP: 30 MIN.
BAKE: 20 MIN. + COOLING
MAKES: 2 DOZEN

- 1 **cup butter, softened**
- 1 **cup sugar**
- 2 **cups all-purpose flour**
- ½ **teaspoon baking soda**
- 1 **jar (10 ounces) lemon curd**
- ⅔ **cup flaked coconut**
- ½ **cup chopped almonds, toasted**

1. Preheat oven to 350°. In a large bowl, cream butter and sugar until light and fluffy. Combine flour and baking soda; gradually add to creamed mixture and mix well.
2. Set aside 1 cup mixture for topping; press remaining mixture onto the bottom of a greased 13x9-in. baking dish. Bake 12-15 minutes or until edges are lightly browned. Cool for 10 minutes.
3. Spread lemon curd over crust. In a small bowl, combine the coconut, almonds and reserved topping mixture; sprinkle over lemon curd.
4. Bake for 18-22 minutes or until golden brown. Cool completely on a wire rack. Cut into bars.

EASY LEMON
CURD BARS

KIWI DESSERT SQUARES

KIWI DESSERT SQUARES
Be ready to share the recipe for this make-ahead dessert. It's a real eye-catcher with a taste to match!

—**MARLENE MUCKENHIRN**
DELANO, MN

PREP: 15 MIN.
BAKE: 20 MIN. + CHILLING
MAKES: 28 SERVINGS

- 2 cups all-purpose flour
- ½ cup confectioners' sugar
- 1 cup cold butter, cubed

CITRUS GLAZE
- 6 tablespoons sugar
- 2 teaspoons cornstarch
- ½ cup cold water
- ¼ teaspoon orange extract

TOPPING
- 16 ounces cream cheese, softened
- ⅔ cup sugar
- 1½ teaspoons orange extract
- 4 kiwifruit, peeled
- 14 fresh strawberries, halved

1. In a large bowl, combine flour and confectioners' sugar. Cut in the butter until crumbly. Press into a greased 15x10x1-in. baking pan. Bake crust at 350° for 16-19 minutes or until golden brown. Cool on a wire rack.

2. In a small saucepan, combine the sugar and cornstarch. Stir in water until smooth. Bring to a boil over medium heat; cook and stir for 2 minutes or until thickened. Remove from the heat; stir in orange extract. Cool completely.

3. In a large bowl, beat the cream cheese, sugar and orange extract until smooth. Spread mixture over the crust. Cover and refrigerate for 45 minutes. Cut into 28 squares.

4. Cut each kiwi into seven slices. Place a kiwi slice in the middle of each square; top each slice with a strawberry half. Brush with citrus glaze; refrigerate until set.

PEAR-APPLE PIE BARS

With two kinds of fruit, these bars from our Test Kitchen have mass appeal. Egg white adds a golden shine to the lovely lattice top crust.

—*TASTE OF HOME* TEST KITCHEN

PREP: 30 MIN. + CHILLING
BAKE: 40 MIN. + COOLING
MAKES: 2 DOZEN

- 4 **cups all-purpose flour**
- 1 **teaspoon salt**
- 1 **teaspoon baking powder**
- 1 **cup shortening**
- 4 **large egg yolks**
- 2 **tablespoons lemon juice**
- 9 **tablespoons cold water**

FILLING

- 1½ **cups sugar**
- 3 **tablespoons all-purpose flour**
- 1 **teaspoon ground cinnamon**
  Dash ground nutmeg
- 4 **cups finely chopped peeled apples**
- 3 **cups finely chopped peeled ripe pears**
- 1 **large egg white, beaten**

1. In a large bowl, combine the flour, salt and baking powder. Cut in shortening until the mixture resembles coarse crumbs. In a small bowl, whisk egg yolks, lemon juice and water; gradually add to flour mixture, tossing with a fork until dough forms a ball. Divide in half, making one portion slightly larger. Chill for 30 minutes.

2. Roll out larger portion of dough between two large sheets of waxed paper into a 17x12-in. rectangle. Transfer rectangle to an ungreased 15x10x1-in. baking pan. Press pastry onto the bottom and up the sides of pan; trim the pastry even with pan top edges.

3. In a large bowl, combine the sugar, flour, cinnamon and nutmeg. Add apples and pears; toss to coat. Spoon over crust.

4. Roll out remaining pastry; make a lattice crust. Trim and seal edges. Brush lattice top with egg white.

5. Bake at 375° for 40-45 minutes or until golden brown. Cool on a wire rack.

PEAR-APPLE
PIE BARS

RASPBERRY PECAN SQUARES

The combination of raspberry and shortbread is a favorite. Even better, this pair is topped with a pecan pie-like filling. Yum!

—DONNA LINDECAMP
MORGANTON, NC

PREP: 15 MIN.
BAKE: 40 MIN. + COOLING
MAKES: 16 SQUARES

- 1¼ cups all-purpose flour
- ½ cup sugar
- ½ cup cold butter
- ⅓ cup seedless raspberry jam

TOPPING
- 2 large eggs
- ½ cup packed brown sugar
- 2 tablespoons all-purpose flour
- 1 teaspoon vanilla extract
- ⅛ teaspoon salt
- ⅛ teaspoon baking soda
- 1 cup chopped pecans

1. In a small bowl, combine flour and sugar; cut in the butter until crumbly. Press into a greased 9-in. square baking pan. Bake at 350° for 15-20 minutes or until lightly browned. Spread with jam.

2. In a small bowl, whisk the eggs, brown sugar, flour, vanilla, salt and baking soda; stir in pecans. Pour over jam. Bake for 20-25 minutes longer or until set. Cool on a wire rack. Cut into squares.

STRAWBERRY OATMEAL BARS

Their fruity filling and crunchy coconut topping make these bars one of a kind. They dress up my trays of Christmas goodies.

—FLO BURTNETT GAGE, OK

PREP: 15 MIN. • **BAKE:** 25 MIN.
MAKES: 2 DOZEN

- 1¼ cups all-purpose flour
- 1¼ cups quick-cooking oats
- ½ cup sugar
- ½ teaspoon baking powder
- ¼ teaspoon salt
- ¾ cup butter, melted
- 2 teaspoons vanilla extract
- 1 cup strawberry preserves
- ½ cup flaked coconut

1. In a bowl, combine first five ingredients. Add butter and vanilla; stir until crumbly. Set aside 1 cup. Press remaining crumb mixture evenly into an ungreased 13x9-in. baking pan. Spread preserves over crust. Combine coconut and reserved crumb mixture; sprinkle over preserves.

2. Bake at 350° for 25-30 minutes or until coconut is lightly browned. Cool. Cut into bars.

RASPBERRY PECAN SQUARES

 **TOP TIP**

REMOVE WITH EASE

For picture-perfect brownies and bars, bake bars in a foil-lined pan and use the foil to lift them out after they're cooled. Trim the edges of the bars and use a ruler to score the lines to cut.

STRAWBERRY
OATMEAL BARS

CHERRY CRUMB
DESSERT BARS

⑤ INGREDIENTS
CHERRY CRUMB DESSERT BARS

Here's a sweet treat that's especially good with a dollop of whipped cream or a scoop of ice cream. The crumb topping has a wonderful nutty flavor, and no one will guess this streusel started with a handy cake mix.

—ANN EASTMAN SANTA MONICA, CA

PREP: 15 MIN. • **BAKE:** 30 MIN.
MAKES: 16 SERVINGS

- ½ **cup cold butter**
- 1 **package yellow cake mix (regular size)**
- 1 **can (21 ounces) cherry or blueberry pie filling**
- ½ **cup chopped walnuts**

1. In a large bowl, cut butter into cake mix until crumbly. Set aside 1 cup for topping. Pat remaining crumbs onto the bottom and ½ in. up the sides of a greased 13x9-in. baking pan.

2. Spread pie filling over crust. Combine the walnuts with reserved crumbs; sprinkle over top. Bake at 350° for 30-35 minutes or until golden brown. Cut into bars.

TOP TIP
EASY AS PIE
Boxed cake mixes, fruit preserves and fruit pie filling are convenient items to have on hand when you want to whip up a treat at a moment's notice. Cherry Crumb Dessert Bars and Raspberry Oatmeal Bars are both versatile recipes, and you can use any flavor of preserves or pie filling to suit your tastes.

⑤ INGREDIENTS
RASPBERRY OATMEAL BARS

Cake mix makes the prep work a snap for these bars. Raspberry jam adds a pop of color and sweetness, and oats lend a homey touch.

—TRISH BOSMAN-GOLATA
ROCK HILL, SC

PREP: 20 MIN.
BAKE: 35 MIN. + COOLING
MAKES: 2 DOZEN

- 1 **package yellow cake mix (regular size)**
- 2½ **cups quick-cooking oats**
- ¾ **cup butter, melted**
- 1 **jar (12 ounces) seedless raspberry preserves**
- 1 **tablespoon water**

1. Preheat oven to 350°. In a large bowl, combine the cake mix, oats and butter until crumbly. Press 3 cups of the crumb mixture into a greased 13x9-in. baking pan. Bake 10 minutes. Cool on a wire rack for 5 minutes.

2. In a small bowl, stir preserves and water until blended. Spread over the crust. Sprinkle with remaining crumb mixture. Bake for 25-28 minutes or until lightly browned. Cool on a wire rack. Cut into bars.

RASPBERRY OATMEAL BARS

MACADAMIA SUNSHINE
BARS, PAGE 121

Caramel, Nuts & More

With caramel, pecans, chocolate chips and other sweet surprises, these irresistible treats are sure to delight!

TIRAMISU NANAIMO BARS

After tasting Nanaimo Bars at a local bakery, I decided to combine them with the flavors of tiramisu, one of my favorite desserts. My friends and I love this creation.

—SUSAN RILEY ALLEN, TX

PREP: 30 MIN. + CHILLING
MAKES: 2½ DOZEN

- ½ cup butter, softened
- ⅓ cup baking cocoa
- ¼ cup sugar
- 2 teaspoons instant coffee granules
- 1 large egg, lightly beaten
- 1½ cups graham cracker crumbs
- 1 cup finely chopped flaked coconut
- ½ cup chopped pecans

FILLING

- ½ cup butter, softened
- 2 tablespoons heavy whipping cream
- 1 tablespoon rum
- 1 teaspoon vanilla extract
- 2 cups confectioners' sugar

GLAZE

- ⅔ cup semisweet chocolate chips
- 2 tablespoons butter
  Baking cocoa

1. In heavy saucepan, combine butter, cocoa, sugar and coffee. Cook and stir over medium-low heat until melted. Whisk a small amount of hot mixture into egg. Return all to the pan, whisking constantly. Cook and stir over medium-low heat until mixture reaches 160°. Remove from heat.
2. Stir in the cracker crumbs, coconut and pecans. Press into a foil-lined 8-in. square baking pan. Refrigerate 30 minutes or until set.
3. For filling, in a large bowl, beat the butter, whipping cream, rum and vanilla until blended. Gradually beat in confectioners' sugar until smooth; spread over crust.
4. In a microwave, melt chocolate chips and butter; stir until smooth. Spread over top. Refrigerate until set. Cut into bars and dust with baking cocoa.

LOADED M&M OREO COOKIE BARS

We're all so busy and pressed for time, and I find myself creating recipes that are fast to prepare but have fabulous results, proving you don't have to spend all day in the kitchen. Here's a favorite of mine that nestles crunchy and gooey chocolate candy into an Oreo-packed blondie.

—AVERIE SUNSHINE SAN DIEGO, CA

PREP: 15 MIN.
BAKE: 25 MIN. + COOLING
MAKES: 9 SERVINGS

- 1 large egg
- 1 cup packed light brown sugar
- ½ cup unsalted butter, melted
- 1 tablespoon vanilla extract
- 1 cup all-purpose flour
- ¼ teaspoon baking soda, optional
- ¼ teaspoon salt, optional
- 18 Oreo cookies, coarsely chopped
- ½ cup milk chocolate M&M's

1. Preheat oven to 350°. Line an 8-in. square baking pan with foil, letting ends extend up sides of pan; grease foil.
2. In a large bowl, whisk egg, brown sugar, butter and vanilla until blended. If desired, mix flour with baking soda and salt; add to brown sugar mixture. Stir in cookies.
3. Spread into prepared pan; sprinkle with M&M's. Bake for 25-30 minutes or until a toothpick inserted in center comes out with moist crumbs (do not overbake). Cool completely in pan on a wire rack. Lifting with foil, remove from pan. Cut into bars. Store in an airtight container.
NOTE *For a chewier texture, add the baking soda and salt.*

TIRAMISU NANAIMO BARS

LOADED M&M
OREO COOKIE BARS

FUDGY MACAROON BARS

FUDGY MACAROON BARS

Folks with a sweet tooth make a beeline for my dessert platter whenever these rich squares make an appearance. They're attractive on the platter and delectable with fudge and coconut.

—**BEVERLY ZDURNE** EAST LANSING, MI

PREP: 25 MIN. • **BAKE:** 35 MIN.
MAKES: 3 DOZEN

- 4 ounces unsweetened chocolate
- 1 cup butter
- 2 cups sugar
- 1 cup all-purpose flour
- ¼ teaspoon salt
- 1 teaspoon vanilla extract
- 3 large eggs, lightly beaten

FILLING

- 3 cups flaked coconut
- 1 can (14 ounces) sweetened condensed milk
- 1 teaspoon vanilla extract
- ½ teaspoon almond extract

TOPPING

- 1 cup (6 ounces) semisweet chocolate chips
- ½ cup chopped walnuts

1. In a microwave, melt chocolate and butter; stir until smooth. Remove from the heat; cool slightly. Stir in the sugar, flour, salt, vanilla and eggs. Spread half of the batter into a greased 13x9-in. baking pan.

2. In a large bowl, combine the filling ingredients. Spoon over chocolate layer. Carefully spread the remaining chocolate mixture over filling.

3. Bake at 350° for 35-40 minutes or until the sides pull away from the pan. Immediately sprinkle with chocolate chips. Allow chips to soften for a few minutes, then spread over bars. Sprinkle with walnuts. Cool the bars completely before cutting.

WHITE CHIP CRANBERRY GRANOLA BARS

These high-energy bars are great for late-night snacks, road trips, lunch boxes and care packages. The tart cranberries balance the sweet white chocolate nicely.

—JANIS LOOMIS MADISON, VA

PREP: 25 MIN.
BAKE: 20 MIN. + COOLING
MAKES: 2 DOZEN

¼ cup maple syrup
¼ cup honey
¼ cup packed brown sugar
2 tablespoons peanut butter
1 large egg white
1 tablespoon evaporated milk
1 teaspoon vanilla extract
1 cup whole wheat flour
½ teaspoon baking soda
½ teaspoon ground cinnamon
2 cups old-fashioned oats
1½ cups crisp rice cereal
½ cup vanilla or white chips
½ cup dried cranberries
¼ cup chopped walnuts

1. In a large bowl, combine the maple syrup, honey, brown sugar, peanut butter, egg white, milk and vanilla; beat until smooth. Combine flour, baking soda and cinnamon; stir into maple syrup mixture. Fold in the oats, cereal, vanilla chips, cranberries and walnuts.

2. Press into a greased 13x9-in. baking pan. Bake at 350° for 18-20 minutes or until golden brown. Cool on a wire rack. Cut into bars. Store in an airtight container.

WHITE CHIP CRANBERRY GRANOLA BARS

PISTACHIO BROWNIE TOFFEE BARS

These brownie bars have a homespun appeal and the surprise of pistachios. Chocolaty awesome, they've been a sought-after staple on Christmas cookie trays for years.
—**MATT SHAW** WARRENTON, OR

PREP: 20 MIN.
BAKE: 30 MIN. + COOLING
MAKES: 3 DOZEN

- ¾ cup butter, softened
- ¾ cup packed brown sugar
- 1 large egg yolk
- ¾ teaspoon vanilla extract
- 1½ cups all-purpose flour
FILLING
- 1 package fudge brownie mix (13x9-inch pan size)
- ⅓ cup water
- ⅓ cup canola oil
- 1 large egg
TOPPING
- 1 package (11½ ounces) milk chocolate chips, melted
- ¾ cup finely chopped salted roasted pistachios

1. Preheat oven to 350°. In a large bowl, cream butter and brown sugar until light and fluffy. Beat in egg yolk and vanilla; gradually add flour to creamed mixture, mixing well.
2. Press dough onto bottom of a greased 15x10x1-in. baking pan. Bake 12-14 minutes or until golden brown. Meanwhile, in a large bowl, combine brownie mix, water, oil and egg until blended.
3. Spread brownie batter over hot crust. Bake 14-16 minutes longer or until center is set. Cool completely in pan on a wire rack.
4. Spread melted chocolate over bars; sprinkle with pistachios. Let stand until set. Cut into bars.

CARAMEL CANDY BARS

Candy or cookie? Whatever you call these decadent bars, they're so rich that a small portion will satisfy almost any sweet tooth.
—**JEANNIE KLUGH** LANCASTER, PA

PREP: 20 MIN.
BAKE: 15 MIN. + CHILLING
MAKES: 2 DOZEN

- ½ cup butter, softened
- ½ cup packed brown sugar
- 1⅓ cups all-purpose flour
CARAMEL LAYER
- 1 package (14 ounces) caramels
- ⅓ cup butter, cubed
- ⅓ cup evaporated milk
- 1⅔ cups confectioners' sugar
- 1 cup chopped pecans
CHOCOLATE DRIZZLE
- ¼ cup semisweet chocolate chips
- 1 teaspoon shortening

1. Preheat oven to 350°. In a large bowl, cream butter and brown sugar until light and fluffy. Beat in flour until blended. Press into a greased 13x9-in. baking dish. Bake 12-15 minutes or until golden brown.
2. In a small saucepan over medium-low heat, melt caramels and butter with milk until smooth, stirring occasionally. Remove from heat; stir in confectioners' sugar and pecans. Spread over crust.
3. In a microwave, melt chocolate chips and shortening; stir until smooth. Drizzle over caramel layer. Cover and refrigerate 2 hours or until firm. Cut into bars.

BIG BATCH
BUTTERSCOTCH PEANUT BARS

The best of three worlds unite when melted butterscotch chips combine with crunchy peanuts over a rich, buttery crust.
—**MARGERY RICHMOND** FORT COLLINS, CO

PREP: 15 MIN.
BAKE: 20 MIN. + COOLING
MAKES: 4 DOZEN

- ½ cup butter, softened
- ¾ cup packed brown sugar
- 1½ cups all-purpose flour
- ½ teaspoon salt
- 3 cups salted peanuts
TOPPING
- 1 package (10 to 11 ounces) butterscotch chips
- ½ cup light corn syrup
- 2 tablespoons butter
- 1 tablespoon water

1. Line a 15x10x1-in. baking pan with aluminum foil. Coat the foil with cooking spray; set aside.
2. In a bowl, cream butter and brown sugar until light and fluffy. Combine flour and salt; gradually add to creamed mixture; mix well.
3. Press into prepared pan. Bake at 350° for 6 minutes. Sprinkle with peanuts.
4. In a large saucepan, combine topping ingredients. Cook and stir over medium heat until chips and butter are melted. Spread over hot crust. Bake for 12-15 minutes longer or until topping is bubbly. Cool on a wire rack. Cut into bars.

TOP TIP
PREVENT CHOCOLATE FROM SEIZING

Before melting chocolate chips, be sure all equipment and utensils are completely dry. Any moisture may cause the chocolate to stiffen, or "seize." Chocolate that has seized can sometimes be saved by immediately adding 1 tablespoon vegetable oil for each 6 ounces of chocolate. Slowly heat the mixture and stir until smooth.—**BRENDA K.** CAMANO ISLAND, WA

PISTACHIO BROWNIE
TOFFEE BARS

CARAMEL CANDY BARS

BUTTERSCOTCH PEANUT BARS

GOOEY CARAMEL
CASHEW BROWNIES

GOOEY CARAMEL CASHEW BROWNIES

These fudgy brownies are simply bursting with chocolate chips, gobs of caramel and plenty of cashews.

—MARILYN MILLER
FORT WASHINGTON, PA

PREP: 25 MIN.
BAKE: 25 MIN. + COOLING
MAKES: ABOUT 2½ DOZEN

- ¾ cup butter, softened
- 1½ cups packed brown sugar
- 3 large eggs
- 3 ounces unsweetened chocolate, melted and cooled
- 3 teaspoons vanilla extract
- 1¼ cups all-purpose flour
- ¼ teaspoon salt
- 1½ cups 60% cacao bittersweet chocolate baking chips
- 1 cup chopped cashews

TOPPING
- 16 caramels
- 3 tablespoons 2% milk

1. In a large bowl, cream butter and sugar until light and fluffy. Add eggs, one at a time, beating well after each addition. Beat in chocolate and vanilla. Combine flour and salt; gradually beat into the creamed mixture just until moistened. Stir in chocolate chips.
2. Pour into two greased 9-in. square baking pans. Sprinkle with cashews. Bake at 325° for 20-25 minutes or until a toothpick inserted in the center comes out with moist crumbs (do not overbake). Cool on wire racks.
3. In a small saucepan, combine caramels and milk. Cook and stir over medium-low heat until the caramels are melted. Drizzle over brownies.

CALGARY NANAIMO BARS

This version may claim roots in Alberta, but the original is said to have originated in Nanaimo, British Columbia. They're three delicious layers of Canadian goodness.

—CAROL HILLIER CALGARY, AB

PREP: 25 MIN. + CHILLING
MAKES: 3½ DOZEN

- ¼ cup sugar
- ¼ cup baking cocoa
- ¾ cup butter, cubed
- 2 large eggs, beaten
- 2 cups graham cracker crumbs
- 1 cup flaked coconut
- ½ cup chopped almonds, optional

FILLING
- 2 cups confectioners' sugar
- 2 tablespoons instant vanilla pudding mix
- ¼ cup butter, melted
- 3 tablespoons 2% milk

GLAZE
- 3 ounces semisweet chocolate, chopped
- 1 tablespoon butter

1. Line an 8-in. square baking pan with foil, letting ends extend over sides by 1 in. In a large heavy saucepan, combine the sugar and cocoa; add butter. Cook and stir over medium-low heat until butter is melted. Whisk a small amount of hot mixture into eggs. Return all to the pan, whisking constantly. Cook and stir until mixture reaches 160°. Remove from heat.
2. Stir in cracker crumbs, coconut and, if desired, almonds. Press into prepared pan. Refrigerate for 30 minutes or until set.
3. For filling, in a small bowl, beat confectioners' sugar, pudding mix, butter and milk until smooth; spread over crust.
4. In a microwave, melt chocolate and butter; stir until smooth. Spread over top. Refrigerate until set. Using foil, lift bars out of pan. Discard foil; cut into bars.

LEBKUCHEN

It's tradition for my family to make these German treats together. The recipe came from my great-grandmother's cookbook, and judging by the number of requests I get, it has certainly stood the test of time.

—ESTHER KEMPKER
JEFFERSON CITY, MO

PREP: 25 MIN.
BAKE: 25 MIN. + COOLING
MAKES: 3 DOZEN

- ½ cup butter, softened
- ½ cup sugar
- ⅓ cup packed brown sugar
- 2 large eggs
- 1 cup molasses
- ¼ cup buttermilk
- ½ teaspoon anise extract
- 4½ cups all-purpose flour
- 1½ teaspoons baking powder
- 1 teaspoon baking soda
- 1 teaspoon ground cinnamon
- ½ teaspoon salt
- ½ teaspoon each ground allspice, cardamom and cloves
- ½ cup ground walnuts
- ½ cup raisins
- ½ cup pitted dates
- ½ cup candied lemon peel
- ⅓ cup flaked coconut
- ¼ cup candied orange peel
- 3 tablespoons candied pineapple

GLAZE
- ½ cup sugar
- ¼ cup water
- 2 tablespoons confectioners' sugar

1. Preheat the oven to 350°. Line a 15x10x1-in. baking pan with parchment paper.
2. In a large bowl, cream butter and sugars until light and fluffy. Add eggs, one at a time, beating well after each addition. Beat in molasses, buttermilk and extract. In another bowl, whisk flour, baking powder, baking soda, cinnamon, salt, allspice, cardamom and cloves; gradually add to creamed mixture and beat well. Stir in walnuts.

3. Place raisins, dates, lemon peel, coconut, orange peel and pineapple in a food processor; pulse until chopped. Stir into batter; press into prepared pan. Bake 25-28 minutes or until lightly browned.
4. For glaze, in a small saucepan, bring sugar and water to a boil; boil 1 minute. Remove from heat; whisk in confectioners' sugar. Spread over warm bars. Cool completely in pan on a wire rack.

APPLESAUCE BROWNIES

Cinnamon-flavored brownies are a cinch to make, even from scratch. This recipe can also be doubled and baked in a jelly-roll pan.

—BERNICE PEBLEY COZAD, NE

PREP: 15 MIN.
BAKE: 25 MIN. + COOLING
MAKES: 16 BROWNIES

- ¼ cup butter, softened
- ¾ cup sugar
- 1 large egg
- 1 cup all-purpose flour
- 1 tablespoon baking cocoa
- ½ teaspoon baking soda
- ½ teaspoon ground cinnamon
- 1 cup applesauce

TOPPING
- ½ cup chocolate chips
- ½ cup chopped walnuts or pecans
- 1 tablespoon sugar

1. In a large bowl, cream butter and sugar. Beat in egg. Combine the flour, cocoa, baking soda and cinnamon; gradually add to the creamed mixture and mix well. Stir in applesauce. Pour into an 8-in. square baking pan coated with cooking spray.
2. Combine topping ingredients; sprinkle over batter. Bake at 350° for 25 minutes or until a toothpick inserted in the center comes out clean. Cool on a wire rack. Cut into squares.

CARAMEL BROWNIES

My family can't possibly eat all of the sweets I whip up, so my co-workers are more than happy to sample them. They're especially fond of these rich, chewy brownies that are full of gooey caramel, chocolate chips and crunchy walnuts.

—CLARA BAKKE COON RAPIDS, MN

PREP: 20 MIN.
BAKE: 35 MIN. + COOLING
MAKES: 2 DOZEN

- 2 cups sugar
- ¾ cup baking cocoa
- 1 cup canola oil
- 4 large eggs
- ¼ cup 2% milk
- 1½ cups all-purpose flour
- 1 teaspoon salt
- 1 teaspoon baking powder
- 1 cup (6 ounces) semisweet chocolate chips
- 1 cup chopped walnuts, divided
- 1 package (14 ounces) caramels
- 1 can (14 ounces) sweetened condensed milk

1. In a large bowl, beat the sugar, cocoa, oil, eggs and milk. Combine the flour, salt and baking powder; gradually add to egg mixture until well blended. Fold in chocolate chips and ½ cup walnuts.
2. Spoon two-thirds of the batter into a greased 13x9-in. baking pan. Bake at 350° for 12 minutes.
3. Meanwhile, in a large saucepan, heat the caramels and condensed milk over low heat until caramels are melted. Pour over the baked brownie layer. Sprinkle with the remaining walnuts.
4. Drop remaining batter by teaspoonfuls over caramel layer; carefully swirl brownie batter with a knife.
5. Bake for 35-40 minutes or until a toothpick inserted in the center comes out with moist crumbs (do not overbake). Cool on a wire rack.

LEBKUCHEN

TOFFEE PECAN BARS

TOFFEE PECAN BARS

Curl up with a hot cup of coffee and one of these treats. The golden topping and flaky crust give way to the heartwarming taste of an old-fashioned pecan pie.

—**DIANNA CROSKEY** GIBSONIA, PA

PREP: 15 MIN.
BAKE: 40 MIN. + CHILLING
MAKES: 3 DOZEN

- 2 cups all-purpose flour
- ½ cup confectioners' sugar
- 1 cup cold butter, cubed
- 1 large egg
- 1 can (14 ounces) sweetened condensed milk
- 1 teaspoon vanilla extract
- 1 package English toffee bits (10 ounces) or almond brickle chips (7½ ounces)
- 1 cup chopped pecans

1. Preheat oven to 350°. In a large bowl, mix flour and confectioners' sugar; cut in butter until mixture is crumbly.

2. Press into a greased 13x9-in. baking pan. Bake 15 minutes. Meanwhile, in a small bowl, mix egg, milk and vanilla. Fold in toffee bits and pecans. Spoon over crust. Bake 24-26 minutes or until golden brown. Refrigerate until firm. Cut into bars.

BIG BATCH
CARAMEL SNICKERDOODLE BARS

What did I do when I couldn't decide between my two favorite desserts? I combined them! This snickerdoodle-blondie hybrid is even better made with another favorite ingredient: caramel.

—**NIKI PLOURDE** GARDNER, MA

PREP: 30 MIN.
BAKE: 25 MIN. + CHILLING
MAKES: 4 DOZEN

- 1 cup butter, softened
- 2 cups packed brown sugar
- 2 large eggs

- 2 teaspoons vanilla extract
- 2½ cups all-purpose flour
- 2 teaspoons baking powder
- 1 teaspoon salt
- ¼ cup sugar
- 3 teaspoons ground cinnamon
- 2 cans (13.4 ounces each) dulce de leche
- 12 ounces white baking chocolate, chopped
- ⅓ cup heavy whipping cream
- 1 tablespoon light corn syrup

1. Preheat oven to 350°. Line a 13x9-in. baking pan with parchment paper, letting ends extend over sides by 1 inch.

2. In a large bowl, cream butter and brown sugar until light and fluffy. Beat in eggs and vanilla. In another bowl, whisk flour, baking powder and salt; gradually beat into creamed mixture. Spread onto bottom of prepared pan.

3. In a small bowl, mix sugar and cinnamon; sprinkle 2 tablespoons mixture over batter. Bake 25-30 minutes or until edges are light brown. Cool completely in pan on a wire rack.

4. Spread dulce de leche over crust. In a small saucepan, combine white baking chocolate, cream and corn syrup; cook and stir over low heat until smooth. Cool slightly. Spread over dulce de leche. Sprinkle with the remaining cinnamon sugar. Refrigerate, covered, at least 1 hour.

5. Lifting with parchment paper, remove from pan. Cut into bars. Refrigerate leftovers.

NOTE *This recipe was tested with Nestle La Lechera dulce de leche; look for it in the international foods section. If using Eagle Brand dulce de leche (caramel flavored sauce), thicken according to the package directions before using.*

CARAMEL
SNICKERDOODLE BARS

CARAMEL APPLE BARS

These bars make a great fall dessert. We like to warm individual servings in the microwave and serve with a scoop of vanilla ice cream. Now one of my family's favorite treats, maybe it will become your family's, too.
—**CAROL STUBER** OSAWATOMIE, KS

PREP: 25 MIN. • **BAKE:** 25 MIN.
MAKES: 15-20 SERVINGS

CRUST
- ½ **cup butter, softened**
- ¼ **cup shortening**
- 1 **cup packed brown sugar**

- 1¾ **cups all-purpose flour**
- 1 **cup old-fashioned or quick-cooking oats**
- 1 **teaspoon salt**
- ½ **teaspoon baking soda**
- ½ **cup chopped pecans, optional**

FILLING
- 4½ **cups coarsely chopped peeled tart apples**
- 3 **tablespoons all-purpose flour**
- 1 **package (14 ounces) caramels**
- 3 **tablespoons butter**

1. In a large bowl, cream butter, shortening and brown sugar until light and fluffy. Add flour, oats, salt and baking soda; mix well. If desired, stir in pecans . Set aside 2 cups. Press the remaining oat mixture into an ungreased 13x9-in. baking pan.

2. For filling, toss apples with flour; spoon over the crust. In a saucepan, melt the caramels and butter over low heat; drizzle over apples. Top with the reserved oat mixture.

3. Bake at 400° for 25-30 minutes or until lightly browned. Cool before cutting into bars.

CARAMEL APPLE BARS

PUMPKIN DELIGHT MAGIC BARS

I improvised these bars as my mother always did, throwing together ingredients to match the flavors of the season. With every bite we honor Mom, the tradition of family and sharing special moments.

—LISA GLASSMAN
BOYNTON BEACH, FL

PREP: 20 MIN.
BAKE: 45 MIN. + COOLING
MAKES: 2 DOZEN

- 1 **package (11 ounces) vanilla wafers**
- ½ **cup butter, melted**
- 3 **ounces cream cheese, softened**
- 1 **can (14 ounces) sweetened condensed milk**
- ½ **teaspoon pumpkin pie spice**
- 1 **can (15 ounces) solid-pack pumpkin**
- 1 **cup dried cranberries**
- 1½ **cups flaked coconut**
- 1 **cup white baking chips**
- 1 **cup chopped pecans**

1. Preheat oven to 350°. Place wafers in a food processor; pulse until coarse crumbs form. Drizzle with melted butter; pulse until blended. Press into bottom of a greased 13x9-in. baking pan.

2. In a large bowl, beat cream cheese, milk and pie spice until smooth. Beat in pumpkin; stir in cranberries. Pour over crust. Layer with the coconut, baking chips and pecans.

3. Bake 45-55 minutes or until golden brown. Cool in pan on a wire rack 10 minutes.

4. Loosen sides from pan with a knife; cool completely. Cut into bars. Refrigerate leftovers.

PUMPKIN DELIGHT MAGIC BARS

PECAN PIE BARS

BIG BATCH

PECAN PIE BARS

Rich and delicious, these bars are perfect for parties and potlucks.

—CAROLYN CUSTER
CLIFTON PARK, NY

PREP: 10 MIN.
BAKE: 35 MIN. + CHILLING
MAKES: 4 DOZEN

- 2 **cups all-purpose flour**
- ½ **cup confectioners' sugar**
- 1 **cup butter, softened**
- 1 **can (14 ounces) sweetened condensed milk**
- 1 **large egg**
- 1 **teaspoon vanilla extract**
  Pinch salt
- 1 **package (8 ounces) milk chocolate English toffee bits**
- 1 **cup chopped pecans**

1. In a large bowl, combine flour and sugar. Cut in butter until mixture resembles coarse meal. Press firmly onto the bottom of a greased 13x9-in. baking dish. Bake at 350° for 15 minutes.
2. Meanwhile, in large bowl, beat milk, egg, vanilla and salt until smooth. Stir in toffee bits and pecans; spread evenly over baked crust.
3. Bake for 20-25 minutes longer or until lightly browned. Cool. Cover and chill; cut into bars. Store in refrigerator.

TOP TIP

CANDY COATING

Candy coating, also known as confectionary coating, is a candy-making product that is tempered, ready for melting and sets up quickly at room temperature. It is available in blocks or discs at grocery stores in white, milk and dark chocolate and butterscotch flavors.

HAWAIIAN JOY BARS

I get rave reviews when I bring these to work or church. With macadamia nuts and hint of rum, every bite is like a trip to the islands.

—JENNIFER NECKERMANN
WENTZVILLE, MO

PREP: 20 MIN.
BAKE: 35 MIN. + COOLING
MAKES: 2 DOZEN

- 1 **cup butter, melted**
- 2 **cups packed brown sugar**
- 2 **large eggs, lightly beaten**
- ⅓ **cup rum**
- 3 **teaspoons vanilla extract**
- 2 **cups all-purpose flour**
- 2 **teaspoons baking powder**
- 1 **teaspoon baking soda**
- ½ **teaspoon salt**
- 2¼ **cups semisweet chocolate chips, divided**
- 1 **package (10 to 12 ounces) white baking chips**
- 1½ **cups flaked coconut**
- 1½ **cups macadamia nuts, chopped**
- 1 **teaspoon shortening**
- 1 **ounce white candy coating, melted**

1. In a large bowl, stir the butter, brown sugar, eggs, rum and vanilla until well blended. Combine the flour, baking powder, baking soda and salt; gradually add to butter mixture. Stir in 2 cups chocolate chips, white chips, coconut and macadamia nuts.
2. Pour into a greased 13x9-in. baking pan. Bake at 350° for 35-40 minutes or until golden brown. Cool on a wire rack.
3. In a microwave, melt the shortening with the remaining chocolate chips; drizzle over bars. Drizzle candy coating over bars. Store in an airtight container.

CANDY BAR BROWNIES

Two kinds of candy bars baked into these brownies make them an extra special treat.

—**SHARON EVANS** CLEAR LAKE, IA

PREP: 15 MIN.
BAKE: 30 MIN. + COOLING
MAKES: 3 DOZEN

- ¾ cup butter, melted
- 2 cups sugar
- 4 large eggs
- 2 teaspoons vanilla extract
- 1½ cups all-purpose flour
- ⅓ cup baking cocoa
- ½ teaspoon baking powder
- ¼ teaspoon salt
- 4 Snickers bars (2.07 ounces each), cut into ¼-inch pieces
- 3 plain milk chocolate candy bars (1.55 ounces each), coarsely chopped

1. In a large bowl, combine the butter, sugar, eggs and vanilla. In a small bowl, combine the flour, cocoa, baking powder and salt; set aside ¼ cup. Stir remaining dry ingredients into the egg mixture until well combined. Toss Snickers pieces with reserved flour mixture; stir into batter.

2. Transfer to a greased 13x9-in. baking pan. Sprinkle with milk chocolate candy bar pieces. Bake at 350° for 30-35 minutes or until a toothpick inserted in the center comes out clean (do not overbake). Cool on a wire rack. Chill brownies before cutting.

BLOND BUTTERSCOTCH BROWNIES

Toffee and chocolate dot the golden brown batter of these delightful brownies. I do a lot of cooking for the police officers I work with, and they always line up for these treats.

—**JENNIFER ANN SOPKO** BATTLE CREEK, MI

PREP: 15 MIN.
BAKE: 20 MIN. + COOLING
MAKES: 2 DOZEN

- 2 cups all-purpose flour
- 2 cups packed brown sugar
- 2 teaspoons baking powder
- ¼ teaspoon salt
- ½ cup butter, melted and cooled
- 2 large eggs
- 1 teaspoon vanilla extract
- 1 cup semisweet chocolate chunks
- 4 Heath candy bars (1.4 ounces each), coarsely chopped

1. In a large bowl, combine the flour, brown sugar, baking powder and salt. In another bowl, beat the butter, eggs and vanilla until smooth. Stir into dry ingredients just until combined (batter will be thick).

2. Spread into a 13x9-in. baking pan coated with cooking spray. Sprinkle with chocolate chunks and chopped candy bars; press gently into batter.

3. Bake at 350° for 20-25 minutes or until a toothpick inserted near the center comes out clean. Cool on a wire rack. Cut into bars.

SALTED PEANUT CHEWS

I took these crunchy treats to an evening reunion. They disappeared fast, and soon people were asking for the recipe.

—**IRENE YODER** MILLERSBURG, OH

PREP: 25 MIN. • **BAKE:** 15 MIN.
MAKES: 2 DOZEN

- 1½ cups all-purpose flour
- ½ cup packed brown sugar
- ¾ cup butter, softened, divided
- 3 cups miniature marshmallows
- 2 cups peanut butter chips
- ⅔ cup corn syrup
- 2 teaspoons vanilla extract
- 2 cups crisp rice cereal
- 2 cups salted peanuts

1. In a large bowl, combine the flour, brown sugar and ½ cup butter. Press into an ungreased 13x9-in. baking pan. Bake at 350° for 12-15 minutes or until crust is lightly browned.

2. Sprinkle with marshmallows and return to the oven for 3-5 minutes or until marshmallows begin to melt; set aside.

3. In a large saucepan, cook and stir the peanut butter chips, corn syrup, vanilla and remaining butter until smooth. Remove from the heat; stir in cereal and peanuts. Pour over prepared crust, spreading to cover. Cool on a wire rack before cutting into bars.

TOP TIP

REMEDY HARD BROWNIE EDGES

If the edges of your brownies or bars are coming out too hard, it may be the baking pan you are using. Dark-colored pans can often cause the edges of baked goods to brown quicker than the rest of the item.

CANDY BAR BROWNIES

BLOND BUTTERSCOTCH BROWNIES

SALTED PEANUT CHEWS

PICNIC BARS

PICNIC BARS

You'll score big points with your crew when you stir together these delicious fudge-like treats. The brownie layer is moist and tender, and chocolate chips and walnuts make a tasty topping.

—FRANK BEE EUGENE, OR

PREP: 10 MIN. • **BAKE:** 25 MIN.
MAKES: 3 DOZEN

- 1¾ cups all-purpose flour
- 1 cup sugar
- ¼ cup baking cocoa
- ½ cup cold butter, cubed
- 2 large eggs
- 1 can (14 ounces) sweetened condensed milk
- 2 cups (12 ounces) semisweet chocolate chips, divided
- 1 cup chopped walnuts

1. In a large bowl, combine flour, sugar and cocoa; cut in butter until mixture resembles coarse crumbs. Stir in eggs. Set aside 1½ cups for the topping.

2. Press remaining crumb mixture into a greased 13x9-in. baking pan. Bake at 350° for 6-8 minutes or until set.

3. Meanwhile, in a saucepan, combine milk and 1 cup of chocolate chips; cook and stir over low heat until melted. Carefully spread over crust. Combine reserved crumb mixture with nuts and remaining chips. Sprinkle over chocolate layer.

4. Bake for 15-20 minutes or until the top is set (chips will not look melted). Cool before cutting.

MACADAMIA SUNSHINE BARS

Your family and friends will be delighted with my bars. They're packed with nuts and dried fruit. Take a bite—it's like a little vacation to a Polynesian paradise. They're pictured on page 100.

—JEANNE HOLT MENDOTA HEIGHTS, MN

PREP: 20 MIN.
BAKE: 35 MIN. + COOLING
MAKES: 2 DOZEN

- 1 package lemon cake mix (regular size)
- ⅔ cup packed light brown sugar
- ½ teaspoon Chinese five-spice powder
- ¾ cup butter, melted
- 2 large eggs
- 4½ teaspoons thawed pineapple-orange juice concentrate
- 2 teaspoons grated orange peel
- 2 teaspoons grated lemon peel
- ½ teaspoon vanilla extract
- 2 jars (3 ounces each) macadamia nuts, coarsely chopped
- ⅔ cup coarsely chopped shelled pistachios
- ⅔ cup chopped dried pineapple
- ⅔ cup chopped dried mangoes
- ⅓ cup flaked coconut, toasted

GLAZE

- 1¼ cups confectioners' sugar
- 1½ teaspoons thawed pineapple-orange juice concentrate
- 4 to 5 teaspoons water

1. In bowl, combine the cake mix, brown sugar and spice powder. Add the butter, eggs, juice concentrate, orange and lemon peels and vanilla; beat mixture on medium speed for 2 minutes. Stir in the nuts, dried fruits and coconut.

2. Spread batter into a greased 13x9-in. baking pan. Bake at 350° for 35-40 minutes or until a toothpick inserted in the center comes out clean. Cool completely on a wire rack.

3. Combine the confectioners' sugar, juice concentrate and enough water to reach desired consistency; drizzle over top. Cut into bars.

TOFFEE CARAMEL SQUARES

Layers of caramel and chocolate cover a shortbread crust in these scrumptious bars. I made several pans for our son's wedding and received many requests for the recipe. They're also great for your holiday cookie exchanges.

—KAREN BOURNE MAGRATH, AB

PREP: 20 MIN. • **BAKE:** 20 MIN.
MAKES: 3 DOZEN

- 1¼ cups all-purpose flour
- ¼ cup sugar
- ½ cup plus 2 tablespoons cold butter

FILLING

- ½ cup butter, cubed
- ½ cup packed brown sugar
- ½ cup sweetened condensed milk
- 2 tablespoons light corn syrup

GLAZE

- 2 cups (12 ounces) semisweet chocolate chips
- 1 tablespoon shortening

1. Preheat oven to 350°. In a large bowl, combine flour and sugar. Cut in butter until crumbly. Press into a greased 9-in. square baking pan. Bake 18-20 minutes or until crust is golden brown.

2. In a small saucepan, combine filling ingredients. Bring to a boil over medium heat; boil and stir 5 minutes. Pour over warm crust.

3. In a microwave, melt chocolate chips and shortening; stir until smooth. Spread over filling. Cool on a wire rack. Cut into squares.

CHOCOLATE CHIP BARS

People are always surprised when I tell them they can bake these sweet treats in the microwave. They're a great recipe to have when you need a quick and easy treat for a busy day.
—**SHIRLEY GLAAB** HATTIESBURG, MS

PREP: 15 MIN. + COOLING
MAKES: ABOUT 1½ DOZEN

- ½ cup butter, softened
- ¾ cup packed brown sugar
- 1 large egg
- 1 tablespoon milk
- 1 teaspoon vanilla extract
- 1¼ cups all-purpose flour
- ½ teaspoon baking powder
- ⅛ teaspoon salt
- 1 cup (6 ounces) semisweet chocolate chips, divided
- ½ cup chopped walnuts

In a bowl, cream butter and brown sugar. Add egg, milk and vanilla; mix well. Combine flour, baking powder and salt; add to creamed mixture. Stir in ½ cup chocolate chips and walnuts. Spread into a greased 8-in. square microwave-safe dish. Sprinkle with remaining chocolate chips. Microwave, uncovered, on high for 3½ minutes or until bars test done, rotating a quarter turn every minute. Cool before cutting.
NOTE *This recipe was tested in a 1,100-watt microwave.*

CHOCOLATE CHIP BARS

CARAMEL PECAN BARS

We had a baking contest at work, and this recipe won first place. Folks love the pecan flavor, and I love that this recipe is quick and easy to make.
—**EMMA MANNING** CROSSETT, AR

PREP: 15 MIN.
BAKE: 20 MIN. + COOLING
MAKES: 4 DOZEN

- 1 cup butter, cubed
- 2¼ cups packed brown sugar
- 2 large eggs
- 2 teaspoons vanilla extract
- 1½ cups all-purpose flour
- 2 teaspoons baking powder
- 2 cups chopped pecans
  Confectioners' sugar, optional

1. In a large saucepan, combine the butter and brown sugar over medium heat until the sugar is dissolved. In a small bowl, beat eggs and vanilla. Gradually add hot sugar mixture, stirring constantly. Combine flour and baking powder; gradually add to the butter mixture and mix well. Stir in pecans.
2. Spread into a greased 13x9-in. baking pan. Bake at 350° for 20-25 minutes or until a toothpick inserted in the center comes out with moist crumbs and edges are crisp. Cool on a wire rack. Dust with confectioners' sugar if desired. Cut into bars.

CARAMEL PECAN BARS

PUMPKIN PIE BARS

PUMPKIN PIE BARS

These bars taste like a cross between pumpkin pie with a pecan bonus. They're rich in fall spices and wonderful alongside a hot cup of coffee or tea.

—SUE DRAHEIM WATERFORD, WI

PREP: 15 MIN.
BAKE: 50 MIN. + CHILLING
MAKES: 16 SERVINGS

- 1 **can (29 ounces) solid-pack pumpkin**
- 1 **can (12 ounces) evaporated milk**
- 1½ **cups sugar**
- 4 **large eggs**
- 2 **teaspoons ground cinnamon**
- 1 **teaspoon ground ginger**
- ½ **teaspoon ground nutmeg**
- 1 **package butter recipe golden cake mix (regular size)**
- 1 **cup butter, melted**
- 1 **cup chopped pecans**
  Whipped topping, optional

1. Preheat oven to 350°. In a large bowl, combine the first seven ingredients; beat on medium speed until smooth. Pour into an ungreased 13x9-in. baking pan. Sprinkle with dry cake mix. Drizzle butter over the top; sprinkle with the pecans.

2. Bake 50-60 minutes or until a toothpick inserted in center comes out clean. Cool bars for 1 hour on a wire rack.

3. Refrigerate for 3 hours or overnight. Remove from the refrigerator 15 minutes before serving. Cut into bars. If desired, serve with whipped topping.

BIG BATCH
CARAMEL PRETZEL BITES

I created this recipe to put my own twist on a pretzel log dipped in caramel, chocolate and nuts that I'd discovered in a popular candy store. These homemade treats are delightful any time of year.

—MICHILENE KLAVER
GRAND RAPIDS, MI

PREP: 45 MIN. + COOLING
MAKES: 6 DOZEN

- 2 **teaspoons butter, softened**
- 4 **cups pretzel sticks**
- 2½ **cups pecan halves, toasted**

- 2¼ **cups packed brown sugar**
- 1 **cup butter, cubed**
- 1 **cup corn syrup**
- 1 **can (14 ounces) sweetened condensed milk**
- ⅛ **teaspoon salt**
- 1 **teaspoon vanilla extract**
- 1 **package (11½ ounces) milk chocolate chips**
- 1 **tablespoon plus 1 teaspoon shortening, divided**
- ⅓ **cup white baking chips**

1. Line a 13x9-in. pan with foil; grease foil with softened butter. Spread pretzels and pecans on bottom of prepared pan.

2. In a large heavy saucepan, combine brown sugar, cubed butter, corn syrup, milk and salt; cook and stir over medium heat until a candy thermometer reads 240°(soft-ball stage). Remove from heat. Stir in vanilla. Pour over pretzel mixture.

3. In a microwave, melt chocolate chips and 1 tablespoon shortening; stir until smooth. Spread over the caramel layer. In microwave, melt the baking chips and the remaining shortening; stir until smooth. Drizzle over top. Let stand until set.

4. Using foil, lift candy out of pan; remove foil. Using a buttered knife, cut candy into bite-size pieces.

CARAMEL PRETZEL BITES

CARAMEL, NUTS & MORE

CHIPPY BLOND BROWNIES

If you love chocolate chip cookies, you won't be able to resist these chip-filled treasures. I often include this recipe inside a baking dish as a wedding present. The bars are even better with a glass of cold milk.
—**ANNA ALLEN** OWINGS MILLS, MD

PREP: 15 MIN. • **BAKE:** 25 MIN.
MAKES: 2 DOZEN

- 6 tablespoons butter, softened
- 1 cup packed brown sugar
- 2 large eggs
- 1 teaspoon vanilla extract
- 1¼ cups all-purpose flour
- 1 teaspoon baking powder
- ½ teaspoon salt
- 1 cup (6 ounces) semisweet chocolate chips
- ½ cup chopped pecans

1. In a large bowl, cream butter and brown sugar until light and fluffy. Add the eggs, one at a time, beating well after each addition. Beat in vanilla. Combine the flour, baking powder and salt; gradually add to creamed mixture. Stir in chocolate chips and pecans.
2. Spread into a greased 11x7-in. baking pan. Bake at 350° for 25-30 minutes or until a toothpick inserted in the center comes out clean. Cool on a wire rack.

BLACK WALNUT BROWNIES

These brownies, studded with big chunks of black walnuts, are crisp on top and chewy on the inside. They always get rave reviews. If you can't find black walnuts, feel free to use any kind.
—**CATHERINE BERRA BLEEM** WALSH, IL

PREP: 10 MIN.
BAKE: 30 MIN. + COOLING
MAKES: 16 SERVINGS

- 1 cup sugar
- ¼ cup canola oil
- 2 large eggs
- 1 teaspoon vanilla extract
- ½ cup all-purpose flour
- 2 tablespoons baking cocoa
- ½ teaspoon salt
- ½ cup chopped black walnuts

1. In a bowl, beat sugar and oil until blended. Beat in eggs and vanilla. Combine the flour, cocoa and salt; gradually add to sugar mixture and mix well. Stir in walnuts.
2. Pour batter into a greased 8-in. square baking pan. Bake at 350° for 30-35 minutes or until a toothpick inserted in the center comes out clean. Cool on a wire rack.

FESTIVE ALMOND BLONDIES

Short on time? Just mix up dough for these easy almond blondies and pop them in the oven. During the holiday season, I sprinkle on red and green sugar before baking.
—**BETSY KING** DULUTH, MN

PREP: 20 MIN.
BAKE: 15 MIN. + COOLING
MAKES: 2 DOZEN

- ⅔ cup butter, softened
- 1 cup packed brown sugar
- 2 large eggs
- 1 teaspoon almond extract
- 1⅔ cups all-purpose flour
- 1½ teaspoons baking powder
- ½ teaspoon salt
- ½ cup unblanched almonds, finely chopped
- ½ teaspoon ground cinnamon
- 2 teaspoons each red and green colored sugars

1. Preheat oven to 375°. In a large bowl, cream butter and brown sugar until light and fluffy. Beat in eggs and extract. In a small bowl, mix flour, baking powder and salt; gradually add to creamed mixture, mixing well.
2. Spread into a greased 13x9-in. baking pan. Sprinkle with almonds, cinnamon and sugars. Bake for 15-20 minutes or until a toothpick inserted in center comes out clean. Cool completely in pan on a wire rack. Cut into bars. Store in an airtight container.

TOP TIP

CHOP NUTS BEFORE OR AFTER MEASURING?

Chopping an ingredient before or after measuring can make a difference in how the recipe turns out. Here's a trick that might help you remember. If the word "chopped" comes before the ingredient when listed in a recipe, then chop the ingredient before measuring. If the word "chopped" comes after the ingredient, then chop after measuring. Using the example of "1 cup nuts, chopped," you should measure 1 cup of nuts and then chop them.

CHIPPY BLOND BROWNIES

BLACK WALNUT BROWNIES

FESTIVE ALMOND BLONDIES

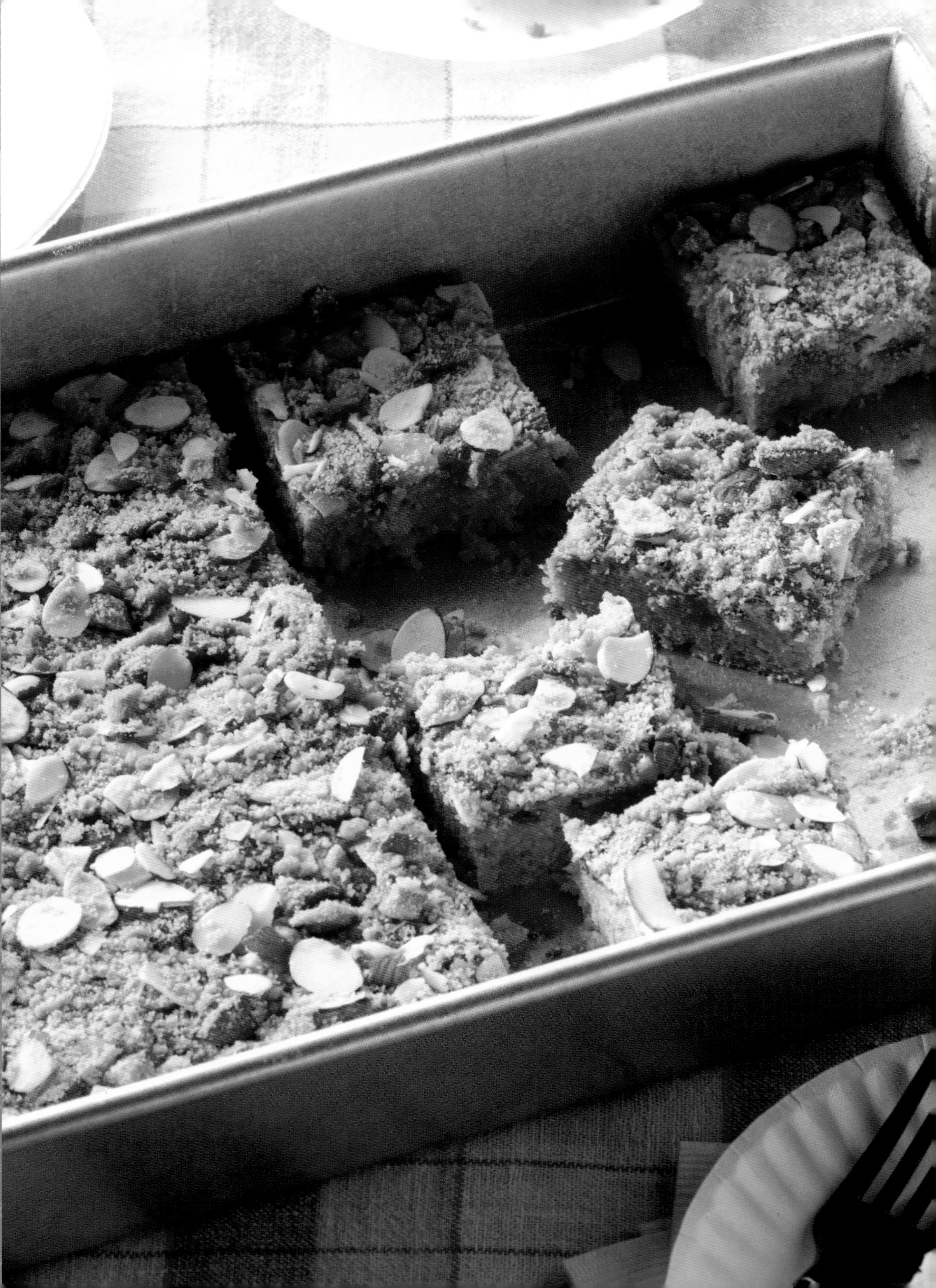

TAILGATE TOFFEE BARS

TAILGATE TOFFEE BARS

Make a one-handed grab for this tender cake studded with toffee bits. Victory is extra sweet with a treat this good.

—NICOLETTE BURNETT, PACKERS WOMEN'S ASSOCIATION
GREEN BAY, WI

PREP: 15 MIN.
BAKE: 30 MIN. + COOLING
MAKES: 2 DOZEN

- 2 **cups all-purpose flour**
- 2 **cups packed brown sugar**
- ½ **cup cold butter, cut into ¼-in. cubes**
- 1 **cup 2% milk**
- 1 **large egg**
- 1 **teaspoon baking soda**
- ½ **teaspoon almond or vanilla extract**
- 3 **Heath candy bars (1.4 ounces each), chopped**
- 1 **cup sliced almonds**
  Sweetened whipped cream or vanilla ice cream, optional

1. Preheat oven to 350°. Using a pastry blender or two forks, combine flour, brown sugar and butter until crumbly. Remove 1 cup of mixture and reserve.
2. In a separate bowl, whisk milk, egg, baking soda and extract. Stir into flour mixture until combined; pour into a greased and floured 13x9-in. pan.
3. Top with chopped Heath bars, almonds and reserved flour mixture. Bake until a toothpick inserted in center comes out clean, about 30 minutes. Cool on a wire rack. Cut into bars. If desired, serve with sweetened whipped cream or vanilla ice cream.

PEANUT BUTTER CARAMEL BARS

When my husband and our three sons sit down to dinner, the first question they ask is, "What's for dessert?" I have a happy group of guys when I report that these rich bars are on the menu.

—LEE ANN KARNOWSKI
STEVENS POINT, WI

PREP: 50 MIN. + CHILLING
BAKE: 20 MIN. + COOLING
MAKES: ABOUT 3 DOZEN

- 1 **package yellow cake mix (regular size)**
- ½ **cup butter, softened**
- 1 **large egg**
- 20 **miniature peanut butter cups, chopped**
- 2 **tablespoons cornstarch**
- 1 **jar (12¼ ounces) caramel ice cream topping**
- ¼ **cup peanut butter**
- ½ **cup salted peanuts**

TOPPING
- 1 **can (16 ounces) milk chocolate frosting**
- ½ **cup chopped salted peanuts**

1. In a bowl, combine the cake mix, butter and egg; beat on low speed for 30 seconds. Beat on medium for 2 minutes or until no longer crumbly. Stir in peanut butter cups.
2. Press into a greased 13x9-in. baking pan. Bake at 350° for 18-22 minutes or until lightly browned.
3. Meanwhile, in a large saucepan, combine the cornstarch, caramel topping and peanut butter; stir until smooth. Cook over low heat for 25-27 minutes or until mixture comes to a boil; stirring occasionally. Remove from heat; stir in peanuts.
4. Spread evenly over warm crust. Bake 6-7 minutes longer or until almost set. Cool completely on a wire rack. Spread with frosting; sprinkle with peanuts. Cover and refrigerate for at least 1 hour before cutting. Store in the refrigerator.
NOTE *Reduced-fat peanut butter is not recommended for this recipe.*

CRAZY HALLOWEEN BLONDIES

I have a sweet tooth, so Halloween is my favorite holiday. I came up with these bars for my kids, but I think I like them even more than they do!

—NANCY HEISHMAN LAS VEGAS, NV

PREP: 20 MIN.
BAKE: 20 MIN. + COOLING
MAKES: 2 DOZEN

- 1 cup butter, melted
- 2 cups packed brown sugar
- 2 large eggs
- 2 teaspoons vanilla extract
- 2 cups all-purpose flour
- ½ teaspoon baking powder
- ¼ teaspoon salt
- 1 cup chopped pecans, divided
- ⅔ cup milk chocolate M&M's, divided
- ⅔ cup chopped candy corn, divided
- ⅔ cup coarsely chopped miniature pretzels, divided
- ⅔ cup miniature semisweet chocolate chips, divided
- ⅔ cup butterscotch chips, divided
- 1 jar (12 ounces) hot caramel ice cream topping

1. Preheat oven to 375°. Line a 13x9-in. baking pan with parchment paper, letting ends extend up sides; grease paper.
2. In a large bowl, beat melted butter and brown sugar until blended. Beat in eggs and vanilla. In a large bowl, mix flour, baking powder and salt; gradually add to brown sugar mixture, mixing well. Stir in half of the pecans, M&M's, candy corn, pretzels, chocolate chips and butterscotch chips.
3. Spread into prepared pan. Bake 20-25 minutes or until a toothpick inserted in the center comes out clean. Cool completely in pan on a wire rack.

4. Spread caramel topping over bars; sprinkle with remaining pecans, M&M's, candy corn, pretzels, chocolate chips and butterscotch chips. Lifting with parchment paper, remove from pan. Cut into bars.

MIXED NUT BARS

One pan of these bars goes a long way. They get a nice flavor from butterscotch chips.

—BOBBI BROWN WAUPACA, WI

PREP: 10 MIN.
BAKE: 20 MIN. + COOLING
MAKES: ABOUT 3½ DOZEN

- 1½ cups all-purpose flour
- ¾ cup packed brown sugar
- ¼ teaspoon salt
- ½ cup plus 2 tablespoons cold butter, divided
- 1 cup butterscotch chips
- ½ cup light corn syrup
- 1 can (11½ ounces) mixed nuts

1. In a small bowl, combine the flour, brown sugar and salt. Cut in ½ cup butter until the mixture resembles coarse crumbs. Press into a greased 13x9-in. baking pan. Bake at 350° for 10 minutes.
2. Meanwhile, in a microwave, melt the butterscotch chips and the remaining butter; stir until smooth. Stir in corn syrup.
3. Sprinkle nuts over crust; top with butterscotch mixture. Bake 10 minutes longer or until set. Cool on a wire rack. Cut into bars.

RICH BUTTERSCOTCH BARS

My husband works second shift, so I spend a few nights each week baking just for fun. He takes half of my sweets to his co-workers, who frequently ask for these tasty bars.

—KATHRYN ROTH JEFFERSON, WI

PREP: 15 MIN.
BAKE: 30 MIN. + COOLING
MAKES: 3 DOZEN

- 1 package (10 to 11 ounces) butterscotch chips
- ½ cup butter, cubed
- 2 cups graham cracker crumbs (about 32 squares)
- 1 package (8 ounces) cream cheese, softened
- 1 can (14 ounces) sweetened condensed milk
- 1 large egg
- 1 teaspoon vanilla extract
- 1 cup chopped pecans

1. Preheat the oven to 325°. In a microwave, melt chips and butter; stir until smooth. Add cracker crumbs; set aside ⅔ cup. Press the remaining crumb mixture into a greased 13x9-in. baking pan.
2. In a small bowl, beat cream cheese until smooth. Beat in milk, egg and vanilla. Stir in pecans.
3. Pour over crust. Sprinkle with reserved crumb mixture. Bake 30-35 minutes or until a toothpick inserted in the center comes out clean. Cool on a wire rack. Store in the refrigerator.

TOP TIP

FREEZE NUTS FOR FUTURE USE

I use lots of nuts in my cooking and baking, but I always seemed to run out of the ones I need at a crucial time. To remedy this, I now buy large bags of walnuts, pecans and other nuts from wholesale stores, pour them into freezer bags, label them and store them in the freezer. When fixing a recipe, I just pour out the amount of nuts called for and put the rest back in the freezer.—DORIS RUSSELL FALLSTON, MD

CRAZY HALLOWEEN
BLONDIES

CARAMEL NUT BARS

CARAMEL NUT BARS

It's hard to resist these rich caramel and chocolate bars with a delightful oat crust and topping. They make a tempting dessert or a special snack for any time. And they're perfect for parties and potlucks because a little goes a long way.

—PATRICIA HILLS SOUTH DAYTON, NY

PREP: 20 MIN. + CHILLING
BAKE: 20 MIN. + COOLING
MAKES: 3 DOZEN

- 1 cup quick-cooking oats
- 1 cup packed brown sugar
- 1 cup all-purpose flour
- ¾ cup butter, melted
- ½ teaspoon baking soda
- ¼ teaspoon salt
- 1 package (14 ounces) caramels
- ⅓ cup milk
- 1 cup (6 ounces) semisweet chocolate chips
- ½ cup chopped walnuts

1. In a large bowl, combine the first six ingredients until crumbly; sprinkle 1 cup into a greased 13x9-in. baking pan (do not press).
2. Bake at 350° for 10 minutes. In a small heavy saucepan, cook and stir caramels and milk until caramels are melted.
3. Pour over the crust. Top with chocolate chips and nuts. Sprinkle with remaining oat mixture. Bake at 350° for 10 minutes. Cool on a wire rack. Refrigerate until set.

HONEY CINNAMON BARS

My Aunt Ellie gave us the recipe for these sweet cinnamon bar cookies. Drizzle with icing, and serve them with coffee or tea.

—DIANE MYERS STAR, ID

PREP: 25 MIN.
BAKE: 10 MIN. + COOLING
MAKES: 3 DOZEN

- 1 cup sugar
- ¾ cup canola oil
- ¼ cup honey
- 1 large egg

- 2 cups all-purpose flour
- 1 teaspoon baking soda
- 1 teaspoon ground cinnamon
- ¼ teaspoon salt
- 1 cup chopped walnuts, toasted

GLAZE
- 1 cup confectioners' sugar
- 2 tablespoons mayonnaise
- 1 teaspoon vanilla extract
- 1 to 2 tablespoons water
  Additional toasted chopped walnuts, optional

1. Preheat oven to 350°. In a large bowl, beat sugar, oil, honey and egg until well blended. In another bowl, whisk flour, baking soda, cinnamon and salt; gradually beat into sugar mixture. Stir in 1 cup walnuts.
2. Spread batter into a greased 15x10x1-in. baking pan. Bake for 10-12 minutes or until golden brown (edges will puff up). Cool bars completely on a wire rack.
3. For glaze, in a small bowl, mix confectioners' sugar, mayonnaise, vanilla and enough water to reach desired consistency; spread over top. If desired, sprinkle top with additional walnuts. Let stand until set. Cut into bars. Refrigerate any leftovers.

HONEY CINNAMON BARS

CARAMEL PEANUT BARS

With goodies like chocolate, peanuts and caramel peeking out from between golden oat and crumb layers, these bars are very popular. They taste like candy bars, but they also have an irresistible homemade goodness.

—ARDYCE PIEHL
WISCONSIN DELLS, WI

PREP: 25 MIN.
BAKE: 15 MIN. + COOLING
MAKES: 3 DOZEN

- 1½ **cups quick-cooking oats**
- 1½ **cups all-purpose flour**
- 1¼ **cups packed brown sugar**
- ¾ **teaspoon baking soda**
- ¼ **teaspoon salt**
- ¾ **cup butter, melted**
- 1 **package (14 ounces) caramels**
- ½ **cup heavy whipping cream**
- 1½ **cups (9 ounces) semisweet chocolate chips**
- ¾ **cup chopped peanuts**

1. In a bowl, combine the oats, flour, brown sugar, baking soda and salt; stir in butter. Set aside 1 cup for topping. Press remaining mixture into a greased 13x9-in. baking pan.

Bake at 350° for 10 minutes or until lightly browned.

2. In a heavy saucepan or the microwave, melt caramels with cream, stirring often. Sprinkle chocolate chips and peanuts over the crust; top with the caramel mixture. Sprinkle with reserved oat mixture. Bake 15-20 minutes or until topping is golden brown. Cool completely on a wire rack. Cut into bars.

CARAMEL PEANUT BARS

BIG BATCH
ALMOND ESPRESSO BARS

If you like coffee, you'll love these mocha morsels dressed up with toasted almonds. Save a few bars for afternoon snacktime—or even for breakfast.

—TAIRE VAN SCOY BRUNSWICK, MD

PREP: 15 MIN.
BAKE: 20 MIN. + COOLING
MAKES: 4 DOZEN

- ¼ cup butter, softened
- 1 cup packed brown sugar
- ½ cup brewed espresso
- 1 large egg
- 1½ cups self-rising flour
- ½ teaspoon ground cinnamon
- ¾ cup chopped slivered almonds, toasted

GLAZE
- 1½ cups confectioners' sugar
- 3 tablespoons water
- ¾ teaspoon almond extract
- ¼ cup slivered almonds, toasted

1. In a large bowl, cream butter, brown sugar and espresso until blended. Beat in egg. Combine flour and cinnamon; gradually add to creamed mixture and mix well. Stir in chopped almonds.

2. Spread batter into a greased 15x10x1-in. baking pan. Bake at 350° for 18-22 minutes or until lightly browned.

3. In a small bowl, combine the confectioners' sugar, water and extract until smooth; spread over warm bars. Sprinkle with slivered almonds. Cool on a wire rack. Cut into bars.

NOTE *As a substitute for 1½ cups of self-rising flour, place 2¼ teaspoons baking powder and ¾ teaspoon salt in a measuring cup. Add all-purpose flour to measure 1 cup. Combine with an additional ½ cup all-purpose flour.*

ALMOND ESPRESSO BARS

CHEWY PEANUT
BUTTER BLONDIES

SALTED PECAN
SHORTBREAD SQUARES

CHUNKY BLOND
BROWNIES

CHEWY PEANUT BUTTER BLONDIES

I enjoy making lots of pies, cakes, breads and other baked goods to share at family gatherings and church potlucks. These peanutty blondies are one of my favorites.

—NICK WELTY SMITHVILLE, OH

PREP: 15 MIN. • **BAKE:** 30 MIN.
MAKES: ABOUT 3 DOZEN

- ¾ cup shortening
- ¾ cup peanut butter
- 2¼ cups sugar
- 5 large eggs
- 1½ teaspoons vanilla extract
- 1½ cups all-purpose flour
- 1½ teaspoons baking powder
- ¾ teaspoon salt
- 1½ cups semisweet chocolate chips
- ¾ cup chopped peanuts

1. In a large bowl, cream the shortening, peanut butter and sugar until light and fluffy. Beat in eggs and vanilla. Combine the flour, baking powder and salt; beat into creamed mixture just until blended. Stir in the chocolate chips and peanuts.
2. Spread the batter into a greased 15x10x1-in. baking pan. Bake at 350° for 30 minutes or until bars are golden brown.

NOTE *Reduced-fat peanut butter is not recommended for this recipe.*

BIG BATCH

SALTED PECAN SHORTBREAD SQUARES

Shortbread squares are the ultimate go-to treat for cookie trays and gift-giving. It's tough to eat just one of the buttery caramel-nut treats.

—DIANA ASHCRAFT MONMOUTH, OR

PREP: 25 MIN.
BAKE: 25 MIN. + COOLING
MAKES: 4 DOZEN

- 1½ cups all-purpose flour
- 1 cup confectioners' sugar
- ½ cup cornstarch
- 1 teaspoon sea salt
- 1 cup cold unsalted butter, cubed

FILLING

- ¾ cup unsalted butter, cubed
- 1½ cups packed brown sugar
- ½ cup dark corn syrup
- ½ teaspoon sea salt
- ½ cup milk chocolate chips
- ¼ cup heavy whipping cream
- 1 teaspoon vanilla extract
- 4 cups coarsely chopped pecans, toasted

1. Preheat oven to 350°. Line two 13x9-in. baking pans with foil, letting ends extend up sides of pan.
2. Place flour, confectioners' sugar, cornstarch and salt in a food processor; pulse until blended. Add butter; pulse until butter is the size of peas. Divide mixture between prepared pans; press onto bottom of pans. Bake 10-12 minutes or until light brown. Cool on a wire rack.
3. For filling, melt butter in a large saucepan. Stir in brown sugar, corn syrup and salt; bring mixture to a boil. Reduce heat to medium; cook and stir until sugar is completely dissolved, about 3 minutes. Remove from heat; stir in chocolate chips, cream and vanilla until smooth. Stir in pecans. Spread over crusts.
4. Bake 12-15 minutes or until filling is bubbly. Cool completely in pans on wire racks. Using foil, lift the shortbread out of pans. Gently peel off foil; cut into bars. Store in an airtight container.

CHUNKY BLOND BROWNIES

Every bite of these chewy bars is packed with big chunks of white and semisweet chocolate plus crunchy macadamia nuts.

—ROSEMARY DREISKE LEMMON, SD

PREP: 15 MIN.
BAKE: 25 MIN. + COOLING
MAKES: 2 DOZEN

- ½ cup butter, softened
- ¾ cup sugar
- ¾ cup packed brown sugar
- 2 large eggs
- 2 teaspoons vanilla extract
- 1½ cups all-purpose flour
- 1 teaspoon baking powder
- ½ teaspoon salt
- 1 cup white baking chips
- 1 cup semisweet chocolate chunks
- 1 jar (3 ounces) macadamia nuts or ¾ cup blanched almonds, chopped, divided

1. Preheat oven to 350°. In a large bowl, cream butter and sugars until light and fluffy. Beat in eggs and vanilla. Combine the flour, baking powder and salt; gradually add to creamed mixture and mix well. Stir in white chips, chocolate chunks and ½ cup nuts.
2. Spoon into a greased 13x9-in. baking pan; spread over the bottom of pan. Sprinkle with remaining nuts. Bake 25-30 minutes or until top begins to crack and is golden brown. Cool on a wire rack. Cut into bars.

TOP TIP

TOASTING NUTS

You can toast chopped nuts in the microwave or in a dry skillet on your stovetop, but one of easiest methods is to toast them in the oven. Spread them in a baking pan and bake at 350° until golden brown, stirring often. Generally, nuts will be toasted in 6-10 minutes. Timing will depend on how finely the nuts are chopped and the thickness of your baking pan.

CREAM CHEESE SWIRL
BROWNIES, PAGE 147

Cream Cheese Marvels

Cream cheese turns an ordinary brownie or bar into a dreamy dessert. You'll love these rich, velvety delights.

MINTY CREAM CHEESE BARS

You'll love the way chocolate and mint come together in these easy, creamy bars. They're sure to be a family favorite.

—PAULA MARCHESI
LENHARTSVILLE, PA

PREP: 25 MIN.
BAKE: 25 MIN. + COOLING
MAKES: ABOUT 2½ DOZEN

- 2 cups (12 ounces) semisweet chocolate chips
- 6 tablespoons butter, cubed
- ¾ teaspoon mint extract
- 2 cups crushed Oreo cookies (about 20 cookies)
- 2 cups chopped walnuts
- 2 packages (8 ounces each) cream cheese, softened
- ½ cup sugar
- 4 large eggs
- 2 tablespoons cold brewed coffee
- ¼ cup all-purpose flour

1. In a large microwave-safe bowl, melt chocolate chips and butter; stir until smooth. Stir in extract until smooth. Stir in cookie crumbs and walnuts (the mixture will be very moist).

2. Set aside 2 cups for topping. Press remaining crumb mixture onto the bottom of an ungreased 13x9-in. baking pan. Bake at 350° for 10-12 minutes or until crust is lightly browned.

3. Meanwhile, in a large bowl, beat the cream cheese and sugar until smooth. Add eggs, one at a time, beating well after each addition. Beat in coffee. Gradually add flour just until combined.

4. Spread over crust. Sprinkle with reserved crumb mixture. Bake for 25-27 minutes or until set. Cool on a wire rack. Cut into bars.

LEMONY CREAM CHEESE BARS

This recipe is special to me because it's been passed down in my family for several generations. I use reduced-fat cream cheese to lighten it up while still keeping the same delicious flavor. Feel free to use regular cream cheese if you prefer—it's wonderful either way!

—PATTI LAVELL ISLAMORADA, FL

PREP: 15 MIN.
BAKE: 25 MIN. + COOLING
MAKES: 2 DOZEN

- 1 package lemon cake mix (regular size)
- ½ cup egg substitute, divided
- ⅓ cup canola oil
- 1 package (8 ounces) reduced-fat cream cheese
- ⅓ cup sugar
- 1 teaspoon lemon juice

1. Preheat oven to 350°. In a large bowl, combine cake mix, ¼ cup of egg substitute and oil; mix until blended. Reserve ½ cup mixture for topping. Press the remaining mixture onto bottom of a 13x9-in. baking pan coated with cooking spray. Bake 11-13 minutes or until edges are light brown.

2. In a small bowl, beat cream cheese, sugar and lemon juice until smooth. Add the remaining egg substitute; beat on low speed just until blended. Spread over crust. Crumble reserved topping over the filling.

3. Bake 11-13 minutes longer or until filling is set. Cool on a wire rack 1 hour. Cut into bars. Refrigerate leftovers.

MINTY CREAM CHEESE BARS

LEMONY CREAM
CHEESE BARS

CRANBERRY EGGNOG
CHEESECAKE BARS

ALMOND CHEESECAKE
BARS

COBBLESTONE BROWNIES

CRANBERRY EGGNOG CHEESECAKE BARS

My family loves cheesecake in all its reincarnations. These bars combine tart cranberries and rich cream cheese, and they taste even better when chilled overnight.
—CARMELL CHILDS FERRON, UT

PREP: 20 MIN.
BAKE: 50 MIN. + CHILLING
MAKES: 2 DOZEN

- 1 package spice cake mix (regular size)
- 2½ cups old-fashioned oats
- ¾ cup butter, melted
- 2 packages (8 ounces each) cream cheese, softened
- ½ cup sugar
- ⅛ teaspoon ground nutmeg
- ½ cup eggnog
- 2 tablespoons all-purpose flour
- 3 large eggs
- 1 can (14 ounces) whole-berry cranberry sauce
- 2 tablespoons cornstarch

1. Preheat oven to 350°. Line a 13x9-in. baking pan with parchment paper, letting ends extend up sides; grease paper. In a large bowl, combine cake mix and oats; stir in melted butter. Reserve 1⅓ cups crumb mixture for the topping; press remaining mixture onto bottom of prepared pan.
2. In a large bowl, beat cream cheese, sugar and nutmeg until smooth. Gradually beat in eggnog and flour. Add eggs; beat on low speed just until blended. Pour over crust.
3. In a small bowl, mix cranberry sauce and cornstarch until blended; spoon over the cheesecake layer, spreading over top. Sprinkle with reserved crumb mixture.
4. Bake 50-55 minutes or until the edges are brown and the center is almost set. Cool for 1 hour on a wire rack.

5. Refrigerate at least 2 hours. Lifting with parchment paper, remove from pan. Cut into bars. **NOTE** *This recipe was tested with commercially prepared eggnog.*

ALMOND CHEESECAKE BARS

My sister-in-law shared the recipe for these delicious bars with me. I've brought them to many parties and potlucks, and someone always requests the recipe.
—MARY COUSER MAPLE PLAIN, MN

PREP: 20 MIN.
BAKE: 35 MIN. + COOLING
MAKES: 3 DOZEN

- 2 cups all-purpose flour
- 1 cup butter, softened
- ½ cup confectioners' sugar
- **FILLING**
- 1 package (8 ounces) cream cheese, softened
- ½ cup sugar
- 1 teaspoon almond extract
- 2 large eggs, lightly beaten
- **FROSTING**
- 1½ cups confectioners' sugar
- ¼ cup butter, softened
- 1 teaspoon almond extract
- 4 to 5 teaspoons milk

1. Combine the flour, butter and confectioners' sugar; press onto the bottom of a greased 13x9-in. baking pan. Bake at 350° for 20-25 minutes or until golden brown.
2. For filling, in a small bowl, beat the cream cheese, sugar and extract until smooth. Add eggs; beat on low speed just until combined. Pour over crust. Bake for 15-20 minutes or until center is almost set. Cool on a wire rack.
3. Combine frosting ingredients until smooth; spread over the bars. Store in the refrigerator.

COBBLESTONE BROWNIES

My family enjoys the combination of chocolate and coconut. So I stirred coconut extract into brownie batter and added flaked coconut to the cream cheese filling. These fudgy bars are the tasty result!
—PHYLLIS PERRY VASSAR, KS

PREP: 15 MIN.
BAKE: 45 MIN. + COOLING
MAKES: 3 DOZEN

- 1 package fudge brownie mix (13x9-inch pan size)
- ½ cup canola oil
- 2 large eggs
- ½ teaspoon coconut extract
- **FILLING**
- 1 package (8 ounces) cream cheese, softened
- 2 large eggs
- 1 teaspoon coconut extract
- 1 teaspoon vanilla extract
- 3¾ cups confectioners' sugar
- 1 cup flaked coconut

1. Preheat oven to 350°. In a large bowl, beat brownie mix, oil, eggs and extract on medium speed until blended (batter will be stiff). Set aside 1 cup for topping.
2. Spread the remaining batter into a greased 13x9-in. baking pan. Bake 10-15 minutes.
3. For filling, in a large bowl, beat cream cheese, eggs and extracts until smooth. Gradually add the confectioner's sugar and mix well. Fold in coconut. Carefully spread over brownies.
4. Drop the reserved batter by teaspoonfuls over filling. Bake 45-50 minutes or until a toothpick inserted near center comes out clean (do not overbake). Cool on a wire rack. Store in the refrigerator.

CHOCOLATE CHIP CREAM CHEESE BARS

These sweet chocolaty bars couldn't be easier to whip up. They make a fun, quick dessert to bring to parties or serve to company.

—**JENNIFER RAFFERTY** MILFORD, OH

PREP: 20 MIN.
BAKE: 20 MIN. + COOLING
MAKES: 2 DOZEN

- 1 package German chocolate cake mix (regular size)
- ⅓ cup canola oil
- 1 large egg

FILLING

- 1 package (8 ounces) cream cheese
- ⅓ cup sugar
- 1 large egg
- 1 cup miniature semisweet chocolate chips

1. In a large bowl, combine the cake mix, oil and egg. Set aside 1 cup for topping. Press remaining crumb mixture into a 13x9-in. baking pan coated with cooking spray. Bake at 350° for 10-12 minutes or until set.

2. For filling, in a large bowl, beat the cream cheese and sugar until smooth. Add egg; beat well. Spread over crust. Sprinkle with chocolate chips and reserved crumb mixture.

3. Bake for 18-20 minutes or until set. Cool on a wire rack. Cut into bars. Store in the refrigerator.

CHOCOLATE CHIP
CREAM CHEESE BARS

CREAM CHEESE PUMPKIN BARS

The first time I brought these to a church function, there was barely a crumb left on the platter when it was time to leave!

—**KIM CHAMBERS** LAURELTON, NY

PREP: 25 MIN.
BAKE: 35 MIN. + COOLING
MAKES: 2 DOZEN

- 1⅓ cups all-purpose flour
- ¾ cup sugar, divided
- ½ cup packed brown sugar
- ¾ cup cold butter, cubed
- 1 cup old-fashioned oats
- ½ cup chopped pecans
- 1 package (8 ounces) cream cheese, softened, cubed
- 2 teaspoons ground cinnamon
- 1 teaspoon ground allspice
- 1 teaspoon ground cardamom
- 1 can (15 ounces) solid-pack pumpkin
- 1 teaspoon vanilla extract
- 3 large eggs, lightly beaten

1. Preheat oven to 350°. In a small bowl, mix flour, ¼ cup sugar and brown sugar; cut in butter until crumbly. Stir in oats and pecans. Reserve 1 cup for topping.

2. Press remaining crumb mixture onto bottom of a greased 13x9-in. baking pan. Bake 15 minutes.

3. In a small bowl, beat the cream cheese, spices and remaining sugar until smooth. Beat in pumpkin and vanilla. Add eggs; beat on low speed just until blended. Pour over warm crust; sprinkle with the reserved crumb mixture.

4. Bake 20-25 minutes or until a knife inserted near the center comes out clean and filling is set. Cool on a wire rack. Cut into bars. Serve the bars within 2 hours or refrigerate, covered.

CREAM CHEESE PUMPKIN BARS

CREAM CHEESE
STREUSEL BARS

CREAM CHEESE STREUSEL BARS

With a chocolaty crust and crispy topping plus a soft, creamy cheese filling, these delectable bars are almost impossible to resist!

—**JANET COOPS** DUARTE, CA

PREP: 20 MIN.
BAKE: 30 MIN. + COOLING
MAKES: 15 SERVINGS

1¼ cups confectioners' sugar
1 cup all-purpose flour
⅓ cup baking cocoa
¼ teaspoon salt
½ cup cold butter
1 package (8 ounces) cream cheese
1 can (14 ounces) sweetened condensed milk
1 large egg, lightly beaten
2 teaspoons vanilla extract

1. In a large bowl, combine the confectioners' sugar, flour, cocoa and salt; cut in butter until crumbly. Set aside ½ cup for topping; press remaining crumb mixture into an 11x7-in. baking pan coated with cooking spray. Bake at 325° for 8-12 minutes or until set.
2. In a small bowl, beat the cream cheese, milk, egg and vanilla until blended. Pour over crust. Bake for 15 minutes. Top with the reserved crumb mixture; bake 5-10 minutes longer or until filling is set. Cool on a wire rack. Store in the refrigerator.

TOP TIP

BAKING COCOA GARNISH

I garnish coffee drinks, cakes and other desserts with sprinkles of baking cocoa for a pretty look. I keep it in a small sugar shaker for easy sprinkling.

—**RENEE Z.** TACOMA, WA

CREAM CHEESE SWIRL BROWNIES

I'm a chocolate lover, and this treat has satisfied my cravings many times. The chewy texture and rich flavor can't be beat. See how delicous they look on page 138.

—**HEIDI JOHNSON** WORLAND, WY

PREP: 20 MIN. • **BAKE:** 25 MIN.
MAKES: 1 DOZEN

3 large eggs, divided use
6 tablespoons butter, softened
1 cup sugar, divided
3 teaspoons vanilla extract
½ cup all-purpose flour
¼ cup baking cocoa
1 package (8 ounces) cream cheese

1. Preheat oven to 350°. Separate two eggs, putting each white in a separate bowl (discard yolks or save for another use); set aside. In a small bowl, beat butter and ¾ cup sugar until crumbly. Beat in the whole egg, one egg white and vanilla until well combined. Combine flour and cocoa; gradually add to egg mixture; stir until blended. Pour into a 9-in. square baking pan coated with cooking spray; set aside.
2. In a small bowl, beat the cream cheese and remaining sugar until smooth. Beat in the second egg white. Drop mixture by rounded tablespoonfuls over the batter; cut through batter with a knife to swirl.
3. Bake 25-30 minutes or until set and edges pull away from sides of pan. Cool on a wire rack.

RASPBERRY CREAM CHEESE BARS

When time is short this recipe fills the bill. An effortless oat mixture forms a crunchy crust and crumbly topping for these sweet bars. You can choose any flavor of preserves to suit your family's tastes.

—LISA CORROO MADISON, WI

PREP: 25 MIN. • **BAKE:** 25 MIN.
MAKES: 2½ DOZEN

- ¾ cup butter, softened
- 1 cup packed brown sugar
- 1½ cups quick-cooking oats
- 1½ cups all-purpose flour
- ½ teaspoon baking soda
- ½ teaspoon salt
- 11 ounces cream cheese, softened
- ½ cup sugar
- 2 large eggs
- 1 teaspoon vanilla extract
- 1 jar (18 ounces) red raspberry preserves
- ⅓ cup chopped slivered almonds

1. In a bowl, cream the butter and brown sugar. Combine the oats, flour, baking soda and salt; add to creamed mixture and mix well. Press three-fourths of the mixture into a greased 13x9-in. baking pan. Bake at 350° for 11-13 minutes or until set and the edges just begin to brown.
2. Meanwhile, in a small bowl, beat cream cheese and sugar. Add eggs and vanilla; mix well. Spread over crust. Drop preserves by spoonfuls over the cream cheese mixture; carefully spread evenly. Combine almonds and the remaining oat mixture; sprinkle over preserves.
3. Bake for 25-30 minutes or until set and edges are golden brown. Cool before cutting. Store bars in the refrigerator.

HONEY CHEESE BARS

If you like cheesecake, you'll love this light dessert. Walnuts lend a subtle nutty taste to the crust, and sweet honey and bright lemon make the creamy topping delicious.

—EDNA HOFFMAN HEBRON, IN

PREP: 25 MIN.
BAKE: 30 MIN. + COOLING
MAKES: 16 BARS

- 1 cup all-purpose flour
- ⅓ cup packed brown sugar
- ¼ cup cold butter, cubed
- ½ cup finely chopped walnuts
FILLING
- 1 package (8 ounces) cream cheese
- ¼ cup honey
- 2 tablespoons milk
- 1 tablespoon lemon juice
- ½ teaspoon vanilla extract
- 1 large egg, lightly beaten
  Additional honey, optional

1. In a small bowl, combine flour and brown sugar. Cut in butter until crumbly. Stir in walnuts. Press onto the bottom of an 8-in. square baking dish coated with cooking spray. Bake at 350° for 10-12 minutes or until lightly browned.
2. For filling, in a large bowl, beat cream cheese, honey, milk, lemon juice and vanilla until blended. Add egg; beat on low speed just until combined. Pour over crust. Bake 20-25 minutes longer or until set. Cool completely on a wire rack. Drizzle with additional honey if desired. Cut into bars. Refrigerate any leftovers.

PATTERNED CHEESECAKE SQUARES

With chocolate-sauce designs piped on top, these sensational squares will bring out your inner artist. They are easy to assemble and so much fun to decorate.

—LAURENE HUNSICKER CANTON, PA

PREP: 15 MIN.
BAKE: 45 MIN. + COOLING
MAKES: 2 DOZEN

- 1 tube (16½ ounces) refrigerated peanut butter cookie dough
- 1 package (8 ounces) cream cheese, softened
- ¼ cup sugar
- 1 cup (8 ounces) sour cream
- 1 large egg
- ½ teaspoon vanilla extract
- 1¼ cups chocolate ice cream topping, divided

1. Cut cookie dough into 24 slices. Arrange slices side by side in an ungreased 13x9-in. baking pan; press together to close gaps. Bake at 350° for 12-14 minutes or until lightly browned.
2. Meanwhile, in a large bowl, beat cream cheese and sugar until smooth. Beat in the sour cream, egg and vanilla; mix well. Spread ¾ cup of chocolate topping over warm crust. Carefully spread cream cheese mixture evenly over topping.
3. Bake for 30-35 minutes or until a toothpick inserted in the center comes out clean. Cool on a wire rack. Cut into bars.
4. Place remaining chocolate topping in a heavy-duty resealable plastic bag; cut a small hole in a corner of bag. Pipe patterns on bars. Refrigerate until serving.

PATTERNED CHEESECAKE
SQUARES

BLUEBERRY
CHEESECAKE DESSERT

CHOCOLATE-CHERRY
CHEESECAKE BARS

CREAM CHEESE BROWNIES

BLUEBERRY CHEESECAKE DESSERT

These creamy bars have a luscious fruit sauce. Indulge in one (or two) now, then pop the rest in the freezer to enjoy later.

—**ARLEEN MAYEDA** ROCKY HILL, CT

PREP: 25 MIN.
BAKE: 15 MIN. + CHILLING
MAKES: 9 SERVINGS

- ⅓ cup all-purpose flour
- ¼ cup old-fashioned oats
- ¼ cup packed brown sugar
- 2 tablespoons chopped walnuts
- 3 tablespoons cold butter, cubed

FILLING

- 11 ounces cream cheese, softened
- ⅓ cup sugar
- 1 large egg
- ¼ cup sour cream
- 1 tablespoon lemon juice
- ½ teaspoon grated lemon peel

SAUCE

- ⅓ cup seedless raspberry jam
- 2 cups fresh blueberries

1. In a food processor, combine the flour, oats, brown sugar and walnuts; cover and process until nuts are finely chopped. Add butter; cover and pulse just until mixture is crumbly. Press into an 8-in. square baking dish coated with cooking spray. Bake at 350° for 9-11 minutes or until set and edges of crust are lightly browned.

2. Meanwhile, for filling, in a food processor, combine the filling ingredients; cover and process until blended. Pour over crust. Bake for 14-18 minutes or until center is just set. Cool on a wire rack. Cover and refrigerate for at least 2 hours.

3. In a microwave-safe bowl, heat jam on high for 15-20 seconds or until warmed; gently toss with blueberries. Cut the dessert into squares; top with blueberry sauce. Refrigerate leftovers.

CHOCOLATE-CHERRY CHEESECAKE BARS

I've had this recipe for as long as I can remember. I make the bars for Christmas, Valentine's Day or any occasion that calls for a yummy treat. The maraschino cherry on top adds a festive touch.

—**DARLENE BRENDEN** SALEM, OR

PREP: 20 MIN.
BAKE: 20 MIN. + CHILLING
MAKES: 15 BARS

- 1 cup all-purpose flour
- ½ cup packed brown sugar
- ⅓ cup cold butter, cubed
- ½ cup finely chopped walnuts
- 1 package (8 ounces) cream cheese, softened
- ½ cup sugar
- ⅓ cup baking cocoa
- 1 large egg, lightly beaten
- ¼ cup 2% milk
- ½ teaspoon vanilla extract
- ½ cup chopped maraschino cherries

  Additional maraschino cherries, halved

1. Place the flour, brown sugar and butter in a food processor; cover and process until fine crumbs form. Stir in walnuts. Set aside ¾ cup for the topping.

2. Press remaining crumb mixture onto the bottom of an ungreased 8-in. square baking dish. Bake at 350° for 10 minutes or until set.

3. Meanwhile, in a small bowl, beat the cream cheese, sugar and cocoa until smooth. Add the egg, milk and vanilla; beat on low speed just until combined. Stir in chopped cherries. Pour over crust; sprinkle with the reserved crumb mixture.

4. Bake for 20-25 minutes or until center is almost set. Cool on a wire rack for 1 hour. Refrigerate for at least 2 hours.

5. Cut into bars; top each with a cherry half. Store in refrigerator.

CREAM CHEESE BROWNIES

A friend from church shared this recipe with me. Cream cheese makes these moist and chewy brownies finger-lickin' good!

—**CAROLYN REED** NORTH ROBINSON, OH

PREP: 20 MIN.
BAKE: 35 MIN. + COOLING
MAKES: 2½ DOZEN

- 2 packages (8 ounces each) cream cheese, softened
- 2 cups sugar, divided
- 3 tablespoons milk
- 1 cup butter, softened
- ⅔ cup instant hot cocoa mix
- 4 large eggs
- 2 teaspoons vanilla extract
- 1½ cups all-purpose flour
- 1 cup chopped nuts

1. In a small bowl, beat the cream cheese, ½ cup sugar and milk until fluffy; set aside. In a large bowl, cream the butter, cocoa mix and remaining sugar until light and fluffy. Beat in eggs and vanilla. Stir in flour and nuts and mix well.

2. Pour half into a greased 13x9-in. baking pan. Spread with the cream cheese mixture. Top with the remaining batter. Cut through batter with a knife to swirl the cream cheese.

3. Bake at 350° for 35-40 minutes or until a toothpick inserted near the center comes out clean. Cool on a wire rack. Cut into bars.

NOTE *This recipe was tested with Swiss Miss instant cocoa.*

TOP TIP

CREAM CHEESE 101

Cream cheese is soft, mild tasting cheese produced from unskimmed cow's milk. It is used to enrich cheesecakes, frosting, dips, spreads and more.

BROADWAY BROWNIE BARS

Broadway brownies are a big hit every time I serve them. They're a little softer than most bars, but they have a gooey factor you will have a hard time resisting.

—ANNE FREDERICK
NEW HARTFORD, NY

PREP: 20 MIN. + CHILLING
BAKE: 30 MIN.
MAKES: 2½ DOZEN

FILLING
- 6 ounces cream cheese, softened
- ½ cup sugar
- ¼ cup butter, softened
- 2 tablespoons all-purpose flour
- 1 large egg, lightly beaten
- ½ teaspoon vanilla extract

BROWNIE
- ½ cup butter, cubed
- 1 ounce unsweetened chocolate
- 2 large eggs, lightly beaten
- 1 teaspoon vanilla extract
- 1 cup sugar
- 1 cup all-purpose flour
- 1 teaspoon baking powder
- 1 cup chopped walnuts

TOPPING
- 1 cup (6 ounces) semisweet chocolate chips
- ¼ cup chopped walnuts
- 2 cups miniature marshmallows

FROSTING
- ¼ cup butter
- ¼ cup milk
- 2 ounces cream cheese
- 1 ounce unsweetened chocolate
- 3 cups confectioners' sugar
- 1 teaspoon vanilla extract

1. Preheat oven to 350°. In a small bowl, combine first six ingredients until smooth; set aside.

2. In a large saucepan over medium heat, melt butter and chocolate. Remove from the heat and let cool. Stir in eggs and vanilla. Add sugar, flour, baking powder and nuts, stirring until blended.

3. Spread brownie batter in a 13x9-in. baking pan coated with cooking spray. Spread filling over batter. For topping, in small bowl, combine chocolate chips and nuts; sprinkle over filling.

4. Bake 28 minutes or until almost set. Sprinkle with marshmallows; bake 2 minutes longer.

5. For frosting, in a large saucepan, heat butter, milk, cream cheese and chocolate until melted, stirring until smooth. Remove from heat; stir in confectioners' sugar and vanilla. Immediately drizzle over marshmallows. Place bars in the refrigerator to chill thoroughly. Cut into squares.

BROADWAY BROWNIE BARS

CHOCOLATE CHIP CHEESECAKE BARS

I got this recipe from a co-worker who made these heavenly bars for a potluck. Since they combine two classic flavors—chocolate chip cookies and cheesecake—in one bite, they are a hit with our three grown children.

—JANE NOLT NARVON, PA

PREP: 20 MIN. • **BAKE:** 45 MIN.
MAKES: 2 DOZEN

- ¾ **cup shortening**
- ¾ **cup sugar**
- ⅓ **cup packed brown sugar**
- 1 **large egg**
- 1½ **teaspoons vanilla extract**
- 1½ **cups all-purpose flour**
- 1 **teaspoon salt**
- ¾ **teaspoon baking soda**
- 1½ **cups miniature semisweet chocolate chips**
- ¾ **cup chopped pecans**

FILLING
- 2 **packages (8 ounces each) cream cheese, softened**
- ¾ **cup sugar**
- 2 **large eggs**
- 1 **teaspoon vanilla extract**

1. In a large bowl, cream the shortening and sugars until light and fluffy. Beat in egg and vanilla. Combine the flour, salt and baking soda; gradually add to the creamed mixture until blended. Fold in the chocolate chips and pecans.

2. Set aside a third of the dough for topping. Press remaining dough into a greased 13x9-in. baking pan. Bake at 350° for 8 minutes.

3. Meanwhile, in a small bowl, beat the cream cheese and sugar until smooth. Beat in eggs and vanilla. Spoon over crust.

4. Drop teaspoonfuls of reserved dough over filling. Bake at 350° for 35-40 minutes or until golden brown. Cool on a wire rack. Cover and store in the refrigerator.

CHOCOLATE CHIP CHEESECAKE BARS

GERMAN CHOCOLATE
DUMP CAKE

GERMAN CHOCOLATE DUMP CAKE

We make this cakey brownie for our Sunday lunches when the whole family gets together. The cream cheese topping is so good it doesn't need additional frosting.

—KRISTY MOORE HIRAM, GA

PREP: 15 MIN.
BAKE: 35 MIN. + COOLING
MAKES: 15 SERVINGS

- 1 cup flaked coconut
- 1½ cups chopped toasted pecans, divided
- 1 package devil's food cake mix (regular size)
- 8 ounces cream cheese, softened
- ½ cup butter, melted
- 2 teaspoons vanilla extract
- 2 cups confectioners' sugar
- ½ cup semisweet chocolate chips

1. Preheat oven to 350°. Grease a 13x9-in. baking pan.
2. Sprinkle coconut and 1 cup pecans into baking pan. Prepare cake mix according to package directions. Pour the w batter into prepared pan.
3. In a large bowl, beat cream cheese, butter and vanilla until smooth; beat in confectioners' sugar. Stir in chocolate chips and remaining pecans. Spoon over batter. Cut through batter with a knife to swirl. Bake 35-40 minutes or until a toothpick inserted in center comes out clean. Cool completely in pan on a wire rack.

ORANGE CHEESECAKE BARS

I remember when my first grade teacher treated our class to little cups of orange sherbet and vanilla ice cream swirled together, so I captured the same delicious flavor in these creamy layered bars.

—CONNIE FAULKNER MOXEE, WA

PREP: 15 MIN. + CHILLING
BAKE: 45 MIN. + COOLING
MAKES: 3 DOZEN

- 2 cups crushed vanilla wafers (about 60 wafers)
- ¼ cup butter, melted
- 3 packages (8 ounces each) cream cheese, softened
- 1 can (14 ounces) sweetened condensed milk
- 3 large eggs, lightly beaten
- 2 teaspoons vanilla extract
- 2 tablespoons orange juice concentrate
- 1 teaspoon grated orange peel
- 1 teaspoon orange extract
- 5 drops yellow food coloring
- 3 drops red food coloring

1. In a large bowl, combine the wafer crumbs and butter. Press into a greased 13x9-in. baking pan.
2. In a large bowl, beat cream cheese until smooth. Add the milk, eggs and vanilla; beat just until combined. Pour half over crust.
3. Add orange juice concentrate, orange peel, extract and food coloring to the remaining cream cheese mixture; beat until combined. Pour over first layer.
4. Bake at 325° for 45-50 minutes or until center is almost set. Cool on a wire rack. Refrigerate for at least 2 hours before cutting.

BLACKBERRY CHEESECAKE BARS

Refrigerated sugar cookie dough makes a tasty and speedy crust for a creamy layer of ricotta and mascarpone cheeses. The bars are even more luxurious with a hint of amaretto and fresh blackberries scooped on top.

—TERRI CRANDALL
GARDNERVILLE, NV

PREP: 30 MIN.
BAKE: 20 MIN. + COOLING
MAKES: 12 SERVINGS

- 1 tube (16½ ounces) refrigerated sugar cookie dough
- 1½ cups ricotta cheese
- 1 carton (8 ounces) mascarpone cheese
- ½ cup sugar
- 2 large eggs, lightly beaten
- 3 teaspoons vanilla extract
- 2 teaspoons grated lemon peel
- 1 teaspoon lemon juice
- 1 teaspoon orange juice
- 1 tablespoon amaretto, optional
- 1 cup seedless blackberry spreadable fruit
- 2⅔ cups fresh blackberries

1. Preheat oven to 375°. Let cookie dough stand at room temperature 5 minutes to soften. Press onto the bottom and 1 in. up the sides of a greased 13x9-in. baking dish. Bake 12-15 minutes or until golden brown. Cool on a wire rack.
2. Meanwhile, in a large bowl, beat ricotta cheese, mascarpone cheese and sugar until blended. Add eggs; beat on low speed just until combined. Stir in vanilla, lemon peel, citrus juices and, if desired, amaretto. Pour into crust.
3. Bake 20-25 minutes or until center is almost set. Cool for 1 hour on a wire rack.
4. Place spreadable fruit in a small microwave-safe bowl; microwave on high for 30-45 seconds or until melted. Spread over cheesecake layer; top with fresh blackberries. Refrigerate until serving.

NUTTY CHEESECAKE SQUARES

These bars are easy to make for everyday occasions but still special enough to serve company.
—RUTH SIMON BUFFALO, NY

PREP: 20 MIN.
BAKE: 20 MIN. + COOLING
MAKES: 16-20 SERVINGS

- 2 cups all-purpose flour
- 1 cup finely chopped walnuts
- ⅔ cup packed brown sugar
- ½ teaspoon salt
- ⅔ cup cold butter
FILLING
- 2 packages (8 ounces each) cream cheese, softened
- ½ cup sugar
- 2 large eggs, lightly beaten
- ¼ cup milk
- 1 teaspoon vanilla extract

1. In a large bowl, combine the flour, walnuts, brown sugar and salt; cut in butter until the mixture resembles coarse crumbs. Set half aside; press the remaining crumb mixture onto the bottom of a greased 13x9-in. baking pan. Bake crust at 350° for 10-15 minutes or until lightly browned.
2. In a bowl, beat filling ingredients until smooth; pour over the crust. Sprinkle with reserved crumbs.
3. Bake at 350° for 20-25 minutes or until a knife inserted near center comes out clean. Cool on a wire rack for 1 hour. Store in the refrigerator.

BLACKBERRY CHEESECAKE BARS

TOP TIP

RICOTTA 101

When milk or cream is separated into curds and whey, the curds are used to make cottage cheese and the whey is used to make ricotta cheese. Ricotta is a soft cheese that has a fine, moist, grainy texture.

NUTTY CHEESECAKE
SQUARES

BACON CHOCOLATE
CHIP CHEESECAKE BLONDIES

APPLE CARAMEL
CHEESECAKE BARS

MINTY
CHOCOLATE
CREAM CHEESE
BARS

BACON CHOCOLATE CHIP CHEESECAKE BLONDIES

What could be better than a cookie, brownie and cheesecake all mixed up together with bacon to top it off? If you're a sweet and savory fan like me, you'll love these.
—**KATIE O'KEEFFE** DERRY, NH

PREP: 30 MIN.
BAKE: 45 MIN. + CHILLING
MAKES: 16 SERVINGS

- 8 bacon strips, cooked and crumbled
- 1 cup butter, softened
- ¾ cup sugar
- ¾ cup packed brown sugar
- 2 large eggs
- 1 teaspoon vanilla extract
- 2¼ cups all-purpose flour
- 1 teaspoon salt
- 1 teaspoon baking soda
- 2 cups (12 ounces) semisweet chocolate chips

CHEESECAKE LAYER

- 2 packages (8 ounces each) cream cheese, softened
- 1 cup sugar
- 2 large eggs
- ¾ cup 2% milk
- 2 teaspoons vanilla extract

1. Preheat oven to 375°. Line a 9-in. square baking pan with foil, letting ends extend up sides of pan; grease foil.
2. Reserve ¼ cup crumbled bacon for top. In a large bowl, cream the butter and sugars until light and fluffy. Beat in eggs and vanilla. In another bowl, whisk flour, salt and baking soda; gradually beat into creamed mixture. Stir in chocolate chips and remaining bacon. Press half of the dough onto bottom of prepared pan.
3. For cheesecake layer, in a large bowl, beat cream cheese and sugar until smooth. Add eggs, milk and vanilla; beat on low speed just until blended. Pour over dough in prepared pan; drop remaining dough by rounded tablespoons over cheesecake layer. Sprinkle with the reserved bacon.
4. Bake 45-50 minutes or until golden brown. Cool in pan on a wire rack. Refrigerate at least 4 hours before cutting. Lifting with foil, remove from pan. Cut into bars.

APPLE CARAMEL CHEESECAKE BARS

Roll a caramel apple, cheesecake and streusel-topped apple pie all into one irresistible dessert.
—**KATHY WHITE** HENDERSON, NV

PREP: 30 MIN.
BAKE: 25 MIN. + CHILLING
MAKES: 3 DOZEN

- 2 cups all-purpose flour
- ½ cup packed brown sugar
- ¾ cup cold butter, cubed
- 2 packages (8 ounces each) cream cheese, softened
- ½ cup plus 2 tablespoons sugar, divided
- 1 teaspoon vanilla extract
- 2 large eggs, lightly beaten
- 3 medium tart apples, peeled and finely chopped
- ½ teaspoon ground cinnamon
- ¼ teaspoon ground nutmeg

STREUSEL

- ¾ cup all-purpose flour
- ¾ cup packed brown sugar
- ½ cup quick-cooking oats
- ⅓ cup cold butter, cubed
- ⅓ cup hot caramel ice cream topping

1. Preheat oven to 350°. In a small bowl, combine flour and brown sugar; cut in butter until crumbly. Press into a well-greased 13x9-in. baking pan. Bake 15-18 minutes or until lightly browned.
2. Meanwhile, in a large bowl, beat cream cheese, ½ cup of sugar and vanilla until smooth. Add eggs; beat on low speed just until combined. Spread over crust.
3. In a small bowl, toss apples with cinnamon, nutmeg and remaining sugar; spoon over cream cheese layer. In another bowl, mix flour, brown sugar and oats; cut in butter until crumbly. Sprinkle over the apple layer.
4. Bake 25-30 minutes or until filling is set. Drizzle with caramel topping; cool in pan on a wire rack 1 hour. Refrigerate at least 2 hours. Cut into bars.

MINTY CHOCOLATE CREAM CHEESE BARS

When I was growing up, I always looked forward to Grandma's gooey rich cream cheese bars. This version includes mint, one of my favorite flavor add-ins.
—**JILL LUTZ** WOODBURY, MN

PREP: 15 MIN.
BAKE: 30 MIN. + COOLING
MAKES: 2 DOZEN

- 1 package chocolate cake mix (regular size)
- ½ cup butter, softened
- 1 teaspoon almond extract
- 1 teaspoon vanilla extract
- 4 large eggs, divided use
- 1 package (10 ounces) Andes creme de menthe baking chips, divided
- 8 ounces cream cheese, softened
- 1⅔ cups confectioners' sugar

1. Preheat oven to 350°. In a large bowl, beat cake mix, butter, extracts and 2 eggs until blended. Spread into a greased 13x9-in. baking pan. Sprinkle with ¾ cup baking chips.
2. In a small bowl, beat cream cheese and confectioners' sugar until smooth. Add remaining eggs; beat on low speed just until blended. Pour over chocolate layer, spreading evenly; sprinkle with remaining baking chips.
3. Bake 30-35 minutes or until edges begin to brown. Cool in pan on a wire rack. Cut into bars. Refrigerate leftovers.

TOFFEE CHEESECAKE BARS

These melt-in-your-mouth treats are absolutely delicious, and just about everyone will want seconds. A must for Christmas gift-giving, they can be made with reduced-fat cream cheese to lighten them up.
—EDIE DESPAIN LOGAN, UT

PREP: 25 MIN.
BAKE: 20 MIN. + CHILLING
MAKES: 2½ DOZEN

- 1 cup all-purpose flour
- ¾ cup confectioners' sugar
- ⅓ cup baking cocoa
- ⅛ teaspoon baking soda
- ½ cup cold butter
- 1 package (8 ounces) cream cheese
- 1 can (14 ounces) sweetened condensed milk
- 2 large eggs, lightly beaten
- 1 teaspoon vanilla extract
- 1¼ cups milk chocolate English toffee bits, divided

1. Preheat oven to 350°. In a small bowl, combine flour, confectioners' sugar, cocoa and baking soda. Cut in butter until mixture resembles coarse crumbs. Press onto the bottom of an ungreased 13x9-in. baking dish. Bake 12-15 minutes or until set.

2. In a large bowl, beat the cream cheese until fluffy. Add milk, eggs and vanilla; beat until smooth. Stir in ¾ cup toffee bits. Pour over crust. Bake 18-22 minutes longer or until center is almost set.

3. Cool on a wire rack 15 minutes. Sprinkle with remaining toffee bits; cool completely. Cover bars and refrigerate 8 hours or overnight.

TOFFEE CHEESECAKE BARS

RASPBERRY CHEESECAKE BARS

My family's love of raspberries and cheesecake make this creamy treat a perfect dessert for us.
—**JILL COX** LINCOLN, NE

PREP: 30 MIN.
BAKE: 35 MIN. + CHILLING
MAKES: 2 DOZEN

- 1 **cup all-purpose flour**
- 1 **cup finely chopped pecans**
- ⅓ **cup packed brown sugar**
- ¼ **teaspoon ground cinnamon**
- ¼ **teaspoon salt**
- ⅓ **cup cold butter**
- 1 **jar (12 ounces) seedless raspberry jam, divided**
- 2 **packages (8 ounces each) cream cheese, softened**
- ¾ **cup sugar**
- ½ **teaspoon grated lemon peel**
- ½ **teaspoon vanilla extract**
- 3 **large eggs, lightly beaten**

TOPPING
- 1½ **cups (12 ounces) sour cream**
- 3 **tablespoons sugar**
- 1 **teaspoon vanilla extract**

1. In a small bowl, combine flour, pecans, brown sugar, cinnamon and salt. Cut in butter until crumbly. Press onto the bottom of a greased 13x9-in. baking dish. Bake at 350° for 10-12 minutes or until lightly browned. Cool on a wire rack for 5 minutes.

2. Set aside 3 tablespoons jam; spread remaining jam over crust. In a large bowl, beat cream cheese and sugar until smooth. Beat in lemon peel and vanilla. Add eggs; beat on low speed just until combined. Spread evenly over jam. Bake for 20-25 minutes or until almost set.

3. In another bowl, combine the sour cream, sugar and vanilla; spread over cheesecake. Warm remaining jam and swirl over top. Bake 5-7 minutes or just until set.

4. Cool on a wire rack for 1 hour. Refrigerate for at least 2 hours. Cut into bars.

RASPBERRY CHEESECAKE BARS

COOKIES 'N' CREAM
BROWNIES

COOKIES 'N' CREAM BROWNIES

You don't need to frost these brownies because the tasty cream cheese layer makes them taste like they're already frosted. The crushed cookies add extra chocolate flavor and a fun crunch.

—DARLENE BRENDEN SALEM, OR

PREP: 15 MIN.
BAKE: 25 MIN. + COOLING
MAKES: 2 DOZEN

- 1 package (8 ounces) cream cheese, softened
- ¼ cup sugar
- 1 large egg
- ½ teaspoon vanilla extract

BROWNIE LAYER
- ½ cup butter, melted
- ½ cup sugar
- ½ cup packed brown sugar
- ½ cup baking cocoa
- 2 large eggs
- 1 teaspoon vanilla extract
- ½ cup all-purpose flour
- 1 teaspoon baking powder
- 12 Oreo cookies, crushed
- 8 Oreo cookies, coarsely chopped

1. In a small bowl, beat the cream cheese, sugar, egg and vanilla until smooth; set aside. For brownie layer, combine the butter, sugars and cocoa in a large bowl. Beat in eggs. Combine flour and baking powder; gradually add to cocoa mixture. Stir in the crushed Oreo cookie crumbs.
2. Pour into a greased 11x7-in. baking pan. Spoon cream cheese mixture over batter. Sprinkle with coarsely chopped cookies. Bake at 350° for 25-30 minutes or until a toothpick inserted in the center comes out with moist crumbs. Cool completely on a wire rack. Cut into bars. Store in the refrigerator.

CHEESECAKE BROWNIE SQUARES

Brownies are my grandson Noah's favorite treat, so we always make some when he comes to visit. These ooey-gooey squares are a definite crowd-pleaser.

—BARBARA BANZHOF MUNCY, PA

PREP: 30 MIN.
BAKE: 30 MIN. + COOLING
MAKES: 3 DOZEN

- 1 package fudge brownie mix (13x9-inch pan size)
- 6 ounces cream cheese, softened
- 6 tablespoons butter, softened
- ½ cup sugar
- 2 tablespoons all-purpose flour
- 1 teaspoon vanilla extract
- 2 large eggs, lightly beaten
- 1 can (16 ounces) chocolate frosting

1. Prepare brownie mix batter according to package directions. Spread 2 cups into a greased 13x9-in. baking dish; set aside.
2. In a small bowl, beat the cream cheese, butter, sugar, flour and vanilla until smooth. Add eggs; beat on low speed just until combined. Spread evenly over brownie batter. Top with remaining brownie batter. Cut through the batter with a knife to swirl.
3. Bake at 350° for 28-32 minutes or until a toothpick inserted in the center comes out with moist crumbs (brownies may appear moist). Cool completely on a wire rack. Spread frosting over brownies.

CHEESECAKE BROWNIE SQUARES

BERRY & GANACHE CHEESECAKE BARS

I put fresh raspberries or blueberries on top of a silky ganache for a rich and satisfying dessert.
—CARMELL CHILDS FERRON, UT

PREP: 35 MIN.
BAKE: 25 MIN. + CHILLING
MAKES: 2 DOZEN

- 1½ cups graham cracker crumbs
- ¼ cup finely chopped pecans
- ¼ teaspoon salt
- ¼ cup butter, melted

CHEESECAKE LAYER
- 2 packages (8 ounces each) cream cheese, softened
- ½ cup sugar
- ½ teaspoon vanilla extract
- 2 large eggs, lightly beaten

TOPPING
- 1½ cups (9 ounces) semisweet chocolate chips
- 1 cup heavy whipping cream
- 2 tablespoons balsamic vinegar
- 1 tablespoon light corn syrup
- 1½ cups fresh berries

1. Preheat oven to 350°. In a bowl, mix cracker crumbs, pecans and salt; stir in melted butter. Press onto bottom of a greased 13x9-in. baking pan. Bake for 8-10 minutes or until lightly browned. Cool on wire rack.
2. In a large bowl, beat the cream cheese and sugar until smooth. Beat in vanilla. Add eggs; beat on low speed just until blended. Spread over crust. Bake 15-20 minutes or until the center is almost set. Cool 1 hour on a wire rack.
3. Place chocolate chips in a small bowl. In a saucepan, bring cream just to a boil. Pour over chocolate; let stand for 5 minutes. Stir with a whisk until smooth. Stir in vinegar and corn syrup; cool slightly, stirring occasionally. Pour over cheesecake layer; let stand for 5 minutes. Top with berries.
4. Refrigerate at least 3 hours, covering when completely cooled. Cut into bars.

MOCHA CHEESECAKE BARS

These no-bake bars are easy to whip up, but they feel sophisticated. You'll want to savor every bite of the silky chocolate filling with a hint of coffee atop a crunchy cookie crust.
—MARY WILHELM SPARTA, WI

PREP: 30 MIN. + CHILLING
MAKES: 24 SERVINGS

- 25 Oreo cookies,
- 3 tablespoons hot fudge ice cream topping
- 3 tablespoons butter, melted

FILLING
- 1 envelope unflavored gelatin
- ½ cup cold strong brewed coffee
- 2 packages (8 ounces each) cream cheese
- ¾ cup sugar
- 1 cup (8 ounces) sour cream
- 3 ounces bittersweet chocolate, melted and cooled
- 24 chocolate-covered coffee beans, optional

1. Place cookies in a food processor. Cover and pulse until fine crumbs form. Add fudge topping and butter; pulse just until blended. Press onto the bottom of a 13x9-in. dish coated with cooking spray. Refrigerate for 10 minutes.
2. Meanwhile, for filling, in a small saucepan, sprinkle gelatin over coffee; let stand for 1 minute. Heat over low heat, stirring until gelatin is completely dissolved. Remove from the heat; set aside.
3. In a large bowl, beat the cream cheese and sugar until smooth. Beat in the sour cream, chocolate and the reserved coffee mixture until blended. Pour over crust. Cover and refrigerate for at least 4 hours or until firm.
4. Cut into bars. If desired, garnish with chocolate-covered coffee beans. Refrigerate leftovers.

CHEESECAKE SQUARES

I lived on a dairy farm when I was young, and my mom always had a lot of sour cream on hand. She put it to good use in this no-crust, all-filling recipe. Top with blackberry sauce for an extra treat if you have it.
—SHIRLEY FOREST EAU CLAIRE, WI

PREP: 10 MIN.
BAKE: 1 HOUR + CHILLING
MAKES: 20 SERVINGS

- 2 packages (8 ounces each) cream cheese, softened
- 1 cup ricotta cheese
- 1½ cups sugar
- 4 large eggs
- ¼ cup butter, melted and cooled
- 3 tablespoons cornstarch
- 3 tablespoons all-purpose flour
- 1 tablespoon vanilla extract
- 2 cups (16 ounces) sour cream
  Seasonal fresh berries

1. In a bowl, beat cream cheese, ricotta and sugar until smooth. Add the eggs, one at a time, mixing well after each addition. Beat in the butter, cornstarch, flour and vanilla until smooth. Fold in sour cream.
2. Pour into a greased 13x9-in. baking pan. Bake, uncovered, at 325° for 1 hour or until almost set. Cool on a wire rack for 10 minutes. Carefully run a knife around edge of pan to loosen; cool 1 hour longer.
3. Chill several hours or overnight. Top each serving with berries.

TOP TIP

BERRIES 101

Fresh berries should be stored covered in your refrigerator. Wash just before needed, and use them within 10 days.

BERRY & GANACHE
CHEESECAKE BARS

MOCHA
CHEESECAKE
BARS

CHEESECAKE
SQUARES

BANANA BARS WITH CREAM
CHEESE FROSTING, PAGE 183

Frosted Treats

It's easy to add a crowning touch to sweet sensations with the smooth glazes and creamy frostings in these recipes.

FUDGY BROWNIES WITH PEANUT BUTTER PUDDING FROSTING

The whole family will love these brownies topped with a double frosting of peanut butter pudding and chocolate fudge. They're a perfect treat for any time.

—AMY CROOK SYRACUSE, UT

PREP: 20 MIN.
BAKE: 25 MIN. + CHILLING
MAKES: 2½ DOZEN

- 1 package fudge brownie mix (13x9-inch pan size)
- 1½ cups confectioners' sugar
- ½ cup butter, softened
- 2 to 3 tablespoons peanut butter
- 2 tablespoons cold 2% milk
- 4½ teaspoons instant vanilla pudding mix
- 1 can (16 ounces) chocolate fudge frosting

1. Prepare and bake brownies according to package directions. Cool on a wire rack.
2. Meanwhile, in a small bowl, beat the confectioners' sugar, butter, peanut butter, milk and pudding mix until smooth. Spread over the brownies. Refrigerate for 30 minutes or until firm. Frost with chocolate fudge frosting just before cutting into squares.

LAYERED GINGERBREAD BARS

Bake a batch of these bars for a truly special dessert. The bottom layer tastes like a gingerbread cookie, the middle layer features smooth buttercream and the top layer is a luscious frosting. What's not to love?

—PATTI ANN CHRISTIAN ARARAT, NC

PREP: 45 MIN. + CHILLING
BAKE: 20 MIN. + COOLING
MAKES: 3 DOZEN

- ½ cup butter, softened
- ⅔ cup packed brown sugar
- 1 large egg
- ⅓ cup molasses
- 1⅔ cups all-purpose flour
- 1⅛ teaspoons ground ginger
- ½ teaspoon salt
- ½ teaspoon baking soda
- ½ teaspoon ground cinnamon
- ½ teaspoon ground allspice
- ¼ teaspoon ground nutmeg
- ⅛ teaspoon ground cloves

BUTTERCREAM LAYER
- ½ cup sugar
- 3 tablespoons all-purpose flour
- ½ cup 2% milk
- ¾ cup butter, softened
- 1 teaspoon lemon extract

ICING
- ½ cup packed brown sugar
- ⅓ cup heavy whipping cream
- ¼ cup butter, cubed
- 2 tablespoons molasses
- ¼ teaspoon ground allspice
- ¼ teaspoon ground ginger
- ⅛ teaspoon salt
- 2½ cups confectioners' sugar
- 2 tablespoons minced crystallized ginger

1. Preheat oven to 350°. In a large bowl, cream butter and brown sugar. Beat in egg and molasses. Combine flour, ginger, salt, baking soda, cinnamon, allspice, nutmeg and cloves; add to creamed mixture. Pour into a greased 13x9-in. baking dish. Bake 20-25 minutes or until a toothpick comes out clean. Cool on a wire rack.
2. In a small saucepan, combine sugar and flour. Whisk in milk until smooth. Cook and stir over medium heat until mixture comes to a boil. Reduce the heat; cook and stir for 2 minutes or until thickened. Remove from heat. Transfer to a small bowl; cover and refrigerate until chilled, about 1 hour.
3. Beat in butter and extract until light and fluffy. Spread over cooled gingerbread. Cover and freeze for 15 minutes.
4. For icing, in a small saucepan, combine brown sugar, cream and butter; bring to a boil. Remove from heat; whisk in molasses, allspice, ginger and salt. Transfer to a large bowl; add confectioners' sugar and beat until smooth. Spread over buttercream layer. Sprinkle with crystallized ginger. Refrigerate any leftovers.

FUDGY BROWNIES WITH PEANUT BUTTER PUDDING FROSTING

LAYERED GINGERBREAD BARS

HARVEST PUMPKIN BROWNIES

BIG BATCH

HARVEST PUMPKIN BROWNIES

These lightly spiced pumpkin brownies are a nice change of pace from typical chocolate brownies. They're the perfect treat when fall is in the air.

—**IOLA EGLE** BELLA VISTA, AR

PREP: 15 MIN.
BAKE: 20 MIN. + COOLING
MAKES: 5-6 DOZEN

- 1 **can (15 ounces) solid-pack pumpkin**
- 4 **large eggs**
- ¾ **cup canola oil**
- 2 **teaspoons vanilla extract**
- 2 **cups all-purpose flour**
- 2 **cups sugar**
- 1 **tablespoon pumpkin pie spice**
- 2 **teaspoons ground cinnamon**
- 2 **teaspoons baking powder**
- 1 **teaspoon baking soda**
- ½ **teaspoon salt**

FROSTING

- 6 **tablespoons butter, softened**
- 3 **ounces cream cheese, softened**
- 1 **teaspoon vanilla extract**
- 1 **teaspoon milk**
- ⅛ **teaspoon salt**
- 1½ **to 2 cups confectioners' sugar**

1. In a large bowl, beat pumpkin, eggs, oil and vanilla until blended. Combine dry ingredients; gradually stir into the pumpkin mixture.

2. Pour into a greased 15x10x1-in. baking pan. Bake at 350° for 20-25 minutes or until a toothpick inserted in the center comes out clean. Cool in pan on a wire rack.

3. In a small bowl, beat the butter, cream cheese, vanilla, milk and salt until smooth. Gradually add the confectioners' sugar until smooth. Frost brownies. Store brownies in the refrigerator.

FROSTED WALNUT BROWNIES

You can't go wrong with a classic walnut-filled brownie. These fudgy frosted squares travel very well to potlucks and picnics and will be one of the first desserts to disappear.

—PAT YAEGER NAPLES, FL

PREP: 20 MIN. + COOLING
BAKE: 25 MIN. • **MAKES:** 2½ DOZEN

- 4 **ounces unsweetened chocolate, chopped**
- 1 **cup canola oil**
- 2 **cups sugar**
- 4 **large eggs**
- 1 **teaspoon vanilla extract**
- 1 **cup all-purpose flour**
- ¼ **teaspoon salt**
- 1 **cup chopped walnuts**

FROSTING
- 2 **tablespoons butter**
- 2 **ounces unsweetened chocolate**
- 2½ **cups confectioners' sugar**
- ¼ **cup milk**
- 1 **teaspoon vanilla extract**

1. Preheat oven to 350°. In a large microwave-safe bowl, heat the chocolate until melted. Add oil and sugar; mix well. Stir in eggs and vanilla. Add flour and salt; mix well. Stir in the nuts. Pour into a greased 13x9-in. baking pan.

2. Bake 25-30 minutes or until a toothpick inserted in the center comes out with moist crumbs (do not overbake). Cool on a wire rack.

3. For frosting, melt the butter and chocolate; stir until smooth. Cool mixture to room temperature. In a medium bowl, combine the chocolate mixture, confectioners' sugar, milk and vanilla until smooth. Frost brownies.

FROSTED WALNUT BROWNIES

BIG BATCH
GLAZED PEANUT BUTTER BARS

Memories of lunchtime at school and my Aunt Shelly's kitchen come to mind when I bite into these sweet, chewy bars. My husband is the biggest fan of these peanut butter and chocolate treats.

—JANIS LUEDTKE WESTMINSTER, CO

PREP: 15 MIN.
BAKE: 20 MIN. + COOLING
MAKES: 4 DOZEN

- ¾ cup butter, softened
- ¾ cup creamy peanut butter
- ¾ cup sugar
- ¾ cup packed brown sugar
- 2 large eggs
- 2 teaspoons water
- 1½ teaspoons vanilla extract
- 1½ cups all-purpose flour
- 1½ cups quick-cooking oats
- ¾ teaspoon baking soda
- ½ teaspoon salt

GLAZE
- 1¼ cups milk chocolate chips
- ½ cup butterscotch chips
- ½ cup creamy peanut butter

1. In a large bowl, cream the butter, peanut butter and sugars until light and fluffy, about 4 minutes. Beat in eggs, water and vanilla. Combine the flour, oats, baking soda and salt; gradually add to creamed mixture and mix well.
2. Spread batter into a greased 15x10x1-in. baking pan. Bake at 325° for 18-22 minutes or until lightly browned.
3. For glaze, in a microwave, melt chips and peanut butter; stir until smooth. Pour over the warm bars; spread evenly. Cool completely on a wire rack before cutting.

CREAMY CASHEW BROWNIES

My sister-in-law dubbed me the "dessert queen" because of treats like this that I take to our family get-togethers. The brownies have a fudge-like texture and a delectable cream cheese topping. Cashews and a hot fudge swirl make these pretty bars extra special.

—KAREN WAGNER DANVILLE, IL

PREP: 15 MIN.
BAKE: 25 MIN. + CHILLING
MAKES: 2 DOZEN

- 1 package fudge brownie mix (13x9-inch pan size)
- ⅓ cup water
- ¼ cup canola oil
- 1 large egg
- 1 cup (6 ounces) semisweet chocolate chips

TOPPING
- 2 packages (8 ounces each) cream cheese, softened
- 1½ cups confectioners' sugar
- 1 teaspoon vanilla extract
- 1 cup salted cashews, coarsely chopped
- ½ cup hot fudge ice cream topping, warmed

1. In a large bowl, combine the brownie mix, water, oil and egg. Stir in chips. Spread into a greased 13x9-in. baking pan. Bake at 350° for 25-27 minutes or until a toothpick inserted in the center comes out clean (do not overbake). Cool on a wire rack.
2. For topping, in a bowl, beat the cream cheese, confectioners' sugar and vanilla until smooth. Spread over brownies. Sprinkle with the cashews; drizzle with hot fudge topping. Refrigerate before cutting. Store in the refrigerator.

TUXEDO FROSTED BROWNIES

I grew up on a farm and liked to help my mother in the kitchen, especially when it came to making desserts. I definitely learned from the best, and now when I'm planning to serve refreshments at one of my social events, these dressed-up brownies are my top pick.

—EDITH AMBURN MOUNT AIRY, NC

PREP: 25 MIN.
BAKE: 20 MIN. + CHILLING
MAKES: 3 DOZEN

- 4 large eggs
- 1 cup canola oil
- 1½ cups sugar
- ½ cup packed brown sugar
- ¼ cup water
- 2 teaspoons vanilla extract
- 1½ cups all-purpose flour
- ½ cup baking cocoa
- 1 teaspoon salt
- ½ cup chopped walnuts

FROSTING
- 1 can (16 ounces) vanilla frosting
- 1 tablespoon rum extract

GLAZE
- 1 cup (6 ounces) semisweet chocolate chips
- 1 tablespoon canola oil

1. In a large bowl, beat the eggs, oil, sugars, water and vanilla. Combine the flour, cocoa, salt and walnuts; stir into egg mixture until blended.
2. Pour into a greased 15x10x1-in. baking pan. Bake at 350° for 20-25 minutes or until center is set. Cool on a wire rack. Combine frosting and extract; spread over brownies. Chill for 30 minutes.
3. In a microwave, melt the chocolate chips and oil; stir until smooth. Drizzle over frosting. Let stand until set before cutting.

GLAZED PEANUT
BUTTER BARS

CREAMY
CASHEW
BROWNIES

TUXEDO FROSTED
BROWNIES

FROSTED
PISTACHIO BARS

FROSTED PISTACHIO BARS

Dare to decorate fast and easy bar cookies as spooky or as pretty as the occasion demands.

—**SHANNON SHEEHY**
CHESTERFIELD, VA

PREP: 20 MIN.
BAKE: 20 MIN. + COOLING
MAKES: 2 DOZEN

- 2 **cups all-purpose flour**
- 2 **packages (3.4 ounces each) instant pistachio pudding mix**
- ½ **cup sugar**
- 1 **teaspoon baking powder**
- ½ **teaspoon salt**
- 1 **large egg**
- ½ **cup butter, melted**
- ½ **cup canola oil**
- ¼ **cup water**
- 1 **teaspoon vanilla extract**
- ½ **cup chopped pistachios**

FROSTING

- 3 **ounces cream cheese, softened**
- ¼ **cup butter, softened**
- 1 **teaspoon vanilla extract**
- ⅛ **teaspoon salt**
- 3 **cups confectioners' sugar**
  Optional decorations: candy eyeballs, M&M's minis, milk chocolate M&M's, Life Savers hard candies and gummies, regular and mini peanut butter cups, licorice twists, shoestring licorice, Starburst fruit chews, mega and regular Smarties, Nerds, Runts, Snaps chewy candies, candy corn, tiny-size Chiclets gum, butterscotch hard candies, Rolo candies, Caramel Creams and PayDay candy bar

1. Preheat oven to 350°. In a large bowl, whisk flour, pudding mix, sugar, baking powder and salt. In another bowl, whisk egg, melted butter, oil, water and vanilla until blended; stir into flour mixture. Stir in pistachios (dough will be stiff).

2. Press dough into a greased 13x9-in. baking pan. Bake 20-25 minutes or until edges begin to brown. Cool completely in pan on a wire rack.

3. In a large bowl, beat cream cheese, butter, vanilla and salt until blended. Gradually beat in confectioners' sugar. Spread over top. Decorate as desired.

4. Cut into bars before serving. Store in the refrigerator.

DOUBLE FROSTED BROWNIES

This recipe is ideal for a quick dessert or bake sale contribution. Dress up a packaged brownie mix with two kinds of frosting, creating a two-toned treat with a luscious look and sweet taste.

—**JEAN KOLESSAR** ORLAND PARK, IL

PREP: 15 MIN. + CHILLING
BAKE: 25 MIN. + COOLING
MAKES: 3 DOZEN

- 1 **package fudge brownie mix (13x9-inch pan size)**
- ½ **cup butter, softened**
- 1½ **cups confectioners' sugar**
- 2 **tablespoons instant vanilla pudding mix**
- 2 **to 3 tablespoons 2% milk**
- 1 **can (16 ounces) chocolate fudge frosting**

1. Prepare brownie mix according to package directions. Spread the batter into a greased 13x9-in. baking pan. Bake at 350° for 25-30 minutes or until a toothpick inserted 2 in. from side of pan comes out clean. Cool completely on a wire rack.

2. In a large bowl, beat the butter, sugar and pudding mix until blended. Add enough milk to reach a spreading consistency. Frost the brownies. Cover and refrigerate for 30 minutes.

3. Spread with fudge frosting. Cut into bars. Store bars in the refrigerator.

ZUCCHINI BROWNIES

A fast-to-fix peanut butter and chocolate frosting tops these moist brownies. They are such a sweet way to use up your green garden squash. You'll love their soft cake-like texture.

—ALLYSON WILKINS AMHERST, NH

PREP: 20 MIN.
BAKE: 35 MIN. + COOLING
MAKES: ABOUT 1½ DOZEN

- 1 cup butter, softened
- 1½ cups sugar
- 2 large eggs
- ½ cup plain yogurt
- 1 teaspoon vanilla extract
- 2½ cups all-purpose flour
- ¼ cup baking cocoa
- 1 teaspoon baking soda
- ½ teaspoon salt
- 2 cups shredded zucchini

FROSTING

- ⅔ cup semisweet chocolate chips
- ½ cup creamy peanut butter

1. In a large bowl, cream butter and sugar until light and fluffy. Add eggs, one at a time, beating well after each addition. Beat in yogurt and vanilla. Combine the flour, cocoa, baking soda and salt; gradually add to the creamed mixture. Stir in zucchini.

2. Pour into a greased 13x9-in. baking pan. Bake at 350° for 35-40 minutes or until a toothpick inserted in the center of brownies comes out clean.

3. For frosting, in a small saucepan, combine the chocolate chips and peanut butter. Cook and stir over low heat until smooth. Spread over warm brownies. Cool on a wire rack. Cut into bars.

ZUCCHINI BROWNIES

RHUBARB CUSTARD BARS

After one taste of these rich, gooey bars, I had to have the recipe to make them for my family and friends. The shortbread crust, rhubarb layer and cream cheese frosting melt in your mouth.

—SHARI ROACH
SOUTH MILWAUKEE, WI

PREP: 25 MIN. + CHILLING
BAKE: 50 MIN. • **MAKES:** 3 DOZEN

- 2 cups all-purpose flour
- ¼ cup sugar
- 1 cup cold butter

FILLING

- 2 cups sugar
- 7 tablespoons all-purpose flour
- 1 cup heavy whipping cream
- 3 large eggs, beaten
- 5 cups finely chopped fresh or frozen rhubarb, thawed and drained

TOPPING

- 6 ounces cream cheese, softened
- ½ cup sugar
- ½ teaspoon vanilla extract
- 1 cup heavy whipping cream, whipped

1. In a bowl, combine the flour and sugar; cut in butter until the mixture resembles coarse crumbs. Press into a greased 13x9-in. baking pan. Bake at 350° for 10 minutes.

2. Meanwhile, for filling, combine sugar and flour in a bowl. Whisk in cream and eggs. Stir in the rhubarb. Pour over crust. Bake at 350° for 40-45 minutes or until the custard is set. Cool.

3. For topping, beat cream cheese, sugar and vanilla until smooth; fold in whipped cream. Spread over top. Cover and chill. Cut into bars. Store in the refrigerator.

RHUBARB
CUSTARD BARS

**FROSTED PEANUT
BUTTER BARS**

BIG BATCH

FROSTED PEANUT
BUTTER BARS

If you're a peanut butter cookie lover, here's the bar for you. This recipe makes a great no-fuss treat to bring to a potluck or bake sale.

—**SHARON SMITH** MUSKEGON, MI

PREP: 20 MIN.
BAKE: 20 MIN. + COOLING
MAKES: 5 DOZEN

- ⅓ cup shortening
- ½ cup peanut butter
- 1½ cups packed brown sugar
- 2 large eggs
- 1 teaspoon vanilla extract
- 1½ cups all-purpose flour
- 1½ teaspoons baking powder
- ½ teaspoon salt
- ¼ cup milk

FROSTING
- ⅔ cup creamy peanut butter
- ½ cup shortening
- 4 cups confectioners' sugar
- ⅓ to ½ cup milk

TOPPING
- ¼ cup semisweet chocolate chips
- 1 teaspoon shortening

1. In a large bowl, cream the shortening, peanut butter and brown sugar until light and fluffy. Beat in eggs and vanilla. Combine the flour, baking powder and salt; gradually add to creamed mixture alternately with milk, beating well after each addition.

2. Transfer to a greased 15x10x1-in. baking pan. Bake at 350° for 16-20 minutes or until a toothpick inserted in the center comes out clean. Cool on a wire rack.

3. For frosting, in a bowl, cream the peanut butter, shortening and confectioners' sugar until light and fluffy. Gradually beat in milk to reach spreading consistency. Frost bars.

4. In a microwave, melt chocolate chips and shortening; stir until smooth. Drizzle over the frosting. Store in the refrigerator.

BIG BATCH

PEPPERMINT CHOCOLATE BARS

I received this treasured recipe from a dear friend years ago. The minty frosting and chocolate drizzle give them extra taste and eye appeal.
—**CHRISTINE HARRELL** CHESTER, VA

PREP: 20 MIN.
BAKE: 20 MIN. + COOLING
MAKES: 4 DOZEN

- ½ **cup butter**
- 2 **ounces unsweetened chocolate**
- 2 **large eggs**
- 1 **cup sugar**
- 2 **teaspoons vanilla extract**
- ½ **cup all-purpose flour**
- ½ **teaspoon salt**
- ½ **cup chopped pecans or walnuts**

FROSTING
- ¼ **cup butter, softened**
- 2 **cups confectioners' sugar**
- 1 **teaspoon peppermint extract**
- 3 **to 4 tablespoons heavy whipping cream**

TOPPING
- 1 **ounce unsweetened chocolate**
- 1 **tablespoon butter**

1. In a microwave, melt butter and chocolate; stir until smooth. Cool slightly. Meanwhile, in a large bowl, beat the eggs, sugar and vanilla. Add the chocolate mixture and mix well. Combine flour and salt; gradually add to chocolate mixture. Stir in the pecans or walnuts.

2. Spread into a greased 13x9-in. baking pan. Bake at 350° for 16-20 minutes or until a toothpick inserted in the center comes out clean. Cool on a wire rack.

3. In a small bowl, cream butter, sugar and extract until light and fluffy. Add enough cream for the frosting to reach spreading consistency. Frost cooled bars. Melt chocolate and butter; drizzle over frosting. Cut into bars.

PEPPERMINT
CHOCOLATE BARS

BIG BATCH
PEANUT BARS

With peanut butter everywhere and chopped nuts on top, this recipe is a triple peanut treat!

—REN REED TAVARES, FL

PREP: 20 MIN.
BAKE: 20 MIN. + COOLING
MAKES: 2 CAKES (24 PIECES EACH)

- 1 cup butter, softened
- 2 cups sugar
- 1 cup creamy peanut butter
- 2 large eggs
- 1 teaspoon vanilla extract
- 2 cups all-purpose flour
- 1 teaspoon baking powder
- 1 cup water
- ½ cup 2% milk

FROSTING

- ¾ cup creamy peanut butter
- ¼ cup butter, softened
- 3¾ cups confectioners' sugar
- 5 to 6 tablespoons 2% milk
- 1 cup chopped unsalted peanuts

1. Preheat oven to 350°. Grease two 13x9-in. baking pans.
2. In a large bowl, cream butter, sugar and peanut butter until light and fluffy. Add eggs, one at a time, beating well after each addition. Beat in vanilla. In another bowl, whisk flour and baking powder; add to creamed mixture alternately with water and milk, beating well after each addition.
3. Transfer to prepared baking pans. Bake 20-25 minutes or until a toothpick inserted in center comes out clean. Meanwhile, for frosting, in a large bowl, beat the peanut butter and butter until blended. Beat in confectioner's sugar alternately with enough milk to reach spreading consistency.
4. Remove cakes from oven; place on wire racks. Spread frosting over warm cakes; sprinkle with peanuts. Cool completely. Cut into bars.

SPIDERWEB BROWNIES

To decorate these moist brownies for Halloween, I drizzle a chocolate spiderweb on their marshmallow icing. They're so delicious that you'll find yourself making them for other gatherings throughout the year—just change the drizzle design.

—SANDY PICHON SLIDELL, LA

PREP: 20 MIN.
BAKE: 30 MIN. + COOLING
MAKES: 2 DOZEN

- ¾ cup butter, cubed
- 4 ounces unsweetened chocolate, chopped
- 2 cups sugar
- 3 large eggs, lightly beaten
- 1 teaspoon vanilla extract
- 1 cup all-purpose flour
- 1 cup chopped pecans or walnuts
- 1 jar (7 ounces) marshmallow creme
- 1 ounce semisweet chocolate

1. In a large microwave-safe bowl, melt the butter and unsweetened chocolate; stir until smooth. Remove from the heat; stir in sugar. Cool for 10 minutes. Whisk in eggs and vanilla. Stir in the flour and nuts. Pour into a greased foil-lined 13x9-in. baking pan.
2. Bake at 350° for 25-30 minutes or until a toothpick inserted in the center comes out clean (do not overbake). Immediately drop marshmallow cream by spoonfuls over hot brownies; spread evenly. Cool on a wire rack.
3. Lift out of the pan; remove foil. For web decoration, melt the semisweet chocolate in a microwave; stir until smooth. Transfer to a small resealable plastic bag. Cut a small hole in one corner of the bag; drizzle chocolate over top in a spiderweb design. Let set before cutting into bars.

ICED BROWNIES

Brownies are a favorite for picnics and gatherings, and these are the best! A dear friend shared the recipe many years ago, and I still make it at least once a month.

—GOLDIE HANKE TOMAHAWK, WI

PREP: 15 MIN. • **BAKE:** 30 MIN.
MAKES: ABOUT 3 DOZEN

- 1 cup sugar
- ½ cup butter, softened
- 4 large eggs
- 1 can (16 ounces) chocolate syrup
- 1 cup all-purpose flour
- ½ cup chopped nuts

ICING

- 1¼ cups sugar
- 6 tablespoons butter
- 6 tablespoons milk or half-and-half cream
- 1 teaspoon vanilla extract
- 1 cup (6 ounces) semisweet chocolate chips

1. In a large bowl, cream sugar and butter until light and fluffy. Add eggs, one at a time, beating well after each addition. Add syrup. Gradually add flour and mix well. Fold in nuts. Pour into a greased 13x9-in. baking pan.
2. Bake at 350° for 30-35 minutes or until top springs back when lightly touched. Cool slightly.
3. Meanwhile, for the icing, combine the sugar, butter and milk in a small saucepan. Cook and stir until mixture comes to a boil. Reduce heat to medium and cook for 3 minutes, stirring constantly. Remove from the heat; stir in vanilla and chocolate chips until chips are melted (mixture will be thin). Immediately pour icing over brownies. Cool completely before cutting.

PEANUT BARS

SPIDERWEB BROWNIES

ICED BROWNIES

FROSTED FUDGE
BROWNIES

FROSTED FUDGE BROWNIES

A neighbor brought over a pan of these rich brownies, along with the recipe, when I came home from the hospital after giving birth to my daughter. Ever since, it's been one of my go-to recipe for family events and work parties.

—SUE SODERLUND ELGIN, IL

PREP: 10 MIN. + COOLING
BAKE: 25 MIN. + COOLING
MAKES: 2 DOZEN

- 1 cup plus 3 tablespoons butter, cubed
- ¾ cup baking cocoa
- 4 large eggs
- 2 cups sugar
- 1½ cups all-purpose flour
- 1 teaspoon baking powder
- 1 teaspoon salt
- 1 teaspoon vanilla extract

FROSTING
- 6 tablespoons butter, softened
- 2⅔ cups confectioners' sugar
- ½ cup baking cocoa
- 1 teaspoon vanilla extract
- ¼ to ⅓ cup milk

1. In a saucepan, melt the butter. Remove from the heat. Stir in cocoa; cool. In a large bowl, beat eggs and sugar until blended. Combine flour, baking powder and salt; gradually add to egg mixture. Stir in vanilla and the cooled chocolate mixture until well blended.

2. Spread into a greased 13x9-in. baking pan. Bake at 350° for 25-28 minutes or until a toothpick inserted in the center comes out clean (do not overbake). Cool on a wire rack.

3. For frosting, in a large bowl, cream butter and confectioners' sugar until light and fluffy. Beat in cocoa and vanilla. Add enough milk until the frosting reaches spreading consistency. Spread over brownies. Cut into bars.

BANANA BARS WITH CREAM CHEESE FROSTING

I make these moist bars whenever I have ripe bananas on hand, then store them in the freezer to share later at a potluck. With creamy frosting and big banana flavor, this treat, shown on page 166, is a real crowd-pleaser.

—DEBBIE KNIGHT MARION, IA

PREP: 15 MIN.
BAKE: 20 MIN. + COOLING
MAKES: 3-4 DOZEN

- ½ cup butter, softened
- 1½ cups sugar
- 2 large eggs
- 1 cup (8 ounces) sour cream
- 1 teaspoon vanilla extract
- 2 cups all-purpose flour
- 1 teaspoon baking soda
- ¼ teaspoon salt
- 2 medium ripe bananas, mashed (about 1 cup)

FROSTING
- 1 package (8 ounces) cream cheese, softened
- ½ cup butter, softened
- 2 teaspoons vanilla extract
- 3¾ to 4 cups confectioners' sugar

1. Preheat oven to 350°. In a large bowl, cream butter and sugar until light and fluffy. Add the eggs, sour cream and vanilla. Combine flour, baking soda and salt; gradually add to the creamed mixture. Stir in the bananas.

2. Spread mixture into a greased 15x10x1-in. baking pan. Bake for 20-25 minutes or until a toothpick inserted in the center comes out clean (do not overbake). Cool.

3. For frosting, in a large bowl, beat cream cheese, butter and vanilla until fluffy. Gradually beat in enough confectioners' sugar to reach desired consistency. Frost bars. Store in the refrigerator.

CARROT CAKE BARS

A friend served these moist, tender cake bars with surprise ingredients at an outdoor party, and everyone raved over the flavor. I'll often freeze some to enjoy another day.

—AGNES WARD STRATFORD, ON

PREP: 35 MIN.
BAKE: 20 MIN. + COOLING
MAKES: 3 DOZEN

    3 large eggs
 1¼ cups canola oil
    2 cups all-purpose flour
    2 cups sugar
    2 teaspoons ground cinnamon
    1 teaspoon baking powder
   ½ teaspoon baking soda
   ¼ to ½ teaspoon salt
    1 jar (6 ounces) carrot baby food
    1 container (3½ ounces) applesauce baby food
    1 container (3½ ounces) apricot baby food
   ½ cup chopped walnuts, optional
FROSTING
    1 package (8 ounces) cream cheese, softened
   ½ cup butter, softened
    1 teaspoon vanilla extract
 3¾ cups confectioners' sugar

1. In a large bowl, beat eggs and oil for 2 minutes. Combine the flour, sugar, cinnamon, baking powder, baking soda and salt; add to the egg mixture. Add baby foods; mix well. Stir in walnuts if desired.
2. Transfer the batter to a greased 15x10x1-in. baking pan. Bake at 350° for 20-25 minutes or until a toothpick inserted near the center comes out clean. Cool the bars on a wire rack.
3. For frosting, in a small bowl, beat cream cheese and butter until light and fluffy. Beat in the vanilla. Gradually beat in confectioners' sugar. Frost; cut into bars. Store in the refrigerator.

SPICE CAKE BARS WITH SALTED CARAMEL ICING

Our family had a full schedule when our kids were growing up. Like many busy moms, I was always looking for baking shortcuts. I hit the jackpot when I stumbled on these easy treats. I still make them for my kids and grandkids.

—ELLEN HARTMAN CHICO, CA

PREP: 20 MIN.
BAKE: 15 MIN. + COOLING
MAKES: 2 DOZEN

    1 package spice cake mix (regular size)
   ¾ cup butter, melted
   ⅓ cup evaporated milk
    1 large egg
FROSTING
   ⅓ cup packed brown sugar
   ⅓ cup evaporated milk
   ¼ cup butter, cubed
    2 cups confectioners' sugar
    1 teaspoon vanilla extract
   ½ teaspoon sea salt

1. Preheat oven to 350°. Grease a 13x9-in. baking pan. In a large bowl, combine cake mix, butter, milk and egg; beat on low speed 30 seconds. Beat on medium 2 minutes (batter will be thick).
2. Transfer to prepared pan. Bake 15-20 minutes or until a toothpick inserted in center comes out clean. Cool in pan on a wire rack.
3. For frosting, in a large saucepan, combine brown sugar, milk and butter over medium heat; bring to a boil, stirring occasionally. Reduce heat; simmer, uncovered, for 3 minutes.
4. Remove from heat. Stir in confectioners' sugar and vanilla. Immediately spread icing over cake; sprinkle with salt. Cool completely. Cut into bars. Store the bars in airtight containers.

BIG BATCH
CRISPY CHOCOLATE SQUARES

Folks think you slaved away on these fast and fudgy squares. When they request the recipe they're surprised how easy the no-bake bars are to make. Even kids can join in the fun of making them.

—KAREN SPEIDEL WHEELING, IL

PREP: 20 MIN. + CHILLING
MAKES: ABOUT 4 DOZEN

    1 package (10½ ounces) miniature marshmallows
    1 cup peanut butter
    1 cup (6 ounces) semisweet chocolate chips
   ½ cup butter, cubed
    2 cups crisp rice cereal
    1 cup salted peanuts
FROSTING
    1 cup (6 ounces) semisweet chocolate chips
   ¼ cup butter, cubed
   ¼ cup milk
    2 cups confectioners' sugar
    1 teaspoon vanilla extract

1. In a large microwave-safe bowl, combine the marshmallows, peanut butter, chocolate chips and butter. Cover and microwave on high for 1½ minutes. Stir until well blended (the mixture will be lumpy). Add cereal and peanuts; stir until well coated. Spread into a greased 13x9-in. pan.
2. For the frosting, combine the chocolate chips, butter and milk in another microwave-safe bowl. Cover and microwave on high for 1 minute. Add sugar and vanilla. With an electric mixer, beat frosting until smooth. Spread over cereal mixture. Cover and refrigerate for 2 hours or until both layers are firm. Cut into squares.
NOTE *This recipe was tested in a 1,100-watt microwave.*

CRISPY CHOCOLATE SQUARES

CINNAMON BROWNIES

CINNAMON BROWNIES

A friend gave us a pan of these delicious brownies for Christmas one year. Half the pan was gone before I figured out that cinnamon was her secret ingredient!

—**GAIL MEHLE** ROCK SPRINGS, WY

PREP: 20 MIN.
BAKE: 30 MIN. + COOLING
MAKES: 3 DOZEN

- ¾ cup baking cocoa
- ½ teaspoon baking soda
- ⅔ cup butter, melted, divided
- ½ cup boiling water
- 2 cups sugar
- 2 large eggs, beaten
- 1 teaspoon vanilla extract
- 1⅓ cups all-purpose flour
- 1½ to 2 teaspoons ground cinnamon
- ¼ teaspoon salt
- 1 cup (6 ounces) semisweet chocolate chips

FROSTING

- 6 tablespoons butter, softened
- ½ cup baking cocoa
- 2⅔ cups confectioners' sugar
- 1 to 1½ teaspoons ground cinnamon
- ⅓ cup evaporated milk
- 1 teaspoon vanilla extract

1. In a bowl, combine cocoa and baking soda; blend in ⅓ cup melted butter. Add boiling water, stirring until thickened. Stir in sugar, eggs, vanilla and remaining butter. Add flour, cinnamon and salt. Fold in chocolate chips. Pour into a greased 13x9-in. baking pan. Bake at 350° for 40 minutes or until brownies test done. Cool.

2. For frosting, cream butter in a bowl. Combine cocoa, sugar and cinnamon; add alternately with the milk. Beat to a spreading consistency; add vanilla. Add more milk if necessary. Spread frosting over the brownies.

PUMPKIN BARS

What's better than a big pan of pumpkin-flavored bars on a cool fall day? We enjoy them the rest of the year, too—not just in autumn!

—**BRENDA KELLER** ANDALUSIA, AL

PREP: 20 MIN.
BAKE: 25 MIN. + COOLING
MAKES: 2 DOZEN

- 4 **large eggs**
- 1⅔ **cups sugar**
- 1 **cup canola oil**
- 1 **can (15 ounces) solid-pack pumpkin**

- 2 **cups all-purpose flour**
- 2 **teaspoons ground cinnamon**
- 2 **teaspoons baking powder**
- 1 **teaspoon baking soda**
- 1 **teaspoon salt**

ICING
- 6 **ounces cream cheese, softened**
- 2 **cups confectioners' sugar**
- ¼ **cup butter, softened**
- 1 **teaspoon vanilla extract**
- 1 **to 2 tablespoons milk**

1. In a bowl, beat the eggs, sugar, oil and pumpkin until well blended. Combine the flour, cinnamon, baking powder, baking soda and salt; gradually add to pumpkin mixture and mix well. Pour into an ungreased 15x10x1-in. baking pan. Bake at 350° for 25-30 minutes or until set. Cool completely.

2. For the icing, beat the cream cheese, confectioners' sugar, butter and vanilla in a small bowl. Add enough milk to reach spreading consistency. Spread over the bars. Store in the refrigerator.

PUMPKIN BARS

CHOCOLATE PEANUT BUTTER BROWNIES

My husband and I have two sons, and I often sent the boys these brownies while they were in college. They told me that they used to hide a few from their roommates just to make sure there would be some left!

—PATSY BURGIN LEBANON, IN

PREP: 30 MIN.
BAKE: 25 MIN. + CHILLING
MAKES: ABOUT 2 DOZEN

- 2 ounces unsweetened chocolate
- ½ cup butter, cubed
- 2 large eggs
- 1 cup sugar
- ½ cup all-purpose flour

FILLING

- 1½ cups confectioners' sugar
- ½ cup creamy peanut butter
- ¼ cup butter, softened
- 2 to 3 tablespoons half-and-half cream or milk

GLAZE

- 1 ounce unsweetened chocolate
- 1 tablespoon butter

1. In a small saucepan, melt the chocolate and butter over low heat; set aside.
2. In a bowl, beat eggs and sugar until light and pale colored. Add flour and melted chocolate; stir well. Pour into a greased 9-in. square baking pan. Bake at 350° for 25 minutes or until the brownies test done. Cool.
3. For filling, beat confectioners' sugar, peanut butter and butter in a bowl. Stir in cream or milk until mixture reaches desired spreading consistency. Spread over cooled brownies; cover and chill until firm.
4. For glaze, melt chocolate and butter in a saucepan, stirring until smooth. Drizzle over filling. Chill before cutting. Store in refrigerator.

GLAZED GINGER BARS

I can't think of the holidays without these luscious bars. The scent and flavor of ginger are just right for the season, and the light glaze adds the perfect amount of sweetness.

—DARLENE BRENDEN SALEM, OR

PREP: 25 MIN.
BAKE: 20 MIN. + COOLING
MAKES: 32 BARS

- ⅔ cup butter, softened
- ¾ cup packed brown sugar
- ½ cup molasses
- 1 large egg
- 2 cups all-purpose flour
- 2 teaspoons ground ginger
- ½ teaspoon baking soda
- ½ teaspoon baking powder
- ½ teaspoon ground cinnamon
- ¼ teaspoon salt
- ½ cup raisins

ORANGE GLAZE

- 1 cup confectioners' sugar
- 5 teaspoons orange juice
- 4 teaspoons butter, melted
- ¾ teaspoon vanilla extract
- ½ teaspoon grated orange peel

1. Preheat oven to 350°. In a large bowl, cream butter and brown sugar until light and fluffy. Beat in the molasses and egg. Combine flour, ginger, baking soda, baking powder, cinnamon and salt; add to creamed mixture and mix well. Stir in raisins.
2. Spread into a greased 13x9-in. baking pan. Bake 20-25 minutes or until a toothpick inserted in the center comes out clean.
3. Combine glaze ingredients until smooth; spread over the warm bars. Cool completely on a wire rack before cutting into bars.

CHOCOLATE PEANUT BUTTER BROWNIES

GLAZED GINGER BARS

**S'MORES CRISPY BARS,
PAGE 199**

Quick & Easy Snacks

When you need a sweet treat but don't have time to spare, try one of these quick-to-fix, no-fuss delights.

CHEWY CHOCO-CARAMEL SQUARES

These rich bars make a quick and easy dessert for holidays and special occasions. They're popular at bake sales and classroom parties, too.

—ROD & SUE BRUSIUS OMRO, WI

PREP: 15 MIN.
BAKE: 30 MIN. + COOLING
MAKES: 2 DOZEN

- 1 package butter recipe golden cake mix (regular size)
- 2 large eggs
- ⅓ cup canola oil
- 2 cups (12 ounces) semisweet chocolate chips
- 1 cup white baking chips
- ½ cup toffee bits
- 1 can (14 ounces) sweetened condensed milk
- 32 caramels
- ½ cup butter, cubed

1. Preheat oven to 350°. In a large bowl, combine cake mix, eggs and oil; beat on low speed 30 seconds. Beat on medium 2 minutes. Fold in chocolate chips, baking chips and toffee bits.
2. Press half of the mixture into a greased 13x9-in. baking pan. Bake 10 minutes. Meanwhile, in a large saucepan, combine milk, caramels and butter. Cook and stir over medium heat until smooth.
3. Pour caramel mixture over crust. Crumble remaining cake mixture over the top. Bake for 20-25 minutes longer or until the edges begin to brown and topping is set. Cool completely in pan on a wire rack. Cut into bars.

⑤ INGREDIENTS *BIG BATCH*
GERMAN CHOCOLATE BARS

My mom gave me this recipe one Christmas when I wanted to make something different and yummy to give as gifts.

—JENNIFER SHARP MURFREESBORO, TN

PREP: 15 MIN.
BAKE: 35 MIN. + CHILLING
MAKES: 4 DOZEN

- 1 package German chocolate cake mix (regular size)
- ⅔ cup cold butter, cubed
- 1 cup (6 ounces) semisweet chocolate chips
- 1 can (15 ounces) coconut-pecan frosting
- ¼ cup milk

1. Place cake mix in a large bowl; cut in butter until crumbly. Press 2½ cups into a greased 13x9-in. baking pan. Bake at 350° for 10 minutes; immediately sprinkle with chocolate chips. Drop frosting by tablespoonfuls over the chips.
2. Stir milk into the remaining crumb mixture; drop mixture by teaspoonfuls over top. Bake 25-30 minutes longer or until bubbly around the edges and top is cracked. Cool on a wire rack. Refrigerate for 4 hours before cutting.

⑤ INGREDIENTS
CHOCOLATY S'MORES BARS

One night, my husband had some friends over to play poker, and he requested these s'mores bars. The boys polished off the pan and asked for more! I shared the recipe with his buddies, and now they make them at home, too.

—REBECCA SHIPP BEEBE, AR

PREP: 15 MIN. + COOLING
MAKES: 1½ DOZEN

- ¼ cup butter, cubed
- 1 package (10 ounces) large marshmallows
- 1 package (12 ounces) Golden Grahams
- ⅓ cup milk chocolate chips, melted

1. In a large saucepan, melt butter over low heat. Add marshmallows; cook and stir until blended. Remove from heat. Stir in the cereal until it is coated.
2. Using a buttered spatula, press evenly into a greased 13x9-in. pan. Drizzle with the melted chocolate chips. Cool completely. Cut into bars. Store in an airtight container.

TOP TIP

TRICK FOR STICKY MARSHMALLOWS

To separate sticky marshmallows, place a spoonful of powdered sugar in the bag and shake well. A few stubborn marshmallows might still need to be separated by hand.

—KERRI W. PROVO, UT

CHOCOLATY
S'MORES BARS

CHOCOLATE PEANUT
TREATS

(5) INGREDIENTS

CHOCOLATE PEANUT TREATS

When I was in high school, I took these sweet and crunchy squares to bake sales—they were the first item to sell out. I still make them for family and friends who love the classic combination of chocolate and peanut butter.

—CHRISTY ASHER
COLORADO SPRINGS, CO

PREP: 20 MIN. + CHILLING
MAKES: ABOUT 2 DOZEN

- ¾ **cup graham cracker crumbs**
- ½ **cup butter, melted**
- 2 **cups confectioners' sugar**
- ½ **cup chunky peanut butter**
- 1 **cup (6 ounces) semisweet chocolate chips**

1. In a bowl, combine the cracker crumbs and butter. Stir in sugar and peanut butter. Press into a greased 8-in. square pan.
2. In a microwave or double boiler, melt the chocolate chips and stir until smooth. Spread over peanut butter layer. Chill 30 minutes; cut into squares. Chill until firm, about 30 minutes longer. Store the bars in the refrigerator.

(5) INGREDIENTS

CHOCOLATE SWIRLED BARS

These swirly chocolate bars make a pretty addition to any cookie or dessert platter. They look like an elegant treat from a bake shop, but they couldn't be easier to make.

—*TASTE OF HOME* **TEST KITCHEN**

PREP: 5 MIN. • **BAKE:** 15 MIN. + STANDING
MAKES: ABOUT 3 DOZEN

1¼ **cups refrigerated cookie dough**
1 **cup (6 ounces) dark chocolate chips**
¼ **cup vanilla or white chips, melted**

1. Press refrigerated cookie dough onto the bottom of an ungreased 13x9-in. baking pan (dough will be thin). Bake the dough at 350° for 11-13 minutes or until the edges begin to brown.

2. Immediately sprinkle with chocolate chips. Allow chips to soften for a few minutes, then spread over bars. Drop spoonfuls of melted vanilla chips over top; cut through chocolate with a knife to swirl. Let stand until set. Cut into bars.

CHOCOLATE
SWIRLED BARS

SPEEDY BROWNIES

Since you "dump" all the ingredients together for these brownies, they take very little time to prepare. But there's no mistaking the homemade goodness of a freshly baked rich and fudgy batch!

—DIANE HEIER HARWOOD, ND

PREP: 15 MIN. • **BAKE:** 30 MIN.
MAKES: ABOUT 3 DOZEN

- 2 cups sugar
- 1¾ cups all-purpose flour
- ½ cup baking cocoa
- 1 teaspoon salt
- 5 large eggs
- 1 cup canola oil
- 1 teaspoon vanilla extract
- 1 cup (6 ounces) semisweet chocolate chips

1. In a large bowl, beat the first seven ingredients. Pour into a greased 13x9-in. baking pan. Sprinkle with chocolate chips.
2. Bake at 350° for 30 minutes or until a toothpick inserted in the center comes out clean. Cool in pan on a wire rack.

STRAWBERRY GRANOLA SQUARES

You likely already have most of the ingredients you need for these delicious squares in your pantry. Make them ahead and freeze for a fast treat anytime.

—TASTE OF HOME TEST KITCHEN

PREP: 5 MIN. • **BAKE:** 25 MIN. + COOLING
MAKES: 16 SQUARES

- 1½ cups granola cereal without raisins
- ¾ cup all-purpose flour
- ⅓ cup packed brown sugar
- ½ teaspoon ground cinnamon
- 5 tablespoons cold butter
- 1 cup strawberry preserves

1. In a large bowl, combine the granola, flour, brown sugar and cinnamon; cut in butter until crumbly. Set aside a third of the mixture for topping. Press the remaining mixture into a well-greased 9-in. square baking pan. Bake at 375° for 10 minutes.
2. Spread preserves over crust; sprinkle with reserved granola mixture. Bake 15 minutes longer or until filling is bubbly around the edges. Cool on a wire rack. Cut into squares. Store in the refrigerator.

5 INGREDIENTS
WHITE CHOCOLATE CEREAL BARS

A friend gave me this fresh take on traditional crispy treats. My husband loves them. They are so quick to make, you can prepare them during a TV commercial and you won't miss much of your program.

—ANNE POWERS MUNFORD, AL

START TO FINISH: 15 MIN.
MAKES: ABOUT 3 DOZEN

- 4 cups miniature marshmallows
- 8 ounces white baking chips (about 1⅓ cups)
- ¼ cup butter, cubed
- 6 cups Rice Krispies

1. In a Dutch oven, combine the marshmallows, baking chips and butter. Cook and stir over medium-low heat until melted. Remove from heat. Add Rice Krispies; stir to coat.
2. Transfer to a greased 13x9-in. pan; gently press mixture evenly into pan. Cut into bars.

DID YOU KNOW?

COLORFUL RICE CEREAL TREATS

To add fun color and a little extra flavor to rice cereal treats, toss in 2 or 3 teaspoons of cherry or strawberry gelatin powder into the marshmallow mixture before adding the cereal.

—BRENDA S. LANDIS, NC

SPEEDY
BROWNIES

STRAWBERRY GRANOLA
SQUARES

WHITE CHOCOLATE
CEREAL BARS

CHEWY SALTED
PEANUT BARS

CHEWY SALTED PEANUT BARS

These rich bars are studded with the all-American peanut. The recipe has been a favorite in my family for several generations. Whenever we get together, someone offers to bring a pan of these crunchy bars.

—ANN MARIE HEINZ STURGEON BAY, WI

PREP: 10 MIN.
BAKE: 20 MIN. + COOLING
MAKES: 2 DOZEN

- 1½ cups all-purpose flour
- ¾ cup packed brown sugar
- ½ cup cold butter, cubed
- 2 cups lightly salted dry roasted peanuts
- 1 cup butterscotch chips
- ½ cup light corn syrup
- 2 tablespoons butter

1. Preheat oven to 350°. Line a 13x9-in. baking pan with foil, letting ends extend up sides; grease foil. In a small bowl, mix flour and brown sugar; cut in butter until crumbly. Press into prepared pan. Bake for 8-10 minutes or until crust is lightly browned. Sprinkle the peanuts over crust.

2. In a small saucepan, melt the butterscotch chips, corn syrup and butter over medium heat; stir until smooth. Drizzle over peanuts. Bake 6-8 minutes longer or until bubbly. Cool completely in the pan on a wire rack. Lifting with foil, remove from pan. Cut into bars.

S'MORES CRISPY BARS

My aunt always brought s'mores-style bars to our summer cottage. They're amazing plain or frosted, and also great for eating on the run. See the photo on page 190.

—BETSY KING DULUTH, MN

PREP: 15 MIN. + COOLING
MAKES: 2 DOZEN

- ¼ cup butter, cubed
- 1 package (10½ ounces) miniature marshmallows
- 6 cups Rice Krispies
- 1½ cups crushed graham crackers
- 1 cup milk chocolate chips

FROSTING
- ¾ cup butter, softened
- 1 cup confectioners' sugar
- 1 jar (7 ounces) marshmallow creme

TOPPING
- ¼ cup crushed graham crackers
- 2 milk chocolate candy bars (1.55 ounces each)

1. In a 6-qt. stockpot, melt the butter over medium heat. Add marshmallows; cook and stir until melted. Remove from heat. Stir in cereal and crushed crackers. Fold in chocolate chips. Press into a greased 13x9-in. baking pan. Cool to room temperature.

2. For frosting, in a small bowl, beat butter and confectioners' sugar until smooth. Beat in the marshmallow creme on low speed just until blended. Spread over bars. Sprinkle crushed crackers over frosting. Cut into bars. Break each candy bar into 12 pieces; place a piece on each bar.

SALTY PEANUT SQUARES

If your gang likes corn chips, they'll love the sweet and salty blend in these bars. They make great treats to take along for picnics or tailgate parties. And they're so easy to whip up, the kids may just want to make their own batch!

—WANDA BORGEN MINOT, ND

PREP: 15 MIN. + COOLING
MAKES: 2 DOZEN

- 1 package (10 ounces) corn chips, lightly crushed, divided
- 1 cup unsalted peanuts, divided
- 1 cup light corn syrup
- 1 cup sugar
- 1 cup peanut butter
- ½ cup milk chocolate chips, melted

1. Place half of the corn chips and peanuts in a greased 13x9-in. pan; set aside. In a large saucepan, bring the corn syrup and sugar to a boil. Stir in peanut butter until blended. Drizzle half over corn chip mixture in pan.

2. Add remaining corn chips and peanuts to remaining syrup; stir until combined. Spoon over the mixture in pan; press down lightly. Drizzle with the melted chocolate. Cool before cutting.

SALTY PEANUT SQUARES

KAHLUA DREAM BARS

I always double this recipe so everyone gets a piece. If the glaze is too sweet, use one square of unsweetened chocolate and two of semisweet.

—LORRAINE CALAND SHUNIAH, ON

PREP: 30 MIN. + CHILLING
MAKES: 6 DOZEN

- 1 cup butter, cubed
- ½ cup baking cocoa
- 1 large egg yolk
- 2 cups graham cracker crumbs
- ½ cup confectioners' sugar
- 1 teaspoon vanilla extract

FILLING
- ½ cup butter, melted
- ⅓ cup Kahlua (coffee liqueur)
- 3 cups confectioners' sugar

GLAZE
- ¼ cup butter, cubed
- 3 ounces semisweet chocolate, chopped

1. In large heavy saucepan, melt butter over medium-low heat; stir in cocoa until blended. Whisk a small amount of hot mixture into egg yolk; return all to the pan, whisking constantly. Cook 2-3 minutes or until mixture thickens and a thermometer reads 160°, stirring constantly. Remove from heat. Stir in the cracker crumbs, confectioners' sugar and vanilla. Press into a greased 13x9-in. pan.

2. For the filling, in a large bowl, combine butter and Kahlua. Stir in confectioners' sugar. Spread over crust. Refrigerate until set.

3. For the glaze, in a microwave, melt butter and chocolate; stir until smooth. Spread glaze over filling. Refrigerate until set. Cut into bars.

KAHLUA DREAM BARS

CHEWY HONEY
GRANOLA BARS

CHEWY HONEY GRANOLA BARS

There's sweetness from the honey, chewiness from the raisins, a hint of chocolate and cinnamon, and a bit of crunch. To save a few for later, wrap individual bars in plastic wrap and place in a resealable freezer bag. When you want a satisfying treat on short notice, just grab one and let it thaw for a few minutes.

—TASHA LEHMAN
WILLISTON, VERMONT

PREP: 10 MIN.
BAKE: 15 MIN. + COOLING
MAKES: 20 SERVINGS

- 3 **cups old-fashioned oats**
- 2 **cups unsweetened puffed wheat cereal**
- 1 **cup all-purpose flour**
- ⅓ **cup chopped walnuts**
- ⅓ **cup raisins**
- ⅓ **cup miniature semisweet chocolate chips**
- 1 **teaspoon baking soda**
- 1 **teaspoon ground cinnamon**
- 1 **cup honey**
- ¼ **cup butter, melted**
- 1 **teaspoon vanilla extract**

1. Preheat the oven to 350°. In a large bowl, combine the first eight ingredients. In a small bowl, combine honey, butter and vanilla; pour over oat mixture and mix well. (Batter will be sticky.)

2. Press into a 13x9-in. baking pan coated with cooking spray. Bake 14-18 minutes or until set and edges are lightly browned. Cool on a wire rack. Cut into bars.

PEANUT BUTTER BROWNIE MIX

I discovered the recipe for this quick mix in our local newspaper. I gave it a whirl, and my family loved it. Pack the dry ingredients in a quart-sized canning jar, then cover the lid with fabric for a heartwarming touch.

—LYNN DOWDALL PERTH, ON

PREP: 15 MIN.
BAKE: 25 MIN. + COOLING
MAKES: 16 BROWNIES

- 1   **cup packed brown sugar**
- ½   **cup sugar**
- ⅓   **cup baking cocoa**
- 1   **cup peanut butter chips**
- 1   **cup all-purpose flour**
- ½   **teaspoon baking powder**
- ¼   **teaspoon salt**
- ½   **cup semisweet chocolate chips**
- ½   **cup chopped walnuts**

ADDITIONAL INGREDIENTS

- 2   **large eggs**
- ½   **cup butter, melted**
- 1   **teaspoon vanilla extract**

In a 1-qt. glass container, layer the first nine ingredients in order listed, packing well between each layer. Cover tightly. Store in a cool dry place up to 6 months.

TO PREPARE BROWNIES *Preheat oven to 350°. In a bowl, combine eggs, butter, vanilla and brownie mix. Spread into a greased 8-in. square baking dish. Bake 25-30 minutes or until set (do not overbake). Cool on a wire rack. Cut into squares.*

PEANUT BUTTER
BROWNIE MIX

(5) INGREDIENTS
PEANUT BUTTER 'N' JELLY BARS

My two young sons are crazy about these simple, fast-to-fix cookie bars. And as a busy mom, thanks to the easy preparation, I can make this scrumptious dessert at the last minute. Feel free to vary the jam or jelly to suit your own family's tastes.
—CAROLYN MULLOY DAVISON, MI

PREP: 10 MIN.
BAKE: 15 MIN. + COOLING
MAKES: 2 DOZEN

- 1 tube (16½ ounces) refrigerated peanut butter cookie dough
- ½ cup peanut butter chips
- 1 can (16 ounces) buttercream frosting
- ¼ cup creamy peanut butter
- ¼ cup seedless raspberry jam or grape jelly

1. Let the dough stand at room temperature for 5-10 minutes to soften. Press into an ungreased 13x9-in. baking dish; sprinkle with peanut butter chips.
2. Bake at 375° for 15-18 minutes or until lightly browned and edges are firm to the touch. Cool on a wire rack.
3. In a small bowl, beat frosting and peanut butter until smooth. Spread over bars. Drop jam by teaspoonfuls over frosting; cut through frosting with a knife to swirl the jam.

CAPPUCCINO CAKE BROWNIES

If you like your sweets with a cup of coffee, this is the recipe for you. These no-nut brownies combine a mild coffee flavor with the richness of semisweet chocolate chips. They're a quick dessert or anytime snack at our house.
—MARY HOUCHIN LEBANON, IL

PREP: 15 MIN.
BAKE: 25 MIN. + COOLING
MAKES: 16 BROWNIES

- 1 tablespoon instant coffee granules
- 2 teaspoons boiling water
- 1 cup (6 ounces) semisweet chocolate chips
- ¼ cup butter, softened
- ½ cup sugar
- 2 large eggs
- ½ cup all-purpose flour
- ¼ teaspoon ground cinnamon

1. In a small bowl, dissolve coffee in water; set aside. In a microwave, melt the chocolate chips; stir until smooth. In a small bowl, cream the butter and sugar until light and fluffy. Beat in the eggs, melted chocolate and the coffee mixture. Combine the flour and cinnamon; gradually add to creamed mixture until blended.
2. Pour into a greased 8-in. square baking pan. Bake at 350° for 25-30 minutes or until a toothpick comes out clean. Cool on a wire rack. Cut into squares.

(5) INGREDIENTS
PEANUT BUTTER POPCORN BARS

If you're looking for a fun treat for kids, try these chewy popcorn bars. They have a mild peanut butter flavor, they're simple to stir up, and they can be pressed into a pan to form bars or shaped into balls.
—KATHY OSWALD WAUZEKA, WI

START TO FINISH: 30 MIN.
MAKES: 2 DOZEN

- 10 cups popped popcorn
- ½ cup sugar
- ½ cup light corn syrup
- ½ cup creamy peanut butter
- ½ teaspoon vanilla extract

1. Place popcorn in a large bowl; set aside. In a saucepan over medium heat, bring sugar and corn syrup to a boil, stirring constantly. Boil for 1 minute. Remove from the heat.
2. Stir in peanut butter and vanilla; mix well. Pour over popcorn and mix until well coated. Press into a buttered 13x9-in. pan. Cool slightly before cutting.

TOP TIP
POPCORN POINTERS

To pop popcorn on the stove, use a 3- or 4-quart pan with a loose-fitting lid to allow the steam to escape. Add ⅓ cup vegetable oil for every cup of kernels. Heat the oil to between 400° and 460° (if the oil smokes, it's too hot). Drop in one kernel, and when it pops, add the rest—just enough to cover the bottom of the pan with a single layer. Cover the pan and shake to spread the oil. When the popping begins to slow, remove the pan from the heat. The hot oil will continue to pop the remaining kernels. If desired, salt the corn after it's popped, not before, to avoid toughening the popcorn. One cup of unpopped kernels equals about 8 cups of popped popcorn.

PEANUT BUTTER
'N' JELLY BARS

CAPPUCCINO CAKE
BROWNIES

PEANUT BUTTER
POPCORN BARS

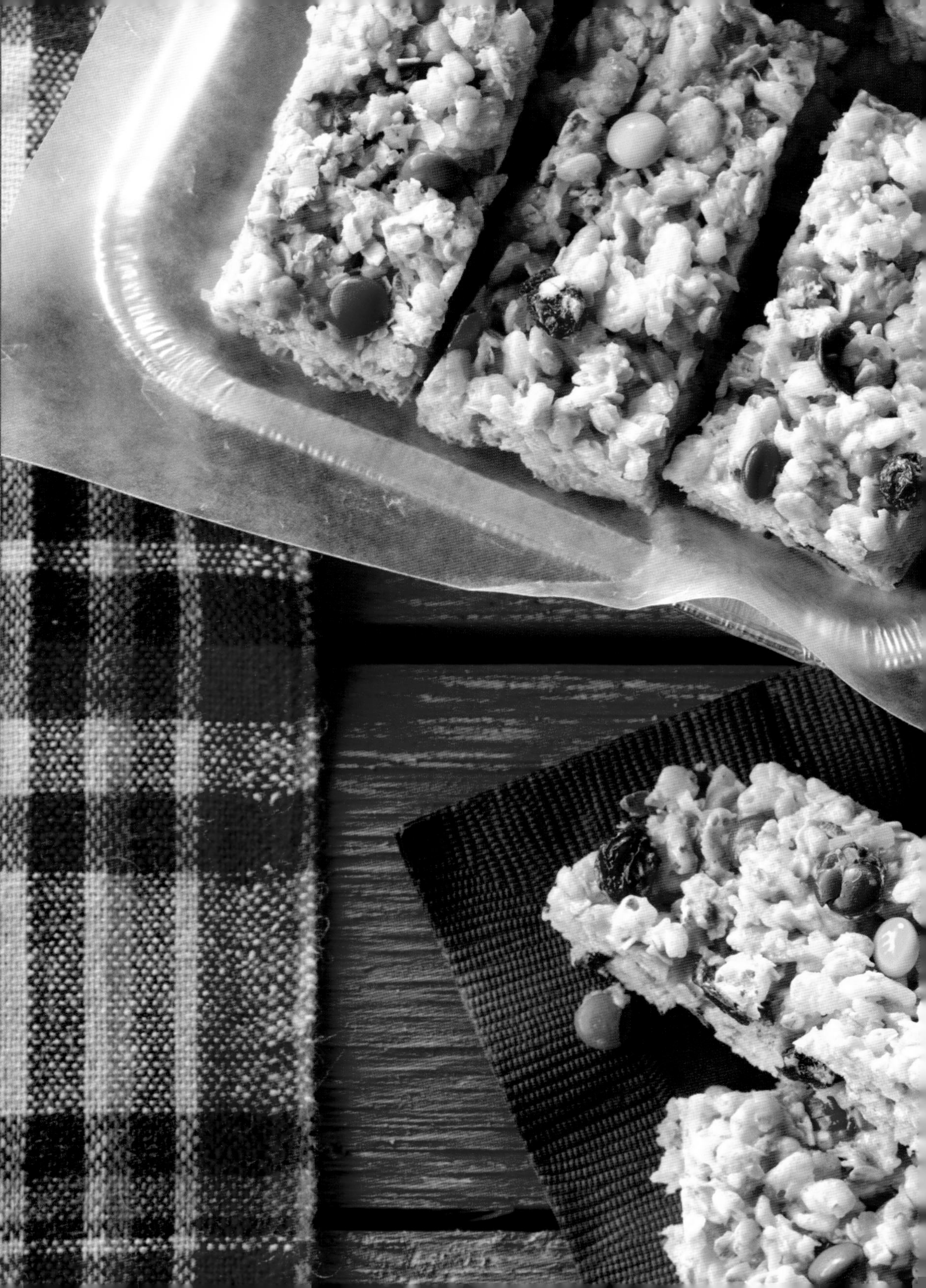

NO-BAKE CEREAL
COOKIE BARS

NO-BAKE CEREAL COOKIE BARS

I toss in raisins, flaked coconut and other goodies in these quick-to-fix bars. For some more color on top, sprinkle on the M&M's once the mixture is in the pan, then gently press them in.
—**CONNIE CRAIG** LAKEWOOD, WA

PREP: 10 MIN.
COOK: 15 MIN. + COOLING
MAKES: 3 DOZEN

- 4½ cups Rice Krispies
- 3¾ cups quick-cooking oats
- ½ cup cornflakes
- ½ cup flaked coconut
- ½ cup butter, cubed
- 1 package (16 ounces) miniature marshmallows
- ¼ cup honey
- ½ cup M&M's minis
- ¼ cup raisins

1. Grease a 15x10x1-in. pan. Place Rice Krispies, oats, cornflakes and coconut in a large bowl; toss the ingredients to combine.
2. In a large saucepan, melt butter over low heat. Add marshmallows; stir until completely melted. Stir in honey until blended. Pour over the cereal mixture; stir until evenly coated. Cool 5 minutes.
3. Stir in M&M's and raisins. Using a greased spatula, press evenly into prepared pan. Let stand 30 minutes before cutting. Store the cut bars between layers of waxed paper in an airtight container.

TRIPLE-LAYER PRETZEL BROWNIES

Imagine a brownie with a salty pretzel crust and an indulgent chocolate-peanut butter topping. Three layers of goodness—that's what you get in these bars.
—**CATHIE AYERS** HILTON, NY

PREP: 30 MIN.
BAKE: 35 MIN. + COOLING
MAKES: 2 DOZEN

- 3 cups crushed pretzels
- ¾ cup butter, melted
- 3 tablespoons sugar
- 1 package fudge brownie mix (13x9-inch pan size)
- ¾ cup semisweet chocolate chips
- ½ cup creamy peanut butter

1. Preheat oven to 400°. In a small bowl, combine pretzels, butter and sugar. Press into an ungreased 13x9-in. baking dish. Bake for 8 minutes. Cool on a wire rack.
2. Reduce heat to 350°. Prepare brownie mix batter according to package directions. Pour over the prepared crust. Bake 35-40 minutes or until a toothpick inserted in the center comes out with moist crumbs (do not overbake). Cool completely on a wire rack.
3. In a microwave, melt chocolate chips and peanut butter; stir until smooth. Spread mixture over top. Refrigerate for 30 minutes or until firm. Cut into bars. Store in an airtight container.

(5) INGREDIENTS
SCOTCH SHORTBREAD BARS

This simple three-ingredient recipe turns out rich, tender bars. Serve them with fresh seasonal berries for a light dessert. They're also great for baby or bridal showers, luncheons or afternoon tea.
—**MARLENE HELLICKSON**
BIG BEAR CITY, CA

PREP: 15 MIN. • **BAKE:** 25 MIN.
MAKES: 4 DOZEN

- 4 cups all-purpose flour
- 1 cup sugar
- 1 pound cold butter, cubed

1. Preheat oven to 325°. In a large bowl, combine the flour and sugar. Cut in the butter until the mixture resembles fine crumbs. Knead the dough until smooth, about 6-10 times. Pat dough into an ungreased 15x10x1-in. baking pan. Pierce with a fork.
2. Bake 25-30 minutes or until lightly browned. Cut into squares while warm. Cool on a wire rack.

SCOTCH SHORTBREAD BARS

(5) INGREDIENTS
BROWNIE SPIDERS

Real spiders petrify me, but I can make an exception for these cute ones made from chocolate. They make perfect Halloween treats.
—**ALI EBRIGHT** KANSAS CITY, MO

PREP: 20 MIN.
BAKE: 30 MIN. + COOLING
MAKES: 9 BROWNIE SPIDERS

- 1 package (15.80 ounces) brownie mix
- ½ cup semisweet chocolate chips
- 2 cups crispy chow mein noodles
- 18 candy eyeballs

1. Prepare and bake brownies according to package directions using an 8-in. square baking pan lined with parchment paper. Cool completely in pan on a wire rack.
2. In a microwave, melt chocolate chips; stir until smooth. Remove 1 tablespoon melted chocolate to a small bowl; reserve for attaching eyes. Add noodles to remaining chocolate; stir gently to coat. Spread onto a waxed paper-lined baking sheet, separating noodles slightly. Freeze until set.
3. Cut nine brownies with a 2¼-in. round cutter for spider bodies. Attach eyeballs using reserved melted chocolate. With a bamboo skewer or toothpick, poke eight holes in top of each spider for inserting legs. Insert a coated noodle into each hole. Store in an airtight container.

TOP TIP
HIGH ALTITUDES
Packaged brownie mixes are a great way to prepare treats at a moment's notice. If you live in a high altitude, add a little extra flour to ensure good results.

BROWNIE SPIDERS

BUTTERSCOTCH
BROWNIE MIX

BUTTERSCOTCH BROWNIE MIX

Most people have butter, eggs and vanilla on hand, and those ingredients are all you'll need to turn this mix into a panful of butterscotch brownies.

—**MACEY ALLEN** GREEN FOREST, AR

PREP: 15 MIN.
BAKE: 20 MIN. + COOLING
MAKES: 2 DOZEN

- 2 **cups all-purpose flour**
- 3½ **teaspoons baking powder**
- ¼ **teaspoon salt**
- ¾ **cup chopped pecans, toasted**
- 1½ **cups packed brown sugar**
- ½ **cup butterscotch chips**

ADDITIONAL INGREDIENTS
- ¾ **cup butter, cubed**
- 2 **large eggs**
- 2 **teaspoons vanilla extract**

In a small bowl, mix flour, baking powder and salt. In a 1-qt. glass jar, layer flour mixture, pecans, brown sugar and butterscotch chips in the order listed. Cover and store in a cool dry place for up to 3 months. Makes 1 batch (about 4 cups mix).

TO PREPARE BROWNIES *Preheat oven to 350°. In a large saucepan, heat butter over medium heat until just melted. Remove from heat. Whisk in eggs and vanilla until blended. Gradually add blondie mix, mixing well. Spread into a greased 13x9-in. baking pan.*

Bake 20-25 minutes or until a toothpick inserted in center comes out with moist crumbs (do not overbake). Cool completely in pan on a wire rack.

BIG BATCH
SNACK BARS

If your family likes granola bars, they're sure to love these tempting treats. Full of hearty ingredients, they're a perfect snack for taking along on picnics and bike trips or for packing in brown-bag lunches.

—CAROLYN FISHER KINZER, PA

PREP: 20 MIN. + COOLING
MAKES: 5 DOZEN

9 cups Rice Chex, crushed
6 cups quick-cooking oats

1 cup graham cracker crumbs
1 cup flaked coconut
½ cup toasted wheat germ
2 packages (one 16 ounces, one 10½ ounces) large marshmallows
1 cup butter, cubed
½ cup honey
1½ cups raisins or M&M's minis or miniature semisweet chocolate chips, optional

1. In a very large bowl, combine the first five ingredients. In a Dutch oven over low heat, cook and stir marshmallows and butter until the marshmallows are melted. Add honey and mix well.

2. Pour over cereal mixture; stir until blended. If desired, add the raisins, M&M's or chocolate chips. Pat two-thirds of mixture into a greased 15x10x1-in. pan and the remaining third into a 9-in. square pan. Cool before cutting into bars.

SNACK BARS

(5) INGREDIENTS

BLACK & WHITE CEREAL TREATS

When my daughter was 7 years old, she came up the great idea of adding Oreo cookies to the rice cereal bars. She's in her 20s now, but it's still a fun treat for us to enjoy.

—TAMMY PHOENIX AVA, IL

PREP: 10 MIN.
COOK: 10 MIN. + COOLING
MAKES: 2 DOZEN

¼ cup butter, cubed
8 cups miniature marshmallows
6 cups Rice Krispies
2½ cups double-stuffed chocolate sandwich cookies (about 16), chopped, divided
1⅓ cups white baking chips, melted

1. In a Dutch oven, melt the butter over medium heat. Add the marshmallows; cook and stir until melted. Remove from heat. Stir in cereal and 2 cups cookies. Press into a greased 13x9-in. baking pan.
2. Spread melted baking chips over top; sprinkle with the remaining cookie pieces, pressing gently to adhere. Cool to room temperature. Cut into bars.

(5) INGREDIENTS

GOOEY CHOCOLATE PEANUT BARS

These bars are quick, easy and delicious. Send a batch to kids away at college or loved ones in the military to remind them of home.

—ELAINE GRIMME SIOUX FALLS, SD

PREP: 10 MIN.
BAKE: 20 MIN. + COOLING
MAKES: 2 DOZEN

1 package (16½ ounces) refrigerated chocolate chip cookie dough
2 cups chocolate-covered peanuts
1 cup miniature marshmallows
½ cup butterscotch ice cream topping

1. Press the cookie dough into an ungreased 13x9-in. baking pan. Bake at 350° for 14-16 minutes or until edges are lightly browned and center is set. Sprinkle with peanuts and marshmallows; drizzle with ice cream topping.
2. Bake 6-8 minutes longer or until the marshmallows are puffed. Cool completely and cut into bars.

CHEWY CHOCOLATE-CHERRY BARS

Colorful dried cherries and pistachios star in this fun take on seven-layer bars. To switch it up even more, try cinnamon or chocolate graham cracker crumbs instead of plain ones. Substitute other nuts—pecans, walnuts or almonds—for the pistachios.

—*TASTE OF HOME* TEST KITCHEN

PREP: 10 MIN.
BAKE: 25 MIN. + COOLING
MAKES: 3 DOZEN

1½ cups graham cracker crumbs
½ cup butter, melted
1 can (14 ounces) sweetened condensed milk
1½ cups dried cherries
1½ cups semisweet chocolate chips
1 cup flaked coconut
1 cup pistachios, chopped

1. Preheat oven to 350°. In a small bowl, mix cracker crumbs and butter. Press into a greased 13x9-in. baking pan. In a large bowl, mix the remaining ingredients until blended; carefully spread over the crust.
2. Bake 25-28 minutes or until edges are golden brown. Cool in pan on a wire rack. Cut into bars.

DID YOU KNOW?

WHITE BAKING CHOCOLATE

White baking chocolate is usually sold in 1-ounce squares in the baking section of grocery stores. You can substitute vanilla baking chips for squares, but be careful to use the same number of ounces the recipe calls for. One cup of vanilla chips is equal to 6 ounces of white baking chocolate.

BLACK & WHITE
CEREAL TREATS

GOOEY CHOCOLATE
PEANUT BARS

CHEWY CHOCOLATE-CHERRY BARS

SOUTH DAKOTA
FRITO TREATS

⑤INGREDIENTS
SOUTH DAKOTA FRITO TREATS

Yep, they're made with corn chips! These salty bars became the go-to after-meeting treat at my quilt guild.

—CAROL TRAMP WYNOT, NE

PREP: 15 MIN. + STANDING
MAKES: 2 DOZEN

- 2 packages (9¾ ounces each) corn chips, divided
- 2 cups semisweet chocolate chips, divided
- 1 cup sugar
- 1 cup light corn syrup
- 1 cup creamy peanut butter

1. Spread 1 package of corn chips on the bottom of a greased 13x9-in. baking pan; sprinkle with 1 cup of chocolate chips.
2. In a large heavy saucepan, combine sugar and corn syrup. Bring to a boil; cook and stir 1 minute. Remove from heat; stir in peanut butter. Pour half of the peanut butter mixture over chip mixture. Top with the remaining corn chips and chocolate chips; drizzle with the remaining peanut butter mixture. Let stand until set. Cut into bars.

STRAWBERRY ALMONDINE

Strawberries are plentiful in this area in early summer. I developed this recipe to use up some berries that had been in my refrigerator for a few days. My crew can't get enough.

—ROBIN PERRY SENECA, PA

PREP: 15 MIN. + CHILLING
BAKE: 10 MIN. + COOLING
MAKES: 16-20 SERVINGS

- 1⅓ cups graham cracker crumbs
- ½ cup confectioners' sugar
- ¼ cup butter, melted
- 2 packages (8 ounces each) cream cheese, softened
- 1 cup sugar
- 1 teaspoon vanilla extract
- 1 cup sliced fresh or frozen strawberries
- 1 carton (8 ounces) frozen whipped topping, thawed
- ½ cup chopped almonds, toasted

In a bowl, combine graham cracker crumbs, confectioners' sugar and butter. Spread on the bottom of a 13x9-in. baking pan. Bake at 350° for 8 minutes. Cool. In a bowl, beat cream cheese, sugar, vanilla and strawberries until smooth. Spread over cooled crust and chill until firm. Spread whipped topping over strawberry mixture and sprinkle with the almonds. Cover pan and refrigerate at least 3 hours.

BIG BATCH
CRISPY PRETZEL BARS

I make a big batch of these peanut butter-flavored cereal bars on days I don't want to heat up the kitchen. Kids love them, so they're great for birthday parties, classroom treats and school bake sales.

—**JANE THOMPSON** EUREKA, IL

START TO FINISH: 20 MIN.
MAKES: ABOUT 3 DOZEN

- 1 cup sugar
- 1 cup light corn syrup
- ½ cup peanut butter
- 5 cups Rice Krispies
- 2 cups pretzel sticks
- 1 cup plain M&M's

In a large microwave-safe bowl, combine the sugar and corn syrup. Microwave on high for 2 minutes or until the sugar is dissolved. Stir in peanut butter until blended. Add the cereal, pretzels and M&M's; stir until coated. Press into a greased 15x10x1-in. pan. Cut into bars.
NOTE *This recipe was tested in a 1,100-watt microwave.*

CRISPY PRETZEL BARS

MONKEY BARS

Mmm—two of my favorite foods together in one dessert! Smooth peanut butter and sweet banana combine to make these thick, muffinlike bars.

—**TINA HAUPERT** WEYMOUTH, MA

PREP: 15 MIN. • **BAKE:** 25 MIN.
MAKES: 16 SERVINGS

- ½ cup butter, softened
- 1 cup packed brown sugar
- ½ cup creamy peanut butter
- 1 large egg
- 1 medium ripe banana, mashed
- 1 teaspoon vanilla extract
- 1 cup whole wheat flour
- 1 teaspoon baking powder
- ⅛ teaspoon salt
  Confectioners' sugar, optional

1. Preheat oven to 350°. In a large bowl, beat butter, brown sugar and peanut butter until blended. Gradually beat in egg, banana and vanilla. In another bowl, whisk flour, baking powder and salt; gradually add to butter mixture, mixing well.
2. Spread into an 8-in. square baking dish coated with cooking spray. Bake 25-30 minutes or until a toothpick inserted in center comes out clean. Cool on a wire rack. Cut into bars. If desired, dust with confectioners' sugar.

MONKEY BARS

EASY FUDGY BROWNIES

EASY FUDGY BROWNIES

I can stir up these moist and chocolaty brownies in a snap. They're oh-so-easy to make and oh-so-scrumptious to eat!

—**EVIE GLOISTEIN** SUSANVILLE, CA

PREP: 15 MIN. • **BAKE:** 35 MIN.
MAKES: 32 BROWNIES

- ½ cup butter, cubed
- 4 ounces unsweetened chocolate, chopped
- 2 cups sugar
- 4 large eggs, lightly beaten
- 1 teaspoon vanilla extract
- ½ cup all-purpose flour
- ½ teaspoon salt
- 2 cups chopped pecans, optional
   Confectioners' sugar, optional

1. In a microwave, melt butter and chocolate; stir until smooth. Cool slightly. In a large bowl, beat sugar and eggs. Stir in the vanilla and chocolate mixture. Combine flour and salt; gradually add to chocolate mixture. Stir in pecans if desired.
2. Spread into two greased 8-in. square baking pans. Bake at 325° for 35-40 minutes or until a toothpick inserted near the center comes out clean. Cool on a wire rack. If desired, dust with confectioners' sugar. Cut into bars.

TOP TIP

DUSTING WITH SUGAR

When a recipe calls for dusting a baked item with confectioners'—also called powdered—sugar, use a mesh tea ball. It keeps the excess sugar dust to a minimum so you won't create a dust storm.

—**NANCY R.** LA PINE, OR

BIG BATCH
BROWNED BUTTER CEREAL BARS

Crispy rice treats were one of the first recipes I ever made as a kid. For this version, I wanted to make something special. Friends and family think using Cap'n Crunch cereal and browned butter is genius, but I just call it delicious.
—**KELLY KRAUSS** LEBANON, NJ

PREP: 15 MIN. + FREEZING
COOK: 20 MIN. + COOLING
MAKES: 5 DOZEN

- **4 cups white fudge-covered miniature pretzels**
- **1 package (10½ ounces) miniature marshmallows**
- **1 package (10 to 12 ounces) white baking chips**
- **2 cups butter, cubed**
- **3 packages (10 ounces each) large marshmallows**
- **2 teaspoons vanilla extract**
- **1 teaspoon salt**
- **8 cups Cap'n Crunch**

1. Line a 15x10x1-in. pan with parchment paper, letting ends extend over sides; set aside. Freeze pretzels, miniature marshmallows and baking chips 1 hour.

2. Remove pretzels, marshmallows and baking chips from freezer; combine in a large bowl. In a Dutch oven, melt butter over medium heat. Heat 10-13 minutes or until golden brown, stirring constantly. Add large marshmallows; cook and stir until blended. Remove from heat; stir in vanilla and salt.

3. Stir in cereal until coated. Stir in pretzel mixture; transfer to prepared pan, pressing evenly with a buttered spatula. Cool completely.

4. Lifting with parchment paper, remove cereal mixture from pan. Cut into bars. Store the bars in airtight containers.

BROWNED BUTTER CEREAL BARS

BROWNIE MOCHA
TRIFLE, PAGE 229

Brownie Desserts

Everyone loves brownies, but when you want something extra special, turn to these luscious desserts.

TOFFEE BROWNIE TRIFLE

This deluxe dessert is a terrific way to dress up brownie mix with other pantry items. Try using different pudding flavors, substitute your favorite candy bar—or do both. Even with low-fat and sugar-free products, it still tastes great.
—**WENDY BENNETT** SIOUX FALLS, SD

PREP: 20 MIN.
BAKE: 25 MIN. + COOLING
MAKES: 16 SERVINGS

1 **package fudge brownie mix (13x9-inch pan size)**
2½ **cups cold milk**
1 **package (3.4 ounces) instant cheesecake or vanilla pudding mix**
1 **package (3.3 ounces) instant white chocolate pudding mix**
1 **carton (8 ounces) frozen whipped topping, thawed**
2 **to 3 Heath candy bars (1.4 ounces each), chopped**

1. Prepare and bake the brownies according to package directions for cake-like brownies, using a greased 13x9-in. baking pan. Cool brownies completely on a wire rack.
2. In a large bowl, beat milk and pudding mixes on low speed for 2 minutes. Let mixture stand for 2 minutes or until soft-set. Fold in whipped topping.
3. Cut the brownies into 1-in. cubes; place half in a 3-qt. glass trifle bowl or serving dish. Cover with half of the pudding. Repeat layers. Sprinkle with chopped candy bars. Refrigerate leftovers.

TOFFEE BROWNIE TRIFLE

LAYERED BROWNIE DESSERT

A tasty brownie is the base for layers of cream cheese and chocolate pudding in this make-ahead dessert.
—**MURIEL LEDEBOER** OOSTBURG, WI

PREP: 20 MIN.
BAKE: 20 MIN. + CHILLING
MAKES: 12-15 SERVINGS

1 **cup butter, softened**
2 **cups sugar**
2 **large eggs**
1 **teaspoon vanilla extract**
2 **cups all-purpose flour**
½ **cup baking cocoa**
½ **teaspoon salt**
½ **teaspoon baking powder**
1 **cup chopped walnuts**
FILLING
11 **ounces cream cheese, softened**
2 **cups confectioners' sugar**
2 **cups whipped topping**
TOPPING
2 **cups cold milk**
1 **package (3.9 ounces) instant chocolate pudding mix**
Whipped topping and chopped walnuts

1. In a large bowl, cream butter and sugar until light and fluffy. Add eggs, one at a time, beating well after each addition. Add vanilla. Combine the flour, cocoa, salt and baking powder; add to creamed mixture just until moistened. Stir in nuts.
2. Transfer batter to a greased 13x9-in. baking pan. Bake at 350° for 20-25 minutes or until a toothpick comes out clean. Cool completely on a wire rack.
3. In a small bowl, beat cream cheese and confectioners' sugar until smooth. Fold in whipped topping; spread over brownies.
4. In a large bowl, whisk milk and pudding mix for 2 minutes. Let stand for 2 minutes or until soft-set. Spread over filling. Refrigerate for 1 hour or until serving.
5. Cut into squares; garnish with whipped topping and nuts.

LAYERED BROWNIE
DESSERT

**FROSTED
BROWNIE PIZZA**

FROSTED BROWNIE PIZZA

It's impossible to eat just one piece of this dessert pizza with its chewy, chocolaty crust, creamy peanut butter frosting and pretty toppings. Folks can't wait to try it.

—**PAULA RIEHL** BOISE, ID

PREP: 10 MIN.
BAKE: 15 MIN. + COOLING
MAKES: 8-10 SERVINGS

- ½ cup butter, cubed
- 2 ounces unsweetened chocolate
- 1 cup sugar
- ¾ cup all-purpose flour
- 2 large eggs, lightly beaten

FROSTING
- 1 cup confectioners' sugar
- ⅓ cup creamy peanut butter
- 1½ teaspoons vanilla extract
- 2 to 4 tablespoons milk

TOPPINGS
- ¾ cup plain M&M's
- ½ cup flaked coconut, toasted
- ½ cup chopped pecans, toasted

1. In a small saucepan over low heat, melt the butter, chocolate and sugar. Remove from the heat; stir in flour until smooth. Add eggs and beat until smooth. Spread onto a greased 12-in. pizza pan.

2. Bake at 350° for 15 minutes or until a toothpick inserted near the center comes out clean. Cool the crust completely.

3. For frosting, in a bowl, beat the sugar, peanut butter, vanilla and enough milk to achieve desired spreading consistency. Spread over brownie crust. Top with M&M's, coconut and pecans.

TOP TIP

CANDY VARIETIES
You can also top this dessert with Reese's Pieces or Peanut Butter M&M's.

BROWNIES A LA MODE

I knew it would be hard to beat the amazing brownie dessert my husband, Merrill, and I tasted at a restaurant. But I'm proud to say my homemade version tops it! Ice cream and homemade hot fudge make it over-the-top delicious.

—LISE THOMSON MAGRATH, AB

PREP: 20 MIN.
BAKE: 30 MIN. + COOLING
MAKES: 1½ DOZEN

- 1 **cup butter, softened**
- 2 **cups sugar**
- 4 **large eggs**
- 2 **tablespoons canola oil**
- 2 **teaspoons vanilla extract**
- 1 **cup all-purpose flour**
- ⅓ **cup baking cocoa**

FUDGE SAUCE

- ½ **cup butter, cubed**
- 2 **cups sugar**
- ½ **cup baking cocoa**
- ½ **cup water**
- ½ **cup light corn syrup**
- 1 **teaspoon vanilla extract**
- ½ **teaspoon salt**
  Vanilla ice cream and maraschino cherries

1. Preheat the oven to 325°. Line a 13x9-in. baking pan with foil, letting ends extend up sides; grease foil. In a large bowl, cream butter and sugar until light and fluffy. Add eggs, one at a time, beating well after each addition. Beat in oil and vanilla. In another bowl, whisk the flour and cocoa; gradually beat into creamed mixture.

2. Spread into prepared pan. Bake 30-35 minutes or until a toothpick inserted near the center comes out clean. Cool on a wire rack.

3. For the fudge sauce, in a large saucepan, melt butter over medium heat. Stir in the sugar, cocoa, water, corn syrup, vanilla and salt until blended. Bring to a boil. Cook sauce, uncovered, for 3-5 minutes or until sugar is dissolved and the sauce is smooth, stirring frequently.

4. Lift the foil to remove brownies from pan. Cut into eighteen 3x2-in. rectangles. Top each brownie with ice cream, fudge sauce and a cherry.

BROWNIES A LA MODE

BIG BATCH
PEPPERMINT BROWNIE CUPS

These cupcakes look fancy, but the recipe is easy. We love the brownie-style texture, loads of peppermint flavor and hint of coffee.

—LINDA BIBBO CHAGRIN FALLS, OH

PREP: 40 MIN.
BAKE: 15 MIN./BATCH + COOLING
MAKES: 4 DOZEN

- 1 cup butter, cubed
- 1 cup plus 3 tablespoons milk chocolate chips
- 3 ounces unsweetened chocolate, chopped
- 3 large eggs
- 1¼ cups sugar
- 1 tablespoon instant coffee granules
- 2 teaspoons vanilla extract
- ½ teaspoon peppermint extract
- ⅔ cup all-purpose flour
- 1½ teaspoons baking powder
- ½ teaspoon salt

FROSTING
- 1½ cups confectioners' sugar
- 1 cup butter, softened
- 1 teaspoon peppermint extract
- 1 jar (7 ounces) marshmallow creme
  Peppermint crunch baking chips

1. Preheat oven to 350°. Line 48 mini-muffin cups with paper or foil liners.
2. In a metal bowl over simmering water, melt butter, chocolate chips and unsweetened chocolate; stir until smooth. Cool slightly.
3. In a large bowl, beat eggs, sugar and coffee granules until blended. Stir in extracts and the chocolate mixture. In another bowl, whisk the flour, baking powder and salt; gradually add to chocolate mixture, mixing well.
4. Fill prepared cups three-fourths full. Bake 12-14 minutes or until a toothpick inserted in center comes out clean (do not overbake). Cool in pans 5 minutes before removing to wire racks to cool completely.
5. For frosting, in a small bowl, beat confectioners' sugar, butter and extract until smooth. Fold in marshmallow creme. Pipe or spread frosting over brownie cups; sprinkle with peppermint baking chips.

CARAMEL FUDGE CHEESECAKE

I combined several recipes in order to satisfy both the chocolate lovers and cheesecake fans in my clan. And the result was even better than anyone expected. A fudge brownie crust, sprinkling of crunchy pecans and gooey layer of caramel make this gem of a dessert hard to resist.

—BRENDA RUSE TRURO, NS

PREP: 30 MIN.
BAKE: 35 MIN. + CHILLING
MAKES: 12 SERVINGS

- 1 package fudge brownie mix (8-inch square pan size)
- 1 package (14 ounces) caramels
- ¼ cup evaporated milk
- 1¼ cups coarsely chopped pecans
- 2 packages (8 ounces each) cream cheese, softened
- ½ cup sugar
- 2 large eggs, lightly beaten
- 2 ounces unsweetened chocolate, melted and cooled

1. Prepare the brownie batter according to package directions. Spread batter into a greased 9-in. springform pan. Place on a baking sheet. Bake at 350° for 20 minutes. Place the pan on a wire rack for 10 minutes (leave oven on).
2. Meanwhile, in a microwave-safe bowl, melt caramels with milk. Pour over brownie crust; sprinkle with pecans.
3. In a large bowl, beat cream cheese and sugar until light and fluffy. Add eggs; beat on low speed just until combined. Stir in melted chocolate. Pour over the pecans. Return pan to baking sheet.
4. Bake for 35-40 minutes or until center is almost set. Cool on a wire rack for 10 minutes. Run a knife around edge of pan to loosen; cool 1 hour longer. Refrigerate overnight. Remove sides of pan.

BANANA CREAM BROWNIE DESSERT

I keep the ingredients for this delish banana-topped brownie on hand because I make it often for potlucks and family gatherings. I'm always asked for the recipe. After one bite, you'll understand why!

—JULIE NOWAKOWSKI LASALLE, IL

PREP: 20 MIN.
BAKE: 30 MIN. + COOLING
MAKES: 12-15 SERVINGS

- 1 package fudge brownie mix (13x9-inch pan size)
- 1 cup (6 ounces) semisweet chocolate chips, divided
- ¾ cup dry roasted peanuts, chopped, divided
- 3 medium firm bananas
- 1⅔ cups cold milk
- 2 packages (5.1 ounces each) instant vanilla pudding mix
- 1 carton (8 ounces) frozen whipped topping, thawed

1. Prepare the brownie batter according to package directions for fudge-like brownies. Stir in ½ cup chocolate chips and ¼ cup peanuts. Spread into a greased 13x9-in. baking pan. Bake at 350° for 28-30 minutes or until a toothpick inserted in the center comes out clean. Cool on a wire rack.
2. Slice bananas; arrange in a single layer over brownies. Sprinkle with ¼ cup chips and ¼ cup peanuts.
3. In a large bowl, beat milk and pudding mixes on low speed for 2 minutes. Fold in whipped topping. Spread over the top. Sprinkle with the remaining chips and peanuts. Refrigerate until serving.

PEPPERMINT
BROWNIE CUPS

CARAMEL FUDGE
CHEESECAKE

BANANA CREAM
BROWNIE DESSERT

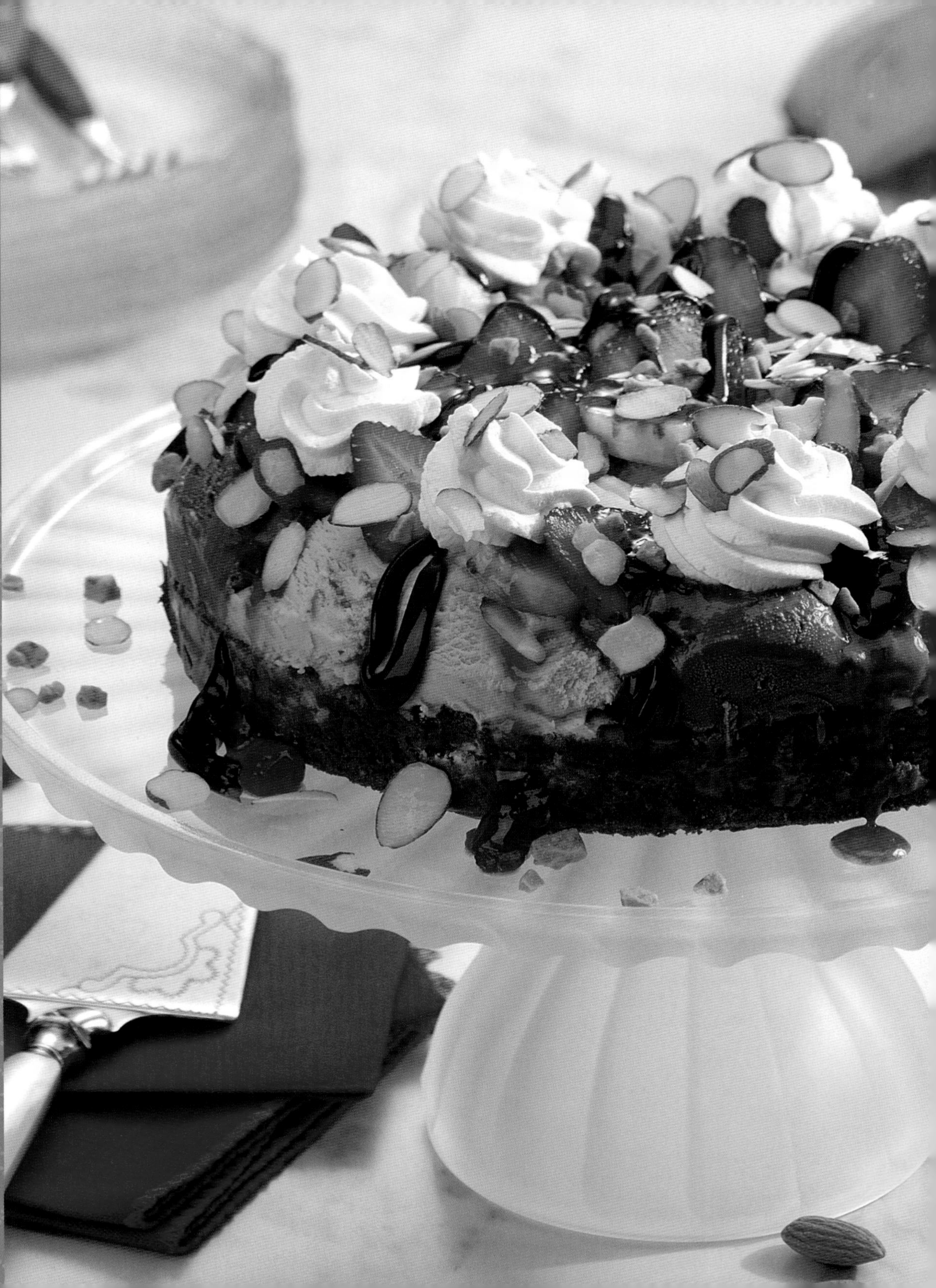

**BANANA SPLIT
BROWNIE PIE**

I often use Neapolitan in place of three different ice cream flavors to make this luscious dessert. You can bake the brownie crust days ahead, top it with the ice cream and freeze until you're ready to serve.
—**TANNA WALKER** SALINA, KS

PREP: 30 MIN. + FREEZING
BAKE: 30 MIN. + FREEZING
MAKES: 10 SERVINGS

- 4 **ounces German sweet chocolate, chopped**
- ½ **cup butter, cubed**
- 3 **large eggs**
- 1 **cup sugar**
- ½ **teaspoon vanilla extract**
- ½ **cup all-purpose flour**
- 1⅓ **cups vanilla ice cream**
- 1⅔ **cups chocolate ice cream**
- 1⅔ **cups strawberry ice cream**
- 2 **medium firm bananas, sliced**
- 1 **cup fresh strawberries, sliced**
- ½ to ¾ **cup hot fudge ice cream topping, warmed**
- ½ to ¾ **cup strawberry ice cream topping**
- ¼ to ½ **cup toffee bits or almond brickle chips**
  Whipped cream and sliced almonds

1. In a microwave, melt chocolate and butter; stir until smooth. Cool. In a small bowl, beat the eggs, sugar, vanilla and the chocolate mixture. Gradually add the flour until well blended. Spread the mixture into a greased 9-in. springform pan.
2. Bake at 350° for 30-35 minutes or until a toothpick inserted in the center comes out clean. Cool crust on a wire rack. Cover and freeze until firm.
3. Using ⅓ cup for each scoop, place four scoops of vanilla ice cream, five scoops of chocolate ice cream and five scoops of strawberry ice cream on a waxed paper-lined baking sheet. Freeze until firm. Place vanilla scoops in center of brownie crust; alternate scoops of chocolate and strawberry around edge. Cover and freeze until firm.
4. Just before serving, remove sides of pan. Arrange bananas and strawberries over ice cream. Drizzle with hot fudge and strawberry toppings. Sprinkle with toffee bits. Garnish with whipped cream and almonds. Cut into wedges.

**BROWNIE MOCHA
TRIFLE**

Instant pudding and a convenient box mix make preparing this trifle, pictured on page 220, a breeze.
—**LOUISE FAUTH** FOREMOST, AB

PREP: 15 MIN. + CHILLING
BAKE: 25 MIN. + COOLING
MAKES: 12 SERVINGS

- 1 **package fudge brownie mix (8-inch square pan size)**
- 1¾ **cups cold 2% milk**
- 2 **packages (3.4 ounces each) instant vanilla pudding mix**
- ¼ **cup cold brewed coffee**
- 2 **cups whipped topping**
- 1 **Heath candy bar (1.4 ounces), crushed**

1. Prepare brownie batter and bake according to the package directions. Cool; cut brownies into 1-in. pieces.
2. In a large bowl, beat milk and pudding mixes for 2 minutes or until thickened. Stir in coffee. Fold in whipped topping.
3. In a trifle bowl or 2-qt. glass bowl, layer a third of the brownie pieces, pudding mixture and crushed candy bar. Repeat layers twice. Chill until serving.

**BANANA SPLIT
BROWNIE PIE**

BROWNIE CRACKLES

Chocolate chips and a convenient brownie mix provide the rich chocolate flavor in these irresistible cookies. Rolling the cookies in confectioners' sugar gives them their inviting crackled appearance.

—ELLEN GOVERTSEN WHEATON, IL

PREP: 15 MIN. + STANDING
BAKE: 10 MIN./BATCH
MAKES: 3 DOZEN

- 1 package fudge brownie mix (13x9-inch pan size)
- 1 cup all-purpose flour
- 1 large egg
- ½ cup water
- ¼ cup canola oil
- 1 cup (6 ounces) semisweet chocolate chips
  Confectioners' sugar

1. Preheat oven to 350°. In a large bowl, beat brownie mix, flour, egg, water and oil until well blended. Stir in chocolate chips. Let stand 30 minutes.

2. Place confectioners' sugar in a shallow dish. Drop dough by tablespoonfuls into sugar; gently roll to coat. Place 2 in. apart on greased baking sheets. Bake for 8-10 minutes or until set. Remove from pans to wire racks to cool.

TOP TIP

COOKIE POINTERS

For even baking, make cookies the same size and thickness. Leave at least 2 inches around the baking sheet and the oven walls for good heat circulation. For best results, bake only one sheet of cookies at a time. If you need to bake two sheets at once, switch the position of the baking sheets halfway through the baking time.

FROZEN CHOCOLATE MINT DESSERT

 This dessert is an adaptation of my great-aunt's recipe for grasshopper pie. I put in too much mint extract, so to cut the minty taste with something chocolaty, I flipped the whole pie upside-down on top of a brownie crust.

—SARAH NEWMAN MAHTOMEDI, MN

PREP: 40 MIN. + FREEZING
MAKES: 24 SERVINGS

- 1 package fudge brownie mix (13x9-inch pan size)
- 2 large egg whites
- ¼ cup unsweetened applesauce
- 2 teaspoons vanilla extract
- ½ cup baking cocoa
- 1½ cups fat-free milk
- 2 packages (16 ounces each) large marshmallows
- ½ teaspoon mint extract
- 1 carton (16 ounces) frozen reduced-fat whipped topping, thawed
- ⅔ cup Oreo cookie crumbs

1. In a bowl, combine the brownie mix, egg whites, applesauce and vanilla. Spread mixture into a 13x9-in. baking dish coated with cooking spray. Bake at 350° for 18-22 minutes or until a toothpick inserted in the center comes out clean. Cool on a wire rack.

2. In a Dutch oven, combine the cocoa and milk. Cook and stir over medium heat until the cocoa is dissolved. Stir in marshmallows until melted. Remove from the heat; stir in extract. Cool mixture completely.

3. Fold in whipped topping. Spread over brownies. Sprinkle with cookie crumbs. Cover and freeze for at least 8 hours. Remove from the freezer 10 minutes before serving.

BLONDIE SUNDAES

Just when we thought rich and chewy blondies couldn't get any better, our Test Kitchen dreamed up a heavenly sundae version. Topped with creamy vanilla ice cream and a sweet butterscotch sauce, this dessert goes from homey to luxurious.

—*TASTE OF HOME* TEST KITCHEN

PREP: 20 MIN.
BAKE: 20 MIN. + COOLING
MAKES: 9 SERVINGS (1½ CUPS SAUCE)

- 1 large egg
- 1 cup packed brown sugar
- ½ cup butter, melted
- 1 teaspoon vanilla extract
- 1¼ cups all-purpose flour
- ⅛ teaspoon salt
- 1 cup butterscotch chips

BUTTERSCOTCH SAUCE

- ½ cup butter, cubed
- 1 cup packed brown sugar
- 1 cup heavy whipping cream
- ½ teaspoon salt
- 1½ teaspoons vanilla extract
- 4½ cups vanilla ice cream

1. In a large bowl, beat the egg, brown sugar, butter and vanilla. Combine flour and salt; gradually beat into egg mixture. Fold in chips.

2. Transfer to a greased 8-in. square baking dish. Bake at 350° for 20-25 minutes or until a toothpick inserted in the center comes out with moist crumbs (do not overbake). Cool on a wire rack.

3. For sauce, in a large saucepan, melt butter. Stir in the brown sugar, cream and salt. Bring to a boil; cook and stir for 5 minutes or until slightly thickened. Remove from the heat. Stir in the vanilla. Cut brownies into squares; serve with ice cream and sauce.

BROWNIE CRACKLES

FROZEN CHOCOLATE
MINT DESSERT

BLONDIE SUNDAES

COCONUT-ALMOND FUDGE CUPS

BIG BATCH

COCONUT-ALMOND FUDGE CUPS

With a coconut filling, these fudgy bites are reminiscent of an Almond Joy candy bar.

—**PRECI D'SILVA** DALLAS, TX

PREP: 30 MIN.
BAKE: 10 MIN./BATCH + COOLING
MAKES: 4 DOZEN

- **1** package chocolate fudge cake mix (regular size)
- **½** cup butter, melted
- **1** large egg

FILLING
- **¼** cup sugar
- **¼** cup evaporated milk
- **7** large marshmallows
- **1** cup flaked coconut

TOPPING
- **¾** cup semisweet chocolate chips
- **¼** cup evaporated milk
- **2** tablespoons butter
- **½** cup sliced almonds

1. In a large bowl, beat the cake mix, butter and egg until well blended. Shape into 1-in. balls; place in foil-lined miniature muffin cups. Bake at 350° for 8 minutes.

2. Using the end of a wooden spoon handle, make a ½-in.-deep indentation in the center of each cup. Bake 2-3 minutes longer or until cake springs back when lightly touched. Remove from pans to wire racks to cool.

3. For filling, in a microwave-safe bowl, heat sugar and milk on high for 2 minutes, stirring frequently. Add the marshmallows; stir until melted. Stir in coconut. Spoon into cooled cups.

4. For topping, in another microwave-safe bowl, combine the chocolate chips, milk and butter. Microwave in 10- to 20-second intervals until melted; stir until smooth. Stir in almonds. Spread over filling. Store in the refrigerator.
NOTE *This recipe was tested in a 1,100-watt microwave.*

TRIPLE LAYER BROWNIE CAKE

A little goes a long way when you bite into this frosted brownie cake. It's rich, lavish and sure to satisfy a chocolate lover's craving.

—BARBARA DEAN LITTLETON, CO

PREP: 30 MIN. + CHILLING
BAKE: 25 MIN. + COOLING
MAKES: 16-20 SERVINGS

- 1½ cups butter
- 6 ounces unsweetened chocolate, chopped
- 3 cups sugar
- 5 large eggs
- 1½ teaspoons vanilla extract
- 1½ cups all-purpose flour
- ¾ teaspoon salt

FROSTING

- 16 ounces semisweet chocolate, chopped
- 3 cups heavy whipping cream
- ½ cup sugar, optional
- 2 milk chocolate candy bars (1.55 ounces each), shaved, optional

1. In a large microwave-safe bowl, melt butter and chocolate; stir until smooth. Stir in sugar. Add eggs, one at a time, beating well after each addition. Stir in the vanilla, flour and salt.

2. Pour into three greased and floured 9-in. round baking pans. Bake at 350° for 23-25 minutes or until a toothpick inserted near the center comes out clean. Cool for 10 minutes; remove from pan to a wire rack to cool completely.

3. For frosting, melt chocolate in a heavy saucepan over medium heat. If desired, gradually stir in cream and sugar until well blended. Heat to a gentle boil; boil and stir for 1 minute. Remove from the heat; transfer to a large bowl. Refrigerate for 2-3 hours or until the mixture reaches a pudding-like consistency, stirring a few times.

4. Beat until soft peaks form. Immediately spread between layers and over top and sides of cake. If desired, sprinkle with shaved chocolate. Store in the refrigerator.

TRIPLE LAYER BROWNIE CAKE

FUDGE BROWNIE PIE

Here's a reason to pull out your cast iron skillet! This pecan-studded brownie pie is delicious topped with whipped cream and strawberries.

—**JOHNNIE MCLEOD** BASTROP, LA

PREP: 15 MIN. • **BAKE:** 25 MIN.
MAKES: 6 SERVINGS

- ½ **cup butter, melted**
- 1 **cup sugar**
- 2 **large eggs**
- 1 **teaspoon vanilla extract**
- ½ **cup all-purpose flour**
- ⅓ **cup baking cocoa**
- ¼ **teaspoon salt**
- ½ **cup chopped pecans**
  Whipped cream, optional
  Strawberries, optional

1. In a large bowl, beat sugar and butter. Add eggs and vanilla; mix well. Add flour, cocoa and salt. Stir in nuts.
2. Pour into a greased 9-in. pie pan or ovenproof skillet. Bake at 350° for 25-30 minutes or until almost set. Serve with whipped cream and strawberries if desired.

CHERRY-COCONUT CHOCOLATE TORTE

I love chocolate-covered cherries and old-fashioned Cherry Mash candy. This showstopping layered torte reminds me of both, and it's sure to satisfy your sweet tooth.

—**DIAN HICKS CARLSON** OMAHA, NE

PREP: 30 MIN.
BAKE: 20 MIN. + CHILLING
MAKES: 12 SERVINGS

- 1 **cup sugar**
- 2 **large eggs**
- ½ **teaspoon vanilla extract**
- ½ **cup butter, melted**
- ½ **cup all-purpose flour**
- ⅓ **cup baking cocoa**
- ¼ **teaspoon salt**
- ¼ **teaspoon baking powder**

CHERRY LAYER
- 4 **jars (10 ounces each) maraschino cherries**
- 4 **cups confectioners' sugar**
- ¼ **cup butter, softened**

COCONUT LAYER
- 1 **package (14 ounces) flaked coconut**
- ¼ **cup sweetened condensed milk**

CHOCOLATE GANACHE
- 12 **ounces semisweet chocolate, chopped**
- 1 **cup heavy whipping cream**
- 1 **cup chopped walnuts, toasted**

1. Preheat oven to 350°. In a large bowl, beat sugar, eggs and vanilla until blended. Beat in the melted butter. In a small bowl, whisk flour, cocoa, salt and baking powder; gradually add dry ingredients to batter and mix well.
2. Spread into a greased 9-in. springform pan. Bake 18-20 minutes or until a toothpick inserted in center comes out clean. Cool brownie layer completely in pan on a wire rack.
3. Drain the cherries, reserving ½ cup juice. Arrange cherries evenly around top edge of brownie; place remaining cherries over top. In a large bowl, beat confectioners' sugar, butter and reserved cherry juice until creamy. Spread evenly over cherries.
4. In a large bowl, combine the coconut and milk. Sprinkle over cherry layer, carefully smoothing down near edges and pressing gently to form an even layer.
5. Place chocolate in a large bowl. In a small saucepan, bring cream just to a boil. Pour over chocolate. Let stand 5 minutes; whisk until smooth. Pour over coconut layer. Refrigerate until set. Loosen sides of pan with a knife. Remove rim from pan. Sprinkle with walnuts.
NOTE *To toast nuts, bake in a shallow pan in a 350° oven for 5-10 minutes, or cook in a skillet over low heat until lightly browned, stirring occasionally.*

FUDGE BROWNIE PIE

CHERRY-COCONUT
CHOCOLATE TORTE

GRILLED BANANA
BROWNIE SUNDAES

GRILLED BANANA BROWNIE SUNDAES

My niece Amanda Jean and I have a lot of fun in the kitchen creating different dishes. One of us will start with a recipe idea and it just grows from there—and so does the mess! That's exactly what happened with our grilled banana sundaes. We always have a blast.

—CAROL FARNSWORTH GREENWOOD, IN

PREP: 10 MIN. • **GRILL:** 5 MIN. + COOLING
MAKES: 8 SERVINGS

- 2 **medium bananas, unpeeled**
- 4 **ounces cream cheese, softened**
- ¼ **cup packed brown sugar**
- 3 **tablespoons creamy peanut butter**
- 8 **prepared brownies (2x2-inch)**
- 4 **cups vanilla ice cream**
- ½ **cup hot fudge ice cream topping, warmed**
- ½ **cup chopped salted peanuts**

1. Cut unpeeled bananas crosswise in half, then lengthwise in half. Place quartered bananas on an oiled grill rack, cut side down. Grill, covered, over medium-high heat 2-3 minutes on each side or until lightly browned. Cool slightly.
2. In a small bowl, beat cream cheese, brown sugar and peanut butter until smooth.
3. To serve, remove bananas from peel; place over brownies. Top with cream cheese mixture, ice cream, fudge topping and peanuts.

MAPLE-MOCHA BROWNIE TORTE

Instead of making regular brownies, I bake brownie mix in cake pans to make a quick torte. Wrapped in a fluffy maple frosting, this sweet dessert is at the top of my list of speedy standbys.

—AMY FLORY CLEVELAND, GA

PREP: 30 MIN.
BAKE: 20 MIN. + COOLING
MAKES: 12 SERVINGS

- 1 **package brownie mix (13x9-inch pan size)**
- ½ **cup chopped walnuts**
- 2 **cups heavy whipping cream**
- 2 **teaspoons instant coffee granules**
- ½ **cup packed brown sugar**
- 1½ **teaspoons maple flavoring**
- 1 **teaspoon vanilla extract Chocolate curls or additional walnuts, optional**

1. Preheat oven to 350°. Prepare batter for brownie mix according to package directions for cake-like brownies. Stir in walnuts. Pour batter into two greased 9-in. round baking pans.
2. Bake 20-22 minutes or until a toothpick inserted 2 in. from the edge comes out clean. Cool 10 minutes before removing from pans to wire racks to cool completely.
3. In a large bowl, beat cream and coffee granules until stiff peaks form. Gradually beat in the brown sugar, maple flavoring and vanilla.
4. Spread 1½ cups over one brownie layer; top with second layer. Spread remaining cream mixture over top and sides of torte. Garnish with chocolate curls or walnuts if desired. Store torte in the refrigerator.

BROWNIE CHEESECAKE SNICKERS PIE

This is the kind of pie you thought existed only in your dreams. Just as the name implies, the triple-threat dessert combines three amazing flavors into one delicious pie. Peanut allergies? Use Milky Ways!

—GENISE KRAUSE STURGEON BAY, WI

PREP: 45 MIN.
BAKE: 20 MIN. + COOLING
MAKES: 10 SERVINGS

- ⅓ cup butter, cubed
- 1 cup sugar
- 2 tablespoons water
- 6 ounces semisweet chocolate, chopped
- 1 teaspoon vanilla extract
- 2 large eggs
- ¾ cup all-purpose flour
- ¼ teaspoon baking soda
- ⅛ teaspoon salt

CREAM CHEESE LAYER
- 10 ounces cream cheese, softened
- ⅓ cup sugar
- 1 large egg, beaten
- 1 teaspoon vanilla extract
- 4 Snickers candy bars (2.07 ounces each), cut into ½-inch pieces

GLAZE
- ½ cup heavy whipping cream
- 4 ounces semisweet chocolate, chopped

1. Preheat oven to 325°. In a heavy saucepan, bring butter, sugar and water to a boil, stirring constantly. Remove from heat. Stir in chocolate until melted; cool slightly. Stir in the vanilla.
2. In a large bowl, beat eggs until lightly beaten. Gradually add the chocolate mixture; mix well. Combine flour, baking soda and salt; gradually add to egg mixture. Spread mixture into a greased 9-in. deep-dish pie plate. Bake for 20 minutes. Cool on a wire rack for 10 minutes.
3. Meanwhile, in a large bowl, beat cream cheese, sugar, egg and vanilla just until blended. Arrange candy bar pieces over the brownie layer; spread cream cheese mixture over top. Bake 18-20 minutes or until top is set and edges are lightly browned. Cool on a wire rack for 1 hour.
4. For the glaze, bring cream to a simmer; remove from heat. Add chocolate and stir until smooth. Cool for 15 minutes; pour over pie. Refrigerate until serving.
MAKE AHEAD *Pie can be made a day in advance. Cover and refrigerate.*

HUGS 'N' KISSES BROWNIE

When I needed a fun dessert in a hurry, I added my own special touches to a basic brownie mix to create this chocolate-lovers treat.

—KRISTI VAN BATAVIA KANSAS CITY, MO

PREP: 20 MIN.
BAKE: 35 MIN. + COOLING
MAKES: 12 SERVINGS

- 1 package fudge brownie mix (8-inch square pan size)
- 1 large egg
- ¼ cup canola oil
- ¼ cup water
- 1½ cups vanilla or white chips, divided
- 14 to 16 milk chocolate kisses
- 14 to 16 striped chocolate kisses
- 1½ teaspoons shortening

1. In a bowl, stir brownie mix, egg, oil and water until well blended. Fold in 1 cup vanilla chips.
2. Pour into a greased 9-in. heart-shaped or round springform pan. Bake at 350° for 35-40 minutes or until a toothpick inserted 2 in. from edge of pan comes out clean.
3. Let stand for 10 minutes; alternate milk chocolate and striped kisses around edge of pan with points toward center. Melt shortening and remaining chips; stir until smooth. Drizzle over brownie. Cool completely. Remove the sides of the springform pan before cutting.

BROWNIE-PEPPERMINT ICE CREAM PIE

Rich, chocolaty brownie crust is a perfect partner to refreshing peppermint ice cream. Holiday guests have come to expect this make-ahead delight.

—CAROL GILLESPIE CHAMBERSBURG, PA

PREP: 30 MIN.
BAKE: 35 MIN. + FREEZING
MAKES: 8 SERVINGS

- 1 package fudge brownie mix (8-inch square pan size)
- ½ cup vanilla or white chips
- ½ cup 60% cacao bittersweet chocolate baking chips
- ⅓ cup caramel ice cream topping
- 1 pint peppermint ice cream, softened
- 1 cup heavy whipping cream
- ¼ cup confectioners' sugar
- ⅛ teaspoon peppermint extract
- ¼ cup crushed peppermint candies

1. Prepare the brownie batter according to package directions; stir in vanilla and bittersweet chips. Spread onto the bottom and up the sides of a greased 9-in. pie plate.
2. Bake at 350° for 35-40 minutes or until a toothpick inserted in the center comes out clean. Cool for 5 minutes. Gently press down the center of crust if necessary. Cool completely on a wire rack.
3. Drizzle caramel topping over crust; spread evenly with ice cream. Cover and freeze for 4 hours or until firm.
4. Remove from the freezer 10 minutes before serving. Meanwhile, in a small bowl, beat cream, confectioners' sugar and extract until stiff peaks form. Spread over ice cream; sprinkle with crushed peppermints.

BROWNIE-PEPPERMINT ICE CREAM PIE

BROWNIE SWIRL
CHEESECAKE

BROWNIE SWIRL CHEESECAKE

It may look rather fancy, but this cheesecake is so simple. You don't need to be a pro to make the elegant chocolate swirls on top.

—JANET BRUNNER BURLINGTON, KY

PREP: 10 MIN.
BAKE: 50 MIN. + CHILLING
MAKES: 8-10 SERVINGS

- 1 package (8 ounces) brownie mix
- 2 packages (8 ounces each) cream cheese, softened
- ½ cup sugar
- 1 teaspoon vanilla extract
- 2 large eggs
- 1 cup milk chocolate chips, melted
  Whipped cream and miniature chocolate kisses, optional

1. Prepare brownie mix according to package directions for chewy fudge brownies. Spread into a greased 9-in. springform pan. Bake at 350° for 15 minutes (brownies will not test done). Cool crust for 10 minutes on a wire rack.
2. Meanwhile, in a bowl, combine the cream cheese, sugar and vanilla. Add eggs, one at a time, beating well after each addition.
3. Pour over the brownie crust. Top with melted chocolate; cut through batter with a knife to swirl the chocolate.
4. Bake at 350° for 35-40 minutes or until center is almost set. Run a knife around edge of pan to loosen; cool completely. Remove sides of pan; refrigerate for at least 3 hours. If desired, garnish with whipped cream and chocolate kisses.

PEANUT BUTTER BROWNIE TRIFLE

This rich, tempting dessert feeds a crowd and features the ever-popular combination of chocolate and peanut butter. Try it for your next party or potluck.

—NANCY FOUST STONEBORO, PA

PREP: 1 HOUR + CHILLING
MAKES: 20 SERVINGS (1 CUP EACH)

- 1 fudge brownie mix (13x9-inch pan size)
- 1 package (10 ounces) peanut butter chips
- 2 packages (13 ounces each) miniature peanut butter cups
- 4 cups cold 2% milk
- 2 packages (5.1 ounces each) instant vanilla pudding mix
- 1 cup creamy peanut butter
- 4 teaspoons vanilla extract
- 3 cartons (8 ounces each) frozen whipped topping, thawed

1. Preheat oven to 350°. Prepare brownie batter according to the package directions; stir in peanut butter chips. Bake in a greased 13x9-in. baking pan 20-25 minutes or until a toothpick inserted in the center comes out with moist crumbs (do not overbake). Cool on a wire rack; cut into ¾-in. pieces.
2. Cut peanut butter cups in half; set aside ⅓ cup for garnish. In a large bowl, whisk milk and pudding mixes for 2 minutes (mixture will be thick). Add peanut butter and vanilla; mix well. Fold in 1½ cartons whipped topping.
3. Place a third of the brownies in a 5-qt. glass bowl; top with a third of the remaining peanut butter cups. Spoon a third of the pudding mixture over the top. Repeat layers twice. Cover with the remaining whipped topping; garnish trifle with the reserved peanut butter cups. Refrigerate until chilled.

PEANUT BUTTER
BROWNIE TRIFLE

PEANUT BUTTER-FILLED BROWNIE CUPCAKES

Folks love brownies and cupcakes, so why not combine them? You'll see these pop-in-your-mouth bites disappear in a flash.

—CAROL GILLESPIE
CHAMBERSBURG, PA

PREP: 15 MIN.
BAKE: 15 MIN. + COOLING
MAKES: 1 DOZEN

- 1 **package fudge brownie mix (8-inch square pan size)**
- ½ **cup miniature semisweet chocolate chips**
- ⅓ **cup creamy peanut butter**
- 3 **tablespoons cream cheese, softened**
- 1 **large egg**
- ¼ **cup sugar**
  Confectioners' sugar

1. Preheat oven to 350°. Prepare brownie batter according to the package directions; stir in chocolate chips. For filling, in a small bowl, beat peanut butter, cream cheese, egg and sugar until smooth.

2. Fill paper-lined muffin cups one-third full with batter. Drop filling by teaspoonfuls into the center of each cupcake. Cover with remaining batter.

3. Bake 15-20 minutes or until a toothpick inserted in brownie portion comes out clean. Cool for 10 minutes before removing from pan to a wire rack to cool completely. Dust the tops with confectioners' sugar. Store in the refrigerator.

PEANUT BUTTER-FILLED BROWNIE CUPCAKES

BROWNIE AFFOGATO SUNDAES

We can't resist brownies and ice cream. We also love coffee and espresso, so I combined an affogato (a coffee-based dessert) with a brownie to get this sundae. Cold, sweet and salty—sensational. This is one recipe to pass along!

—JULIE MERRIMAN SEATTLE, WA

START TO FINISH: 20 MIN.
MAKES: 6 SERVINGS

- ½ **cup heavy whipping cream**
- ¼ **cup marshmallow creme**
- 6 **prepared brownies**
- 6 **tablespoons fudge ice cream topping**
- 2 **cups coffee ice cream**
- ¾ **cup hot brewed espresso**
- 6 **tablespoons Kahlua (coffee liqueur), optional**
  Chocolate-covered coffee beans
  Sea salt or smoked salt

1. In a small bowl, beat whipping cream and marshmallow creme until soft peaks form. Refrigerate until serving.

2. To serve, place each brownie in a dessert dish; top with fudge topping and ice cream. Pour espresso and, if desired, Kahlua over ice cream. Top with cream mixture and coffee beans; sprinkle with salt. Serve desserts immediately.

BROWNIE AFFOGATO SUNDAES

BROWNIE ICE
CREAM CONES

BANANA SPLIT
BROWNIE CAKE

GREAT AMERICAN
BROWNIE PIE

BROWNIE ICE CREAM CONES

My husband is in the Air Force, so we've moved around a lot. I've been fortunate to make new friends in each place we've been stationed. When they share their interesting recipes, I like to put my own twist on them. Here's one—serving these fun treats to kids is a sure way to create friendships anywhere!

—MARLENE RHODES PANAMA CITY, FL

PREP: 20 MIN.
BAKE: 20 MIN. + COOLING
MAKES: 2 DOZEN

- 4 ounces German sweet chocolate, chopped
- ¼ cup butter, cubed
- ¾ cup sugar
- 2 large eggs
- ½ cup all-purpose flour
- ½ cup chopped walnuts, optional
- 1 teaspoon vanilla extract
- 24 ice cream cake cones (about 3 inches tall)
- 24 scoops ice cream
  Colored sprinkles

1. In a microwave, melt chocolate and butter; stir until smooth. Cool slightly; pour into a large bowl. Add sugar and eggs until well blended. Stir in the flour, walnuts if desired and vanilla.

2. Place the ice cream cones in muffin cups; fill half full with batter. Bake at 350° for 20-22 minutes or until brownies are set on top and a toothpick inserted near the center comes out with moist crumbs (do not overbake). Cool completely.

3. Just before serving, top each cone with a scoop of ice cream and garnish with sprinkles.

BANANA SPLIT BROWNIE CAKE

Brownies, ice cream, bananas, hot fudge, nuts—everything we love about a banana split is beautifully layered into what may be the most awesome cake ever.

—TASTE OF HOME TEST KITCHEN

PREP: 20 MIN. + FREEZING
MAKES: 14 SERVINGS

- 2 packages (13 ounces each) fudge brownies
- 1 quart strawberry ice cream, softened
- 3 large firm bananas, halved lengthwise
- 1 cup hot fudge ice cream topping, warmed
- 1 quart vanilla ice cream, softened
- ¾ cup chopped pecans

1. Arrange brownies in a greased 9-in. springform pan, cutting to fit and filling in small holes. Spread with strawberry ice cream. Cover and freeze for 3 hours or until firm.

2. Arrange bananas over ice cream, cutting to fit as needed. Spread with fudge topping and vanilla ice cream. Sprinkle with pecans. Cover tightly and freeze overnight. (May be frozen for up to 2 months.)

3. Remove cake from the freezer 10 minutes before serving. Carefully run a knife around the edge of the pan to loosen; remove sides of pan.

NOTE *This recipe was prepared with Little Debbie fudge brownies.*

GREAT AMERICAN BROWNIE PIE

Why settle for a square brownie when you can have a whole slice of brownie pie? Pair it with a glass of cold milk for a refreshing treat.

—EDIE DESPAIN LOGAN, UT

PREP: 30 MIN.
BAKE: 30 MIN. + COOLING
MAKES: 8 SERVINGS

- ½ cup butter, softened
- ¾ cup sugar
- 2 large eggs
- 2 tablespoons corn syrup
- 1½ teaspoons almond extract
- ⅔ cup all-purpose flour
- ⅓ cup baking cocoa
- ¼ teaspoon baking powder
- ⅓ cup chopped maraschino cherries
- ⅓ cup coarsely chopped almonds
- 1 cup white baking chips
  Whipped topping and maraschino cherries with stems, optional

1. In a small bowl, cream butter and sugar. Add the eggs, corn syrup and extract; mix well. Combine the flour, cocoa and baking powder. Add to creamed mixture and mix well. Drain chopped cherries on paper towels. Fold the cherries, almonds and chips into batter.

2. Transfer mixture to a greased and floured 9-in. pie plate. Bake at 325° for 30-35 minutes or until a toothpick inserted near the center comes out clean. Cool on a wire rack. If desired, garnish with whipped topping and cherries.

TOP TIP

SOFTEN ICE CREAM

If your ice cream is too hard to scoop, put the entire container in the microwave on high for 15-20 seconds. It'll soften just enough to make it easy to scoop.

—SUE B. APOLLO, PA

GENERAL RECIPE INDEX

This handy index lists recipes by food categories and major ingredients so you can find recipes that suit your needs.

ALPHABETICAL RECIPE INDEX

Find every recipe by title.